The California Missions

A Sunset Book

The California Missions
A PICTORIAL HISTORY

BY THE SUNSET EDITORS
Editor, Soft Cover Edition: Dorothy Krell
Editor, Original Edition: Paul C. Johnson
Chief Photographer: John S. Weir
Historical and Architectural Consultant: Harry Downie
Book Design: Adrian Wilson
Color Section Design: Joe Seney
Cover Photograph: Philip Spencer
Watercolor Paintings: France Carpentier

SUNSET BOOKS
MENLO PARK, CALIFORNIA

San Miguel Arcángel
PHILIP SPENCER

El Camino Reál—The Royal Road

El Camino Reál (The Royal Road) was pioneered by the Spaniards in the late 1700's when they colonized California in the name of their king. The road started as a foot trail connecting the chain of missions established between San Diego in the south and Sonoma in the north. As the mission settlements grew, traffic increased, and the narrow trail became a well-traveled road. After the Americans acquired California, they used the old road as the main north-south stage route, and when the Concord coach was replaced by the automobile, the road became the principal highway linking northern and southern California. The modern highway is called El Camino Reál in recognition of its historic importance, and it follows the original path of the padres with only a few deviations. For many years it carried the designation US 101, and although it still carries this identification for much of its way, portions have been renumbered.

Vice-President, Editorial Director, Sunset Books:
Bob Doyle

12 13 14 15 16 17 18 19 20 QPD 9 8 7 6 5 4 3 2 1 0

Map labels:

San Francisco Solano — Sonoma
San Rafael Arcángel — San Rafael
San Francisco de Asís — SAN FRANCISCO
San José
Santa Clara de Asís — San Jose
Santa Cruz — Santa Cruz
San Juan Bautista — Hollister
San Carlos Borromeo de Carmelo — Soledad
Nuestra Señora de la Soledad — Carmel
San Antonio de Padua
San Miguel Arcángel — Paso Robles
San Luis Obispo de Tolosa — San Luis Obispo
La Purísima Concepción — Santa Maria
Santa Inés
Santa Bárbara — Santa Barbara
San Buenaventura — Ventura
San Fernando Rey de España — San Fernando
San Gabriel Arcángel — LOS ANGELES
San Juan Capistrano — San Juan Capistrano
San Luis Rey de Francia — San Luis Rey
San Diego de Alcalá — San Diego

Modern Highway U. S. 101

Original Route of the *Padres*

Acknowledgments

In preparing the original hard cover edition of this book, we were privileged to work closely with a number of experts on the California missions who helped us find our way through the maze of information and misinformation about this complex subject. We wish to express special appreciation to the one-and-only Harry Downie, veteran restorer of missions and a walking encyclopedia of mission fact and lore, who generously gave of his time to help us from start to finish of the book.

We also wish to acknowledge our gratitude to the eminent Father Maynard Geiger, O.F.M., and Dr. Edward Planer for their helpful criticisms of the manuscript and captions. In addition, we wish to thank the individuals at each of the missions who kindly checked manuscript and pictorial details.

Thanks are due to Dr. Rexford Newcomb for granting permission to adapt material from his classic book on mission architecture, *The Old Mission Churches and Historic Houses of California*, on pages 75, 132, 157, 189, 194, 252, 264, and 288. Special thanks also go to the following for their direct participation in compiling this work: John S. Weir, whose fine photographs form the core of the book; Henry T. Conserva, who prepared the draft for the appendix; Marian Goodman, who wrote the initial manuscript for the individual mission chapters; Richard Pik, whose line drawings grace the book; and Vance Jonson, whose color photographs of mission details appear on the first seven pages.

In the assembling of historical photographs, prints, and drawings, we gratefully acknowledge the help of Ruth I. Mahood, Robert Weinstein, Dr. George P. Hammond, Dr. John Barr Topkins, Jerry MacMullen, Joseph LaBarbera, Helen S. Giffen, Richard Dillon, Ralph Hansen, James Abajian, Howard Willoughby, and Mrs. Madie Brown for the loan of illustrative materials from their personal collections.

Contents

Portraits of the

The twenty-one missions depicted in the color section that follows are watercolor impressions by artist France Carpentier. The paintings were done to honor California's bicentennial of the establishment of the first mission, San Diego de Alcalá, in 1769.

Missions

1769-1770

TWO SPANISH OUTPOSTS 650 MILES APART

The beginning of the mission chain: two widely separated mission settlements established a year apart at the major ports of San Diego and Monterey. Between them lay an untracked wilderness peopled with hostile Indians.

SAN DIEGO DE ALCALÁ

Founded July 16, 1769. On Presidio Hill, overlooking the bay of San Diego, a handful of dedicated Spaniards established the first permanent settlement in California. In 1774, the mission was moved five miles up the San Diego Valley. The adobe church on the site today is a restoration of one dedicated in 1813.

SAN CARLOS BORROMEO DE CARMELO

*Founded June 3, 1770. Founded first at the presidio of Monterey, the mission was moved
to Carmel Valley the following year. Most beautiful of all the missions, today's Carmel Mission
church is the seventh in a series that began with a crude shelter of logs.*

1771-1772

THREE NEW MISSIONS LINK THE PORTS

With two missions established, the work of settling the frontier province could now proceed. The chosen sites for new missions radiated outward from San Diego and Monterey. The chain developed in two clusters: one in the north and one in the south.

SAN GABRIEL ARCÁNGEL

Founded September 8, 1771. It sat astride three well-traveled trails: two from Mexico to Alta California, and one from the East Coast of the United States to California.

SAN LUIS OBISPO DE TOLOSA

Founded September 1, 1772. Its simple, almost stark façade was restored to its original form in the 1930s. The clay roofing tiles devised by the padres to protect the mission from flaming arrows were said to be the first such tiles made in California.

SAN ANTONIO DE PADUA

Founded July 14, 1771. In its prime, it was the home of thirteen hundred Indians, who worked at a score of handicrafts, produced bountiful crops, and herded some 17,000 livestock.

1775-1776

A PROSPEROUS MISSION FOUNDED TWICE

Indian unrest caused a year's delay between dedication of the ground and the reciting of the founding service. During the interim, the mission bells were buried and the founding party took shelter in the presidio at San Diego.

SAN JUAN CAPISTRANO

Founded November 1, 1776; previously established October 30, 1775. In its prime, the mission was one of the most prosperous in the chain. Considered the oldest church in California, it is called "Father Serra's Church" because it holds one of two remaining chapels where he is known to have said Mass.

1776-1777

GUARDIANS OF SAN FRANCISCO BAY

A bay was discovered north of Monterey that was seen to be large enough to "hold all the ships of Spain." Plans were rapidly made for two new mission settlements to secure the strategic port against foreign colonizing or attack.

SAN FRANCISCO DE ASÍS

Founded June 29, 1776. Though founded as Mission San Francisco de Asís, it has long been known as Mission Dolores, so-named for a stream, the Arroyo de los Dolores, that fed a lake near the mission.

SANTA CLARA DE ASÍS

Founded January 12, 1777. After a delay of several months because of an Indian uprising at San Luis Obispo, the second of the missions to be founded to protect the great port of San Francisco was laid out on a site chosen by Juan Bautista de Anza about forty miles southeast of Mission Dolores.

SAN BUENAVENTURA

Founded March 31, 1782. It was the dream of Father Serra to establish three Channel missions, protected by a presidio, to bridge the gap between San Luis Obispo and San Gabriel, but he lived only long enough to preside over the founding of the first, San Buenaventura.

1782-1787

THE SANTA BARBARA CHANNEL MISSIONS

After a wait of several years, which allowed the existing missions to become self-supporting, the gap between the northern and southern clusters was closed by the opening of three new missions along the Santa Barbara Channel.

SANTA BÁRBARA

Founded December 4, 1786. Father Fermín Francisco de Lasuén established the noble landmark that today is called the "Queen of the Missions."

LA PURÍSIMA CONCEPCIÓN

Founded December 8, 1787. In a quiet, rural setting, La Purísima was a flourishing outpost where friendly Indians and energetic padres worked successfully together.

1791

TWO MORE LINKS IN THE CHAIN

As fast as supplies, soldiers, and missionaries arrived to support them,
new missions were founded to fill the gaps between existing settlements.
Where once there were only empty fields, great structures of adobe
and stone sprang up, built by the Indians under the padres' supervision.

SANTA CRUZ

Founded August 28, 1791. A modern replica of Mission Santa Cruz, about one-third the size of the original, stands as a reminder of the twelfth mission. Already weakened by several severe earthquakes, the original church collapsed following a devastating quake in 1857.

NUESTRA SEÑORA DE LA SOLEDAD

Founded October 9, 1791. When Father Lasuén dedicated the mission to Our Lady of Solitude in 1791, the members of the little company were the only figures to break the monotony of a treeless, sun-baked landscape.

SAN JOSÉ

Founded June 11, 1797. When the good news was received that the number of missions could be increased, four expeditions were dispatched in a search for suitable sites. The first site selected was a point northeast of San Jose from which Mission Dolores and Yerba Buena Island could be seen.

SAN JUAN BAUTISTA

Founded June 24, 1797. On a site selected only 13 days after the founding of Mission San Jose, a new mission was dedicated to John the Baptist. The town that grew up around it has become a shrine to the romantic past.

1797

FOUR MISSIONS IN ONE SUMMER

Able to draw upon the surplus foodstuffs produced by the operating
missions, more links were added to the chain. In the busy summer of
1797, four new missions got under way under the direction of the
energetic Father Lasuén.

....IN ONE SUMMER

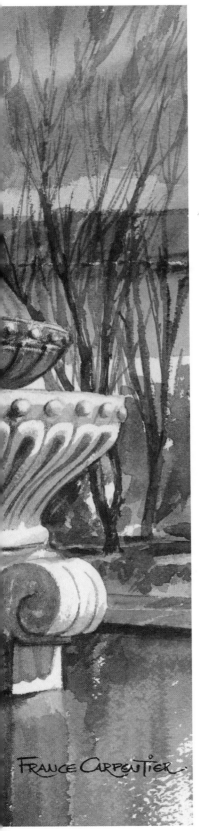

FRANCE CARPENTIER

SAN FERNANDO REY DE ESPAÑA

Founded September 8, 1797. Friendly Indians and the presence of four springs that flowed as if they would never run dry influenced the padres' decision to settle here.

SAN MIGUEL ARCÁNGEL

Founded July 25, 1797. The third mission founded in the summer months of 1797 filled in the long gap between San Antonio and San Luis Obispo.

1798-1804

THE LAST OF THE SOUTHERN MISSIONS

These two missions completed the chain between San Francisco and San Diego. The seventeen missions already established were at the height of their prosperity. The mission system appeared to be thriving.

SAN LUIS REY DE FRANCIA

Founded June 13, 1798. The last mission to be founded by Father Lasuén, San Luis Rey closed a critical gap between San Diego and San Juan Capistrano. One of the most extensive of the missions, its buildings covered nearly six acres and were arranged around a patio 500 feet square.

SANTA INÉS

Founded September 17, 1804. The nineteenth mission was favored with fertile lands excellent for crops and grazing. Its craft work was known and used throughout the province.

SAN RAFAEL ARCÁNGEL

Founded December 14, 1817. Illness and death that had plagued Mission Dolores for nearly forty years led to the founding of Mission San Rafael on a sunnier slope across San Francisco Bay.

1817-1823

THE TWO NORTHERNMOST MISSIONS
ENDED THE CHAIN

Within a few years of the founding of these two missions north of San Francisco, the orchards, herds, fields, and foodstocks that grew under the mission system disappeared into private hands as secularization of the missions progressed. Soon there was little left to indicate the prosperity and industry of the once-thriving settlements.

SAN FRANCISCO SOLANO

Founded July 4, 1823. Within sight of this mission, the last in the chain, the Bear Flag was raised in 1846, declaring the province a republic, independent of Mexico—it lasted about a month.

Last Outposts of Empire

Spaced along the California coast a stiff day's march apart, stand twenty-one mission churches, simple and massive structures of adobe and stone that draw more travelers to their mellowed cloisters than any other historical attraction in this tourist-minded state. Some of these old buildings are smothered in the metropolitan embrace, enclosed on all sides by the structures of a newer day. Others stand free in open valleys, still retaining some measure of the pastoral charm that was their original setting. Nearly all of them are merely token survivals of once-widespreading structures that were miniature cities in themselves, teeming with activity. Like shells found on the beach, the missions that stand in varying degrees of restoration seem washed up on the shores of time, the life within long since departed.

Perhaps best viewed in the gentle gold of predawn, the fiery afterglow of sundown or under the silver cast of the moon, the missions look their best when their harsh new surroundings are least visible or when the slick surfaces and rigid lines of restoration cannot be seen or sensed. Simple and forthright in design, the missions everywhere reveal the touch of the hands of men in the uneven textures of wall and roof, the whimsical variations in the span of arches marching down the arcades, and in the ingenuous decorations that wreathe windows and doorways. The solid proportions of pillar, arch, and wall convey a sense of permanence and shelter, reinforced by the simplicity of the building materials themselves—earth and stone, seashell mortar, trees and reeds, and rawhide bindings.

For one reason or another, the missions exert a spell over those who stroll through their gardens and cloisters. To some, the appeal is that of antiquity, for collectively these are the oldest historic relics along the Pacific shore of the United States. To others, the fascination is in seeing bits of old Europe transplanted into a raw young civilization. The massive tile-roofed churches remind

From the soil around them, the padres gathered the materials to build simply and honestly. The handsome old doorway at San Juan Bautista reveals mission hallmarks: simple forthright design and hand-textured workmanship.

the beholder that this land was once a remote colonial province of the mighty Spanish empire, established here in the dying days of its two and a half centuries of world dominion. To many viewers, the appeal lies in the visual evidence of what a handful of dedicated and resourceful men can create in a hostile wilderness sans adequate tools, artisans, or building materials. Some feel the poignancy of indoctrinating Native Americans with a Christian message and of introducing Indian tribes to a brief—and often bitter—taste of a more modern life. To the viewers who know the end of the story, the patched and dismembered mission quadrangles bear mute testimony to the despoliation of a prospering institution and the betrayal of the Indians once the hand of authority was lifted.

To the history-minded onlooker, the missions recall one final fact—the success of the missions as an institution not only sealed their doom with the covetous colonists who at the first opportunity seized the vast mission acreages, crops, herds, and manufactured goods; but it also sealed the fate of the whole colony as word of the mission prosperity seeped out to foreign nations. Trading vessels that had stopped to exchange merchandise for the raw materials produced by the missions carried home the word that here was a bountiful land, ably developed by the padres but poorly protected by an inadequate soldiery; in short, a prize ripe for plucking by the first nation to reach it with an adequate force. England and France had consuls in Monterey, and the United States maintained an unofficial representative there. But of the three nations that tried to get their hands on California, the United States got here first and wrested the land from the Spanish-Mexican colonists two years before the Gold Rush changed the course of western history.

It is perhaps one of the crowning ironies of history that the Spaniards who had unsuccessfully sought gold for two hundred and fifty years should have missed discovering the California bonanza by such a scant margin. Coloma, where Marshall found the historic flakes, is 90 miles from Sonoma, where the last mission was founded. Was California prevented from becoming a prosperous gold-supported province of the Spanish-Mexican complex, perhaps an independent Spanish-American nation in its own right, by a gap of only two years and a few miles? The question is one that challenges the imagination.

When Half the World Belonged to Spain

The story of the Spanish missions of California stretches back two hundred years before the first crude shelter was erected at San Diego in the summer of 1769.

In the 15th and 16th centuries, Spain dominated the New World. After recovering from a series of internal wars and power struggles, lasting for centuries, Spain became a unified nation under Ferdinand and Isabella. Having drained the surrounding lands of their wealth, the Spanish aristocracy, trained in warfare and imbued with crusading spirit, pushed back the rim of the known world to find new sources of wealth and luxury. Exploring parties ventured on uncharted seas in search of spices, silks, pearls, and precious metal. Wherever they found an abundance, they claimed the land in the name of the Crown. In due time colonies were planted to restrain the natives and to serve as depots for the accumulation of natural wealth for trans-shipment to Spain. Within a century, Spanish ambition had taken title to half the world, a fact that was recognized in 1493 by Pope Alexander VI, who divided the world into two parts, one assigned to Spain and the other to Portugal, her principal colonial rival.

Within its half, Spain aggressively pursued a colonial course that brought all of present-day Mexico, Central America, the Caribbean, half of South America, and much of the United States into her grasp, until by 1531 the Crown reigned over a vast global domain, covering a great deal more territory than that later governed by the British.

Spain's colonies were developed under a complex and clumsy system. Authority was centralized in the king and his counsellors in Spain and partly delegated to viceroys (vice-kings) who were appointed for one year at a time and were held responsible for civil, religious, and military affairs within vast overseas dominions. The planting of the missions in California was under the Viceroy of New Spain (Mexico), located in Mexico City. Since all transactions were conducted in writing, the governmental machinery operated with glacial slowness. Letters and requests sent from colonial outposts took months to make the round-trip to the viceroy and back, and if matters had to be referred to Madrid, a year or more was often consumed before a decision could be relayed to the patient petitioner. Well aware of the delays inherent in their communications, the Spaniards compensated by painstakingly working out plans for action well ahead of time. Exploring and colonizing ventures were usually provided with instructions that covered every conceivable contingency, down to the color of the cloth to be given to the Indians. In theory, the pioneers would have little need to refer problems to higher authority—all they had to do was consult their voluminous set of rules.

Colonial settlement was developed under close cooperation between the clergy and the military. In its first stages of take-over, an alien land was either reduced by the sword or the cross, or by both in combination. Sometimes, military invasion set the stage, as in Mexico, and the conquered land was later consolidated under the clergy and, ultimately, civil authority. In some areas, where the natives were known to be docile, the clergy opened the frontier with only a military escort for protection. This was the method used in establishing the colony in California.

A Great Dream Is Pigeonholed

Although Spain had claimed title to California long before the arrival of the missionaries in San Diego, the Crown had only authorized exploration of the sea coast, and very little was known about the land that was to become the last outpost of the empire.

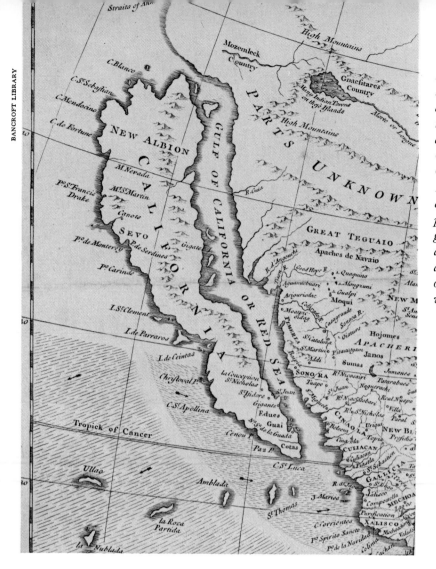

So little was known about California that it was mapped as an island as late as mid-18th century. Explorers had traveled partway up the western and eastern coasts of Baja (Lower) California and had assumed that the Gulf of California was a strait. Even after the island myth was disproved by explorations of several padres in the early 1700's, the Spanish government still mapped California as an island for several decades. The map at the left was published in England only 24 years before the first mission was founded in San Diego.

Two sea expeditions—one in 1542 and the other 60 years later—had sailed up the coast from New Spain in search of a shortcut to the Orient and to find suitable harbors and sites for colonizing, but neither party had made a systematic survey of the natural and human resources hidden behind the cliffs that lined the California shore. Both stopped briefly to take on water, repair storm damage, and communicate with the natives, but neither one discovered the great harbor of San Francisco concealed behind fogbound bluffs, and both contented themselves with recording observations about the coastline, charting water depths, and assigning saints' names to every topographical feature in sight.

One half-hearted attempt at colonizing came not from the Spaniards but from the English during this period. The famous explorer-pirate, Francis Drake, on his way home from a successful raid on Spanish treasure galleons, made port north of San Francisco to repair his storm-damaged ship in 1579. Impressed by the land, he claimed it for Queen Elizabeth and named it New England (Nova Albion). After his return to the British Isles, a colonizing party was dispatched to settle California; but the fleet was betrayed and dispersed by the Spanish off the coast of Brazil, and no further attempts were made by the English to take over the land.

Between the visit of the last Spanish sailing vessel in 1602 and the coming of the padres, California was largely ignored. Spanish treasure ships from Manila sailed past the coast once a year, but made no attempts to land, and no expeditions penetrated the unexplored interior. Plans to colonize the area were frequently advanced, and one almost got under way. The last explorer to land in California, Sebastián Vizcaíno, had described Monterey Bay in such glowing terms that every proposal for colonizing California in the next 160 years aimed at founding a settlement on the shores of this fine "sheltered" harbor. Vizcaíno himself was authorized to establish such a settlement, but his plan was shelved in 1611 and he was sent on a search for mythical islands near Japan. Over the decades, proposals, memoranda, reports, and letters recommending development of the northwestern province drifted into the Viceroy's files, where for various reasons they were firmly pigeonholed.

In the first place, the land was remote from the bases of supply in New Spain. Planting a settlement by ship was a dangerous and uncertain venture, and sending a colonizing party by land was fraught with hazard. No land routes existed, the hypothetical pathway was beset with hostile Indians, and the distance was so great that a small party would fall prey to Indian arrows before it could reach its destination and a large party would succumb to starvation because it would be unable to live off the barren land through which it would have to pass. Further, whether approached by land or sea, the task would be costly, and in the declining years of the Spanish empire, the government was reluctant to underwrite any venture that did not offer a good return on the money invested in it. California's riches were unknown, and neither private nor royal capital was likely to be spent to find out what was there. Legendary wealth, such as the Seven Cities of Cíbola that had lured earlier generations of conquistadores, no longer mesmerized the frugal Spaniards of the late 16th century.

Thus, the latent riches of California and the simple life of its inhabitants were left untouched for a century and a half after the last European stepped ashore at Monterey. In this interval, Spanish settlements were being founded east of the mountains in present-day Arizona, Texas, and New Mexico, and English colonies were springing up on the opposite shore of the continent, but California slumbered undisturbed.

But this peaceful twilight came to an abrupt end. The change was signalled innocently enough by the arrival of a pair of white-sailed ships and two dusty caravans in San Diego in the year 1769.

The Precarious Beginnings of California

On a day late in June in 1769, a straggling packtrain led by a doughty little friar on a mule picked its way slowly along the marshy shore of San Diego bay. As the procession filed up and down the gullied shoreline, they could catch occasional glimpses of the blue water of the landlocked bay and the masts of two ships anchored offshore. Ahead lay the end of a long march and the beginning of a dream. Unknown to the party, there also awaited them a struggle with disease, starvation, and death that would try their souls.

The friar on muleback was Father Junípero Serra, a man destined to go down in history as the founder of California and in the annals of his Church as a man of saintly attainments. Born in Mallorca, Spain, in 1713, he had already served the Christian cause for many years as a brilliant teacher, a devout missionary, and a skilled administrator. He had been chosen by his government to serve as head of the missions in Baja California, which had just been transferred from the Jesuits to his order, the Franciscans. He had hardly had time to begin his new responsibilities when the newer assignment reached him. He was ordered to turn over Baja to other hands and to assist in the founding of a new settlement to the north in Alta California. Although his superiors protested the assignment, Serra welcomed it as the opportunity for which he had longed all his life, to bring the Christian message to the unenlightened.

As he jogged toward San Diego bay, he joyfully looked forward to a reunion with the other members of the colonizing party with whom the great work would be accomplished. "Thanks be to God," he wrote his close friend Fr. Palóu, "I arrived here at the Port of San Diego. It is beautiful to behold, and does not belie its reputation. Here I met all who had set out before me whether by sea or by land—but not the dead."

The sight that met his eyes was saddening—and profoundly discouraging—for of those who had left New Spain a few months before, only a small number were alive, many of them having succumbed to scurvy on the long voyage from La Paz. By the time Serra's party arrived, all but two of the crew of one ship had died and all the sailors on the other were ill. More than a third of the individuals who had reached San Diego three months before had died and most of the remainder were ill. The little encampment was virtually a hospital.

In the face of this tragic situation, plans so carefully made some months earlier had to be re-examined. The little group now stranded so far from aid and reinforcement, was utterly on its own and in a desperate state to carry out its mission, let alone survive. The sailors' dread disease was endangering the whole project. This little-understood affliction that rotted the gums and affected joints and muscles had a high mortality rate. A scourge of the seaways for centuries, it was accepted as a grim but unavoidable hazard of the sailors' life, and its simple prevention and cure by adding fresh fruit and vegetables to the diet was not widely known at the time of the founding of San Diego. Besides, there were no fruits or vegetables in San Diego.

"To Guard the Dominion from Insult and Injury"

The great project now hanging in the balance had been launched auspiciously as the culmination of a long-held dream. Following the discovery of Alta California and the mapping of its two principal ports, San Diego and Monterey, 160 years previously, the missionary orders had clamored for aid and permission to found missions at the two ports. But the Viceroy was not to be interested. Indeed, upper California might never have been settled by the Spaniards had it not been menaced by a foreign power—Czarist Russia.

Russian fur traders and explorers had poked in and out of the inlets along the Alaskan coast between 1740 and 1765, and the Czarina had ordered the establishment of colonies on the eastern shores of the Bering Sea. In quest of seals, the Russian fur trappers worked their way down the coast and set up temporary outposts as far south as the Farallon Islands off San Francisco. Word of the Russian actions and intentions filtered to Madrid, and countermeasures were ordered "to guard the dominions from all invasion and insult."

Plans for colonizing Alta California were dusted off. Twin expeditions by land and sea were to be sent from a base in Baja California to colonize the port of Monterey. The port of San Diego, discovered and mapped in 1542 by the Columbus of California, Juan Rodríguez Cabrillo, was selected as an intermediate stopping point, halfway between Monterey and Loreto in Baja California. A combination of soldiers and settlers was to be dispatched to hold the country and missionaries were to convert the Indians.

Under the direction of the King's personal agent in New Spain, Inspector-General José de Gálvez, the detailed plans for the expedition were drawn. Leadership of the project was assigned to a Catalonian soldier of noble rank, Don Gaspár de Portolá, who had recently been appointed governor of Baja California. Since there was little in Baja to govern, Portolá was delighted to lead the party as an escape from what amounted to virtual political exile. Under him, in charge of the missionaries, was Father Serra, relieved of his presidency of the Baja missions to supervise this more important work.

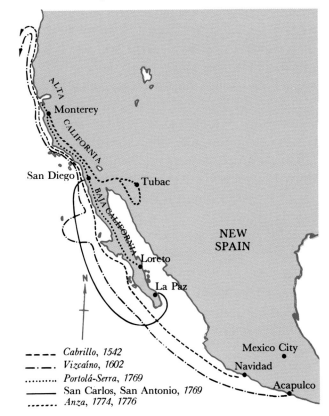

The lines of supply stretched a long, long way from remote California to the home bases in New Spain (Mexico). Whether reached by land or sea, the northern outpost was weeks and months away from relief. Land parties had to travel through arid country, held by hostile natives. Sea parties braved storms, adverse winds, and the terrors of scurvy. The faraway colony in Alta California had to become self-supporting or perish.

- - - - Cabrillo, 1542
- · - · - Vizcaíno, 1602
· · · · · · Portolá-Serra, 1769
———— San Carlos, San Antonio, 1769
- - - - - Anza, 1774, 1776

The group was divided into four parties with San Diego as a common destination. Two were to go by land, two by sea. After several months of preparation the first contingent left in the packet *San Carlos*, which sailed out of La Paz January 7, 1769, with soldiers and supplies on board. A month later, a second vessel, the *San Antonio*, embarked for Alta California; and as matters turned out, it sailed into San Diego bay 17 days before the first ship arrived. Both encountered perpetual headwinds—the *San Carlos* was blown 200 leagues off course by one storm—and both captains were misled by faulty charts that placed San Diego 100 miles above its actual location. Both ships made landfalls near San Pedro. The *San Antonio* found its way to port in a few days, but the unfortunate *San Carlos* wandered up the coast as far as Point Conception, turned back, and eventually reached San Diego after 110 days at sea.

A third ship, the *San José*, was crammed full of supplies and dispatched northward in June, but it ran into trouble and returned after three months at sea. It set sail again the following spring, loaded with ten thousand pounds of dried meat, eight casks of good wine, two casks of brandy, twelve hundred and fifty pounds of dried figs, many bushels of beans, quantities of raisins and dried fish, with a church bell, vestments for the padres, and trading materials for the Indian converts. These supplies, so desperately needed by the struggling colony, never reached San Diego. After it left La Paz, the ship was never heard from.

The two land expeditions departed after the ships had left. The first one set out from El Rosario on Good Friday, 1769. Under Captain Rivera and accompanied by Fr. Juan Crespí, diarist of the expedition, the packtrain of 180 mules and 500 domestic animals headed north to San Diego, 350 miles away. The party of leatherjackets and Christian Indians made its way slowly up the peninsula, which Fr. Crespí described as "sterile, arid, lacking grass and water, and abounding in stones and thorns." Two months later, minus most of the Indians who had either died or deserted en route, the party reached San Diego.

The fourth and final contingent under Captain Portolá and Father Serra left in mid-May. Along the way, they stopped at the mission settlements in Baja to pick up supplies for Alta California. As Portolá remembered it, "In consideration of the great deserts into which I was going, and of the Russian hunger with which I foresaw we were going to contend, I was obliged to seize everything I saw as I passed through those poor missions, leaving them, to my keen regret, scantily provided for." The party soon ran out of food and "as a result," Portolá wrote, "some of the Indians died, and the rest of them deserted from natural necessity." The remainder lived off the land, subsisting on game and fish, and reached San Diego on July 1. Portolá rode on ahead when they were within a day's march and left the contingent in Serra's hands.

Although now united, the California expedition was in a sorry state. Of the 219 individuals who had made up the original contingents only half had reached Alta California. Many had deserted on the way and a quarter had died. The doleful situation would have discouraged a less stout-hearted soldier than Portolá, but he was not the man to be deflected from fulfilling his orders. The Viceroy expected him to plant a colony at Monterey Bay, and plant it he would.

When the San Carlos *left La Paz for California in 1769, flags were broken
out and cannon roared a farewell salute. The ill-fated voyage took 110 days
to reach San Diego and lost all but two of the crew to scurvy. In ensuing years,
she shuttled back and forth between Alta and Baja California carrying supplies.
She was the first ship to sail into the great harbor of San Francisco.*

First, though, help had to be secured for the weakened colony. The *San Antonio* was ordered to return to San Blas with a report on conditions in San Diego and to bring back badly needed supplies. The ship sailed with a crew of eight, all that remained alive of its original complement of twenty-eight, and eventually arrived in San Blas with only two living souls aboard!

A few days after the ship sailed, Portolá assembled a small company of "skeletons who had been spared by scurvy, hunger, and thirst" and set off overland to guess their way to Monterey through uncharted wilderness.

Shortly after Portolá's party left, on July 16, 1769, Father Serra triumphantly raised the cross on the site of the first mission in California. On the slope of a hill overlooking the tranquil bay, he sang High Mass and preached a sermon before the handful of survivors. He dedicated the mission to St. Didacus of Alcalá, a Franciscan friar who had been sainted in 1588. The few Indians who watched at a distance were suspicious and cautious. They were probably faintly aware that these strange ceremonies, conducted by men who had arrived in "floating houses" or ridden on the backs of animals never before seen in this land, somehow meant drastic changes in their timeless way of life.

The natives did not respond to the appeals of the padres to enter the mission life, but they eagerly accepted all the gifts of beads and clothing that were offered them. Food they refused because they reasoned it was the cause of the illness in camp. They mingled freely with the settlers, observing their activities with rapt attention. At length, their curiosity satisfied, they became increasingly bold. They ignored the exhortations of the padres and reportedly resorted to thievery even taking blankets off the sick. A small boarding party rafted out to the *San Carlos,* still anchored in the bay, and attempted to make off with the sails. The nuisance campaign soon erupted into an attack on the weakened colony that was repulsed with the death of three natives and one Spaniard. As a protection against further assaults, the soldiers built a stockade around the thatch-roofed missions and forbade the Indians to enter. An uneasy truce prevailed.

The Myth of Monterey Bay

While the colony was nursing its sick, burying its dead, and keeping a wary eye on recalcitrant natives, Governor Portolá was struggling through "rocks, brushwood, and rugged mountains covered with snow" on his way to Monterey. Foodless, lost most of the time, the party took thirty-eight days to reach the long-sought harbor but did not recognize it from the description of its discoverer, Sebastián Vizcaíno.

Vizcaíno had been sent on an expedition in 1602 to find ports of refuge for the Manila galleons, which sailed past California on the final leg of their seven months' voyage from the Philippines, and to discover sites for colonial settlement. A man of ability and courage, Vizcaíno was also one of lively imagination, as history later proved. He was greatly impressed by Monterey Bay, which he discovered and named for his Viceroy, the Conde de Monterey, but he described it in such exaggerated terms that Portolá walked right by it.

Those who are today familiar with the wide open arc of Monterey Bay or who have seen a storm lash the exposed fishing fleet anchored there will wonder at Vizcaíno's description of it as a fine *sheltered* port. He wrote: "We found ourselves to be in the best port that could be desired, for besides being sheltered from all the winds, it has many pines for masts and yards, and live oaks and white oaks, and water in great quantity, all near the shore." Portolá found the pines and oaks all right, but the open roadstead certainly did not match Vizcaíno's repeated references to it as "very secure against all winds." Certain he had missed it, Portolá nevertheless erected a large cross on the shore of the unrecognized bay and put up another near Carmel, where it could easily be seen from the sea. The cross at Monterey bore the dour inscription: "the overland expedition from San Diego returned from this place . . . starving."

Disappointed, the party turned back, subsisting for the last 12 days on their pack animals at the rate of one barbecued mule a day, which they ate "like hungry lions." After six weeks they reached San Diego, "smelling frightfully of mules," to be chided by Father Serra for missing Monterey. "You come from Rome," he complained to Portolá, "and you did not see the pope!"

If conditions were crucial before Portolá left on his six-months' trip, they now became more desperate as time wore on. The Governor ordered Captain

Rivera to return to the south and bring back a pack-train of supplies. Absence of these men reduced the drain on the dwindling food supply, but there was little to go around, and the colonists waited anxiously for the supply ship *San José*, unaware that she had been lost at sea.

For seven months the survivors waited for relief, and finally Portolá announced abandonment of the project and ordered preparations for a return to Baja. The missionaries protested the decision and vowed to remain on their own, even if the rest of the party returned. They prayed for the arrival of a vessel, and on the eve of the day of departure, their prayers were answered. The *San Antonio* sailed into the bay amid great rejoicing with a cargo of rice, beans, and flour.

With the colony saved from disaster, Portolá and Serra completed plans for moving on to their grand objective, the Port of Monterey, which they were now convinced was the harbor where Portolá had planted a cross. Portolá took a small party overland and Serra, having turned the San Diego Mission over to two other padres, followed a few days later on board the *San Antonio*. When Portolá's group reached Monterey, they hastened to the cross they had erected the previous winter. To their astonishment they found it surrounded with a strange array of articles: meat, shellfish, feathers, arrows stuck in the ground, and a string of sardines. The Indians had observed the reverence with which the Spaniards held the cross and had made propitiatory offerings to their gods.

The *San Antonio* anchored in the bay a week after Portolá's arrival, and at last, on June 3, 1770, the dramatic scene took place that history had so long postponed. In keeping with the august importance of the event, the ceremonies were conducted with all the pomp and pageantry that the group could improvise. To the wondering Indians, shyly watching from the woods, the display of power and glory was awe-inspiring and troubling. Bells were hung and blessed and an altar erected under an oak tree that Vizcaíno had used as a setting for services held in 1602. On the altar was placed the statue of the Virgin (now in the Carmel Mission) which had been given to the expedition by the Viceroy and had been used in the dedication of Mission San Diego. The uniformed troops and sailors formed a hollow square facing the altar, and Father Serra consecrated the site of the new mission and dedicated it to St. Charles of Borromeo. Throughout the services, volleys of musketry and the booming of cannon on the *San Antonio* served in lieu of musical accompaniment. The devout padre delivered an eloquent sermon and when he was finished, Governor Portolá ceremonially claimed the land for the Crown.

The formalities completed, the party at once set to building a presidio and a mission. Within a month, the royal fortress and a mission structure of earth and poles were completed. The fort was armed with a few cannon and staffed with a small garrison of leatherjackets. His job completed, Portolá turned the reins of authority over to Lieutenant Don Pedro Fages, and set sail for Mexico in the *San Antonio*. When the news of the occupation of Monterey reached Mexico City, bells of the great cathedral heralded the welcome tidings—certain bells never rung except upon occasions of joy and thanksgiving—and these chimes were answered as was the custom by the bells of all the other churches.

The Missions Get Under Way

With the two missions established in San Diego and Monterey, the work of settling the frontier province could now proceed. Father Serra, designated as Father-President of the missions, and Don Pedro Fages, appointed provincial Governor, set to work on the task of colonizing additional territory between the widely separated outposts.

It was a back-breaking, discouraging task, complicated by insufficient supplies, bureaucratic red tape (of which the Spanish government had an abundance), conflicts in authority between religious and civil agencies, and the uncertain state of the Indians who could at any time have turned upon the newcomers and driven them into the sea. Nevertheless, under the protection of the military and with the assistance of capable missionaries and artisans, Serra managed to establish nine thriving missions before he died in 1784. His able successors added twelve more to the chain before the mission period drew to a close.

It was obvious at the start that more missions would have to be established if the colony were to survive, let alone succeed. Two missions 650 miles apart could hardly make much of an impression on the estimated 100,000 natives in Alta California. The settlements were too remote from each other to maintain contact, for between them lay an untracked wilderness inhabited with Indians who could waylay messengers or attack supply trains. The padres were forbidden to leave the mission compound without armed escort.

Furthermore, the padres and their protective guard were not in themselves good colonizing agents. Barely able to support themselves off the land, they were incapable of expanding the outposts without the help of colonists or converted natives who could cultivate crops and tend livestock in the volume needed to make a colony truly self-supporting. In time, hundreds of Native Americans would be trained to these tasks, but the time required to teach them rendered this prospect years in the future.

The equation was simple; more missions were needed to convert the Indians and to support a frontier colony. But more missions required more priests, artisans, soldiers, and more equipment and foodstuffs. Existing means of supply were inadequate to maintain a large colony. Alta California was literally months

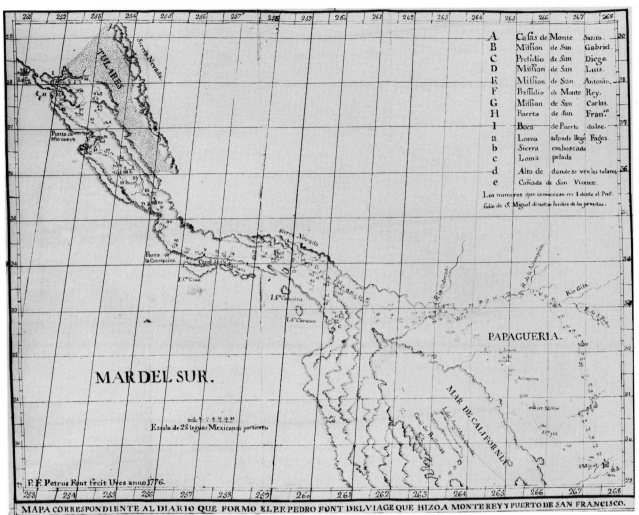

MAPA CORRESPONDIENTE AL DIARIO QUE FORMO EL P.F. PEDRO FONT DEL VIAGE QUE HIZO A MONTEREY Y PUERTO DE SAN FRANCISCO.

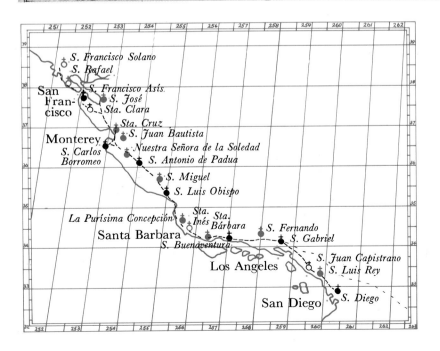

Earliest contemporary map of the missions and the El Camino Reál (*the King's Highway*) was drawn by Fr. Pedro Font, diarist of the Anza overland expedition, who left this record of the province in 1776.

At the time, only six missions were in operation, but sites had been chosen for subsequent foundings. Within 47 years, 15 more missions were established. Father-Presidents Serra and Lasuén each founded 9, and their successors, 3.

Founder	Period
Fr. Serra	Pre-1776
	1777-1784
Fr. Lasuén	1785-1803
Others	1804-1823

El Camino Reál -----

away from the nearest base in New Spain, and yet for years the settlers were precariously dependent on imported materials. Famine twice struck the province when foodstocks ran low, once at the beginning in San Diego and again in 1772, when only a massive bear hunt near San Luis Obispo kept the Monterey and San Antonio missions from starving to death.

Cargo ships were too small (under 200 tons) to carry more than a few months' rations in their holds. At the mercy of the weather, they were often blown off course and delayed for weeks, and sometimes they were never heard from after they sailed from New Spain. The land route also presented formidable obstacles. The long overland trail that ran 800 leagues down the spine of Baja passed through a continuous wasteland, lacking in water and grass to sustain large pack trains. Father Serra calculated that supplying Alta California would take 1,500 mules, more than the known mule population in all the northern provinces of New Spain! Baja itself was too poor in natural and cultivated foodstuffs to serve as a source of food for the northern colony, and the impoverished missions there could spare nothing from their meager stocks. Furthermore, the route passed through the homeland of Indian tribes that would not take long to acquire a taste for the cargo carried by the plodding caravans. Not until 1774, when a new overland route from the east was pioneered by Juan Bautista de Anza, was it considered possible to satisfy all the needs of the colony by packtrain.

One Mission—Two Masters

In addition to the critical problems of supply, the Father-President and the Governor had to cope with a confusion of authority that hampered the development of the missions. Officially, the entire project was authorized by the Visitador-General, Gálvez, and all the leaders were responsible to him. It was he who ordered the Franciscans to establish missions in Alta California, and his civil representative in the province, the Governor, was technically the superior of Father Serra in all matters except the spiritual. But the dividing line between spiritual and civil matters in the operation of a chain of missions was sometimes razor-thin, and the possibility of friction existed from the start. Under the first governor, Don Gaspár de Portolá, affairs ran smoothly because of his tact and understanding. But under his less-than-diplomatic successors, disputes arose.

The principal source of irritation was the unrestrained conduct of the soldiers, who were responsible solely to the Governor. Although many of the soldiers were reputable men who later helped in the development of California, most of them were a brutish lot, recruited from the lower levels of New Spain, many of them jailbirds, and their pursuit of the Indian women caused continual unrest and occasional armed conflict with the native men, crippling the efforts of the missionaries to attract converts. The Governor was unable to discipline the guards, and the padres had no authority over them, and the baleful conflict hampered one mission after another. Partly to separate the Indians from the presidial garrisons, the Monterey Mission was moved five miles to a new site

Military operations centered in the presidios (forts), such as the one at
San Francisco sketched in 1816 by Louis Choris. Each was enclosed by a high
wall of logs and adobe; each mounted 6 or 8 brass cannon, housed a small
garrison of leatherjackets. Mission guards were under commanders of four
military districts, headquartered at the presidios.

on the Carmel River and San Diego was moved six miles upriver from its original site.

Bickering even occurred over the authority for establishing new missions. The Governor, for instance, refused to permit Serra to found a mid-point mission at Ventura, even though it was to have been founded at the same time as San Diego and Monterey, because he could not spare troops for a garrison. Thus, the two padres, corporal's guard, and all the goods consigned to the middle mission were held at another mission for ten years before the Commandant would permit the founding. The Governor took the position that the Indians throughout Alta California could not be trusted to remain peaceful indefinitely, and an effective defensive force was essential for the protection and success of each mission. Some of Serra's superiors agreed with the Governor and chided the zealous padre for over-eagerness. The Governor of the two Californias wrote sternly that Serra's "vehement desire to establish missions additional to those of San Diego and Monterey was, in the dearth of troops, nothing less than the temptation of the evil one."

The question of authority went all the way to the top via voluminous correspondence, memorials, petitions, and reports. In time, Father Serra became so vexed by the interference that he journeyed to Mexico City to present his case personally to the Viceroy. He found the latter receptive, won his points, and departed for Alta California with the promise of supplies and men for five new missions and a commitment that the Governor would be replaced. Unfortunately, the replacement later proved to be more of a nuisance than the man replaced.

Rapid Growth of the Mission Chain

When the way was finally cleared to complete the chain of missions, new ones were founded as fast as supplies, soldiers, and missionaries arrived to support them. Being dependent on shipping, the first missions were located near the ocean. The chosen sites radiated outward from the two major ports, San Diego and Monterey, and the chain developed in two clusters, one in the north, the other in the south. The discovery of San Francisco Bay at the time of the founding of the Monterey colony caused it to be selected as a site for two strategic settlements to hold it against enemy attack.

After a wait of several years, which allowed the existing missions to become self-supporting, the gap between the northern and southern clusters was closed by the opening of three new missions along the Santa Barbara Channel. From then on, at widely spaced time intervals, new missions were founded to close the gaps between existing establishments. Able to draw upon the surplus foodstuffs produced by the operating missions, the new ones were no longer dependent on waterborne supplies, and they were built farther and farther inland.

Actually, Spanish settlements never did penetrate deeply into Alta California, and the mission chain was confined to a strip of coastal valleys. In time, the mission authorities felt enough confidence in the self-sufficiency of the settlements to plan for a second string far inland in the great Central Valley. Explorations were made and sites chosen and mapped for the additional group, but political upheavals prevented their founding.

During the years of growth, the reins of top authority changed hands without affecting the development of the missions. Upon the death of Father Serra in 1784, the building of the mission chain soon fell to his successor as Father-President, Fermín Lasuén. An extremely able man, well liked by all who knew him, Fr. Lasuén had already distinguished himself in administering missions beset with problems. He had revitalized a run-down mission in Baja before being ordered north, and after arriving in Alta California, he had successfully operated in turn two missions—San Gabriel and San Diego—that had been plagued by Indian troubles. As Father-President, Lasuén carried forward Serra's great dream with skill and energy. Though outshone in history by the greater light of Father Serra, Lasuén is considered by some authorities to have been every bit as dedicated and capable as Serra—indeed, there are a few historians who consider him the greater man of the two. Be that as it may, he came into the picture when the tasks of the Father-President had changed. The pioneering days were over and nine missions were already in operation. Before Lasuén died 18 years later, he added nine more to the chain, and as the number increased, the job of administering them became progressively more complex. The task called for a man with executive and administrative ability—qualities that Lasuén had in abundance. Like Serra, Lasuén died in harness, at the age of 67. He was buried in 1803 alongside his illustrious predecessor in the Carmel Mission.

For a total of 34 years, these two men had controlled the destiny of the California missions. In the remaining 31 years before secularization, the chain was administered by a half dozen capable successors—notably Frs. Tápis and Durán—but none of them approached the stature of this pair.

And so it was that over a span of half a century, the New World representatives of the Spanish King planted a chain of twenty missions on this coast and the Mexicans added one more before the end of the mission era. The Indians who had lived here for 10,000 years had not asked to have these settlements established on their ancestral lands, nor had they requested the gray-robed padres to bring them the word about a new God. They had had intimations that their way of life might someday change. Some had seen the tall-masted ships sail down the coast, some had actually met the white man in his resplendant raiment, and many had heard tales carried over the mountains from the east about his fearsome weapons, his horses, and his cruel ways of dealing with Indians.

As the Indians watched the industrious colonists fashion their settlements and observed their fellows coming under the spell of the new life growing up around the missions, the seers among them must have sensed that this was the beginning of the end for their age-old way of life. For several thousand natives, life was fated to change drastically. For some, it would be better than before; for many others, worse.

What was the existence of California's Native Americans like before the advent of the missionaries? And just what kind of an institution was "The Mission" that the newcomers introduced into the fabric of Indian life? Answers to these two questions help to reveal the true significance of the mellowed old relics standing today in modern California.

California Native American Culture

The Indians whom the padres encountered may well have seemed the most unpromising of prospects for conversion. Short of stature, swarthy and unkempt by European standards, they were living a life far different from the Spaniards. The men went naked, although the women were clothed "with becoming modesty" in knee-length smocks of deerskin.

For diet the tribes lived off the land. Along the coast, they ate shellfish, shore birds, and small game, or feasted on the carcasses of dead whales that occasionally washed ashore. Inland, they lived on small game, birds, and acorns. Capable hunters with bow and arrow, they stalked deer and smaller game, but they would not kill bears (evil omen) or coyotes (considered poisonous). They ate insects,

*Many of the California tribes practiced cremation. When an Indian died, his
body and all his personal effects were consumed in a blazing fire.*

occasionally as a delicacy, sometimes as emergency rations when other sources
of food were low.

California's Native Americans have often been criticized because they lived
idly, not stirring themselves to raise crops, herd flocks, or practice other disciplined forms of food production characteristic of other cultures. However, in a
land that offered ample game and great natural orchards of oaks, there was no
need to develop more sophisticated forms of food supply, and it was little wonder that this bountiful land was crowded with more Indians per square mile
than any other part of what is now the United States. Over the centuries the
natives had evolved a sensible pact with nature and they were able to support
themselves off the land with great success. Ironically, the Spaniards, who
looked down upon the more unwordly natives, suffered famines after they first
settled in the same environment when their imported foodstuffs failed to
arrive on time.

The Indians had no written language and no forms of political organization.
Although they indulged in brief, bloody raids on neighboring villages, they had

no concepts of organized warfare. Their religious concepts were linked to basic natural phenomena, but were unusually complex and subtle, as sometimes occurs in primitive societies that do not have to struggle to supply their daily needs.

As a group they were generally quite healthy. Among the 4,771 adult Indians first baptized at the Santa Bárbara Mission, the padres were able to find only 30 cases of chronic disease, blindness, lameness, or mental illness. The Indians entrusted their health to the quackery of medicine men and the use of home remedies, derived from roots, herbs, and berries, that were sometimes more effective than those brought by the Spanish doctors. At least three remedies first used by the California Indians have found their way into the Pharmacopoeia.

Unfortunately, the natives had no natural immunity against the white man's diseases, and simple childhood ailments such as measles and chickenpox swept through the villages, killing hundreds. Some of the Indian graveyards at the missions contain the tightly packed bones of thousands of Indians who died in such epidemics. In addition, venereal disease brought in by the soldiers and sailors in later years also killed hundreds.

The Indians lived in villages, located near streams, the ocean, or groves of live oaks. Their homes were formed of brush or tules, bent and tied to form conical or hemispherical shelters; and when these became too filthy or verminous, the Indians cleaned house by simply burning the hut to the ground.

Unfamiliar with metals, they fashioned all their weapons, tools, and appliances from stone, bone, and wood. Fine baskets, especially those made by the coastal tribes, were so tightly woven that they would hold water. Along the channel off Santa Barbara, the Indians built plank boats, precisely joined, well caulked, and sewn together with fiber, that have been judged the finest boats made by the Indians in the United States. These vessels could hold ten or twelve passengers and were rowed over the open sea with great speed.

One feature of Indian village life was the *temescal*, or sweat house, a kind of early-day sauna. A men-only institution, the temescal was an airtight structure in which a fire was kept burning, and where the men would gather inside to work up a sweat. When they were perspiring heavily they would run out and dash into the ocean, lake, or stream. This practice was considered a cure for many ailments—and it did prevent certain skin diseases—but its use by the panicky Indians as a cure for measles helped to increase the death toll from this disease.

Basically individualistic, many of California's Native Americans resisted the highly organized life of the mission. Some refused to listen to the padres' appeals, fought mission guards, or harrassed Indians who had already accepted Christianity. Even those who accepted the mission way of life sometimes rebelled against their stern regimentation within the compound and attempted to escape to their villages. In the first five years of the first five missions, only 491 infants had been baptized, 462 members enrolled, and 62 marriages performed (less than 3 per year per mission). Conversion of the Indian was no easy matter for the dedicated padres.

In their prime, the missions were miniature cities that housed, fed, clothed, and occupied Indians by the hundreds. Where once there were only empty fields and quiet hills, great rambling buildings sprang up, built from the earth by the natives under the padres' supervision. As at Mission La Purísima, the church with its belltower was only one part of a complex of buildings that contained shops, offices, warehouses, living quarters, infirmaries, and cooking and dining facilities.

The Meaning of the Missions

The missions that the visitor strolls through today offer little visible evidence of the importance that they once held in the life of California. Fully restored missions, such as La Purísima, convey some idea of the immense amount of activity that took place in a busy mission, but even here the visitor has to read into the exhibits more than meets the eye to appreciate fully the meaning of the missions in history.

The mission was much more than the adobe chapel and workshops that many people mistakenly assume to be the whole mission. It was a colonial institution of great importance in the spread of the Spanish Empire of the 15th to 17th centuries, which reached its final hour in the twenty-one missions of California. Along with the presidio (fort) and the pueblo (town), the mission was one of the three major agencies used by Spain to extend its borders and consolidate its colonial territories. In California, as in many other parts of the empire, it was the most important single agency, far outweighing the other two.

Although without question the primary purpose of the mission system in the eyes of the padres who served it was to spread Christian doctrine among the Indians, to the government that paid for it, its true values were usually political. As the distinguished historian of the California missions, Father Engelhardt, put it, perhaps a bit sweepingly: "The men who presumed to guide the destinies of Spain cared not for the success of Religion or the welfare of its ministers except in so far as both could be used to promote political schemes." It is highly significant that the establishment of missions in California, urged by the clergy for 150 years, was not authorized until the threat of foreign invasion by Czarist Russia prompted the government to find the money to pay for the troops, supplies, and personnel and to send the expeditions northward that founded California.

Spain had learned in the 250 years of its colonial adventure that the mission offered one of the most economical means of settling a new territory. A mission was inexpensive to launch—one or two padres, a handful of soldiers, and a load of supplies—and once established, it soon became self-supporting and later served as the nucleus for permanent settlement. It was also economical in the need for Spanish colonizers. As historian Herbert E. Bolton pointed out, "Spain laid claim to the lion's share of the two Americas, but her population was small and little of it could be spared to people the New World. On the other hand, her colonial policy, equalled in humanitarian principles by that of no other country, perhaps, looked to the preservation of the natives, and to their elevation to at least a limited citizenship. Lacking the Spaniards to colonize the frontier, she would colonize it with aborigines. Such an ideal called not only for the subjugation and control of the natives, but their civilization as well. To bring this end about the rulers of Spain made use of the religious and humanitarian zeal of the missionaries, choosing them to be to the Indians not only preachers, but also teachers and disciplinarians. To the extent that this work succeeded it became possible to people the frontier with civilized natives, and thus to supply the lack of colonists. This desire was quite in harmony with the religious aims of the friars, who found temporal discipline indispensable to the best work in Christianization."

The missions were characteristically frontier institutions; that is, they were intended to be temporary. As soon as their work was finished, the missionaries were expected to move on to fresh fields. Legally, each mission was expected to complete its assignment in ten years, by which time the natives would be sufficiently civilized to run a pueblo, subject to civil law and under the spiritual guidance of the regular clergy. Where the tribes were culturally advanced before the Spaniards arrived, as in Mexico, Central America, and Peru, such a turn over was practical. But along the northern frontier, especially in California, the tribal cultures were too primitive to be advanced to semi-civilization within such a short time, and at none of the twenty-one missions were the Indians ready to take over their own affairs when the order came through to secularize the missions after sixty-five years of missionary rule, although many individual Indians had been settled on mission lands by the padres.

As an arm of the State, the missions derived their chief financial support from government funds. By the time the California missions were founded, however, the government was running low on capital funds, and the money was appropriated from a large private endowment known as the Pious Fund, which had been established in Baja California by the Jesuits and taken over by the government when they were banished. An annual stipend in goods of $300 to $400 was sent to each padre. In addition, the State paid the expenses of the military cadres posted at each mission and the presidial forces.

At the start, each new mission received a grant of $1,000 from the Pious Fund to purchase bells, tools, seeds, vestments, and other needs. In addition, the established missions nearby were expected to donate breeding stock, fowl, grain, seeds, cuttings, wine, or whatever else could be spared. The mission properties were held in trust by the padres for the Indians, to whom they were expected to revert when the Indians were sufficiently civilized to run them. Although some of the missions amassed considerable wealth thanks to skillful administration of the crops and herds, none of the profits from the transactions ever accrued to the padres, who had no financial stake whatsoever in the economic

*When the Spanish round-the-world voyage of Alejandro Malaspina stopped
in Monterey in 1791, two years before work on the present church was begun,
the mission was then 20 years old, had thatch-roofed church and monastery.
The Indians lived in ranchería of brush huts west of the mission.*

life of the missions. Also, detailed accounts of the economic dealings of the
mission's receipts and expenditures were sent to the nearest presidio commander.

As one of its basic purposes, the mission was expected to civilize and educate
the native. In frontier areas where the Indians were amenable to education,
schools were established and the Indians were taught to read and write Spanish.
Originally, the intent had been to educate the natives in their own language, but
the padres encountered a babel of dialects—there were six distinct languages
between Sonoma and San Diego and each language had a number of dialects—
all of them inadequate to accommodate the concepts of modern life and the tenets
of Christianity. The native vocabularies contained few words for things that
could not be seen, heard, touched or tasted. The padres had no choice but to
teach Spanish to the natives—a decision that had far-reaching effects in the
Spanish empire, for it explains why Spanish is today the native tongue for
Mexico, Central America, and much of South America and a second language in
pockets of California and all of the Southwest.

Where the Indians were not sufficiently advanced to profit from regular
schooling, the emphasis was directed toward manual training. Skill in a trade
or the simple arts of agriculture was for the Indian a first step to becoming
civilized, and it was also a necessary element in the development of the missions

as self-sustaining units. The culture of California's Native Americans was so different from that of the Spaniards that the padres never did have time, in their few years of dominion, to educate them to European standards; only a few bright natives were taught to read and write. Training rarely got beyond industrial school, of which the largest sometimes oversaw more than 2,000 Native Americans.

The mission compounds were hives of activity. Tanning, blacksmithing, wine making, stock tending, and the care of fields and crops occupied the native men. Women from the tribe learned to cook, sew, spin, and weave. In 1834, on the eve of the destruction of the missions, the Indians at the 21 missions herded 396,000 cattle, 62,000 horses, and 321,000 hogs, sheep, and goats, and harvested 123,000 bushels of grain. Sixty-five years before, there had not been a single cow, horse, hog, sheep, goat, or grain of wheat in the entire province of Alta California.

It is perhaps ironic that the unworldly men who came here to Christianize and educate natives should have had to devote so much of their energies to the production of worldly goods. As Father Engelhardt wrote: "It must be remembered that the friars came to California as messengers of Christ. They were not farmers, mechanics, or stock breeders. As an absolutely necessary means to win the souls of these savages these unworldly men accepted the disagreeable task of conducting huge farms, teaching and supervising various mechanical trades, having an eye on the livestock and herders, and making ends meet generally."

In their heyday, the missions comprised the sole industrial plant of Alta California. They conducted a flourishing commerce with trading vessels from the east coast and from foreign countries. Trading hides, tallow, grain, wine, brandy, olive oil, leatherwork for manufactured goods, the padres were able to acquire badly needed tools, furniture, glass, nails, hardware, cloth, chests, rendering pots, cooking utensils, lighting fixtures, musical instruments, and a host of other items. This picturesque exchange of goods is graphically described in Dana's *Two Years Before the Mast*.

During the Spanish regime, the Californians were forbidden to trade with foreigners and a good deal of smuggling was openly conducted. In time, the restrictions were lifted and customs inspectors were set up in San Diego and Monterey, and later under the Mexicans, in San Francisco. Theoretically, all foreign goods had to flow through these channels, but some genteel smuggling persisted almost to the American occupation.

Missions Were Founded by the Rule Book

The development of an individual mission followed long-established rules and time-honored sequences. The founding was not a matter of priestly whim—the paperwork was likely to involve virtually the entire bureaucracy of the viceroyalty and would require months if not years of correspondence.

The padres were usually assigned in pairs to each mission, with one of them designated as the superior. In theory, they divided responsibilities: one watched over temporal and the other spiritual affairs, but they frequently interchanged tasks. The assignment of two men to each mission had sound psychological values because it kept them from becoming too lonely in their wilderness outposts. More than one padre, stranded alone for years in a frontier mission, lost his sanity under the crushing weight of isolation from his fellows. Although he rejoiced in the attainments of his charges, he was likely to look upon them as children who offered little companionship for a highly educated man. Nor could he count on his military escort for much personal communion.

Empowered to found a mission within a general area, the padres assigned to it journeyed thence, chose a specific site that afforded good wood and water and ample fields for grazing herds and raising crops. The padres blessed the chosen site and with the help of their military escort erected temporary shelters of boughs, followed soon by structures formed of driven stakes and roofed with thatch or reeds, and ultimately by the buildings of stone or adobe that are still standing.

Except in the few instances where the entire original structure and all its shops and outbuildings have been faithfully restored, most of the mission buildings now standing are merely the chapel or church portion of the original structure and the rest have long since returned to the soil or been swallowed by metropolitan encroachment.

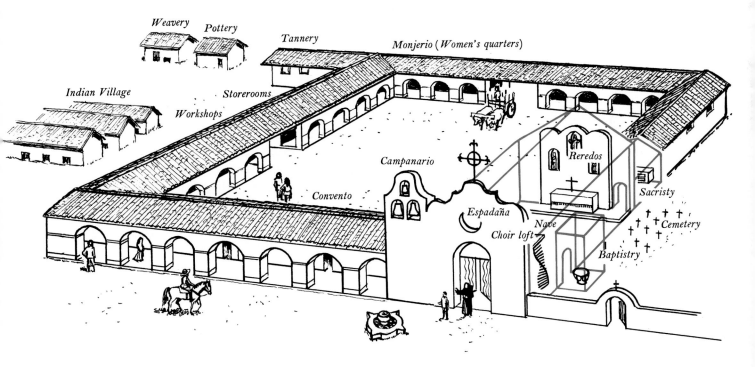

The completed mission was usually built in the form of a quadrangle with a church in one corner and shops, storerooms, living quarters around the square.

The typical structure, which was the core of the mission, was a large rambling, four-sided building formed around a square. Along the inner side of the square ranged an arcade that served as an outdoor hallway connecting a series of rooms devoted to workshops, priest's quarters, dining and cooking facilities, storage and office space, and living quarters for the young maidens, who were kept sequestered until they were married. The outside of the building had only one or two doors, and these were locked at night as a protection against marauders and to keep the inmates inside the compound until the alabado, or morning hymn, started the day.

Capstone of the quadrangle was always the church, the largest and most imposing building in the structure, usually located on the northeast corner. Designed in massive scale, and decorated with the best that could be obtained from New Spain or improvised on the spot, the church took four or five years to construct, and it symbolized the majesty and glory of God's word. Rising above the church, a campanile carried the great bells brought from Mexico City or Peru whose sonorous voices rolled over the countryside, summoning the Indians to work or to pray.

Mission Indians Led a Regimented Life

The padres attracted the natives to the mission by offering them gifts of bright glass beads, clothing, blankets, and food, and when they had secured their trust, they induced them to abandon their lifestyle and move into the mission compound or one of the villages close by.

Once the Indians had consented to join the mission community, they could never again leave it without permission, and they were henceforth subject to rigid authoritarian discipline. They were taught the externals of Christian worship and were expected to attend divine services several times a day. Schooled in the basic skills of building and farming by the artisans, the Indians were assigned to specialties in which they showed proficiency. Each Indian was required to devote a specified number of hours per week to making adobe blocks or roof tiles, building walls, working at a handcraft, or tilling the fields. The women were expected to meet daily quotas of woven cloth, ground meal, carded wool, or whatever other seasonal products needed to be processed.

To relieve the monotonous round, the Spaniards encouraged the observance of nearly every feast day on their calendar; hence processions, fiestas, games, and celebrations were frequent occurrences. The Indians were well fed with three substantial meals a day, which freed them for the first time in their lives from the perpetual search for food that had been their preoccupation in pre-mission days. In many of the missions, the Indians were granted a two-week vacation every five weeks for visiting their villages.

Although the majority of the Indians were content with their new way of life, there were many who did not appreciate the benefits of regimented living. The men had long been accustomed to alternating between periods of intense activity,

Mission discipline was not strict enough to stop the neophytes (Christianized Indians) from a favorite vice: gambling. A popular game, as depicted by the artist with the Russian ship Rurik *in 1816, was to toss handfuls of sticks into the air and bet on whether the number to fall would be odd or even.*

when they were hunting or raiding neighboring villages, and intervals of absolute torpor, when some were wont to lie face down in the grass for hours on end. Some of the older men chafed under the restrictions of the daily mission grind, and they resisted it openly or covertly. The histories of the individual missions are peppered with instances of runaways being hunted down and returned to the compound for discipline, usually a day or two in the stocks, and with cases of large-scale revolts that resulted in setting fire to the buildings, destroying crops, or scattering herds. On the outskirts of nearly every mission domain there lived unconverted Indians who liked to harass the mission Indians and to encourage the rebellious among them to escape.

To maintain order and return runaways, a corporal's guard of five or six soldiers was assigned to each mission. If more troops were needed in an emergency, they were brought in from the presidios at Monterey, San Francisco, San Diego, and Santa Bárbara. For several years, Mission San José served as a military base for launching punitive campaigns against the Indians living in the marshlands of the San Joaquin River, where the intricate windings of the delta channels provided haven for warlike tribes, who sallied forth to attack the

Christian Indians at the mission and who offered refuge to runaways from all over the San Francisco Bay Area.

Although the mission guard and the padres were often in conflict—over methods of discipline or the unrestrained conduct of the soldiers themselves—the guard was indispensable to the missions for protection of the lives of the padres themselves, as a means of impressing the childlike natives with the steel of authority, and, often, to furnish straw bosses for harvesting and shop work.

That the mission guard was effective is certainly proven by the fact that a mere 300 soldiers, dispersed over 650 miles, were able to keep in check an Indian population of 100,000. The Indians were basically peace-loving and lacked traditions of organized warfare, but they did resent the intrusion into their way of life and in some localities they forcefully resisted the foreigners, principally along the Santa Barbara Channel and in the delta area of the San Joaquin River. The tribes along the Colorado River massacred Spanish colonists in 1781 at Yuma, demonstrating what an aroused native population could do if sufficiently provoked.

In Alta California, however, the soldiers were generally able to keep the Indians under control. The Indians' arrows and spears were usually no match for the Spanish firearms. The soldiers carried shields of tough bull hide to deflect arrows and spears, and they wore leather jackets made of seven plies of deerskin that could stop an arrow. Furthermore, some of the soldiers rode horses, an animal that had never been seen in California before the arrival of the Spanish, and this gave them a psychological as well as tactical advantage over the unmounted Indians. The individualistic Indians had no experience in disciplined battle; indeed the various tribes were unaccustomed to cooperate in any venture, and they were easily subdued by the trained guard whose tactics embodied Spain's experience in centuries of conflict with native populations.

Discipline within the mission was not wholly under the control of the guards, however, for the padres appointed a small number of carefully chosen native police to assist in keeping order. Christianized Indians from earlier missions were also imported to help maintain discipline.

Of course the troops and their assistants could not have held back the natives if the padres had not performed their task with skill and devotion. The fact that the natives did not revolt on a large scale is a tribute to the success of the padres in teaching them the rudiments of European civilization. At the close of the mission period, there were 31,000 Christianized natives peaceably existing within 21 missions under the control of 60 padres and 300 soldiers.

Mission System: Good or Evil?

This, then, was the complex institution that the Spaniards had interjected into the simple lifestyle of California's natives. Often called a form of "benevolent despotism," the mission system has divided historians into two camps—those who consider it a good institution for its day and those who look upon it as a malevolent one. The arguments for both sides have filled historical literature for decades—some of the noteworthy books and articles are cited in the bibliography of this book—but they can be summarized briefly.

In defense of the mission system, the proponents point out that the padres, with only a few exceptions, were devoted to their charges, trained them in the ways of European civilization with the sincere conviction that they were helping them to a better life, and defended them against the demoralizing influences of the presidio and pueblo. In many missions, natives enjoyed the new life and revered the padres in charge. The basic notions behind the whole scheme were idealistic, aimed at the salvation of the Indians and their education so they could take their place in modern life, living in communal villages run by their own members. Indeed, many natives were later able to sustain themselves after the missions closed by pursuing crafts and trades learned in the mission compound. Fundamentally humanistic, the system offered a peaceable method of settling new territory for colonial expansion. And finally, the Spaniards always recognized the Indians' legal right to their ancestral land, did little to interfere with village existence, and expected to turn over enough land to the Indians when their period of tutelage was completed to permit them to be self-supporting.

Critics of the mission system charge that it was a thinly disguised form of slavery, masquerading under a pious front. The culture that it forced upon the natives was alien to their traditions, and no attempts were made by the padres to retain any of the rich native heritage of the past. The stated objectives of the system were obviously impractical: the Indians trained to the mission life were ill-adapted to live under any other system and could never again return to their old ways. Most of those who tried after the missions closed failed and were reduced to thievery. And finally, the introduction of the system brought with it diseases that destroyed thousands of natives because they had no immunity to outside ailments.

Balancing up the two arguments, it can also be pointed out that the treatment of natives by the Spaniards, though open to criticism by modern standards of political morality, was certainly no worse than that practiced in other colonial empires of the time. Slavery was condoned by all the world empires until late in the 19th century and it was a persistent evil in the southern United States for 30 years after the California missions were closed. Basically, the conflict of Spaniard vs. Indian was that of two cultures widely separated in style but fated to collide, and the reduction of the weaker by the stronger was inevitable. In comparison with their treatment by later immigrants, the doomed natives were better off under the Spaniards than under their successors. The newcomers wiped out the natives beyond the range of the mission chain, introduced similar diseases to those of the Spaniards, drove the Indians off their ancestral land, and herded survivors into reservations located on the most useless land in the new state. Ironically, when the federal government finally took a belated interest in the welfare of Native Americans, the program adopted for their betterment was very close to the system introduced by the Spaniards.

Decay and Rebirth

The bustling life of the missions, developed over seven decades of toil and devoted work, sputtered to an inglorious end in the middle of the last century. Signs of the end had long been apparent for the farsighted.

To those with the vision, the visits of the trading vessels from New England were the first indication that Alta California was doomed as a province of Spain. These ships were the advance agents of a restless young republic of four million citizens, separated from the colony on the Pacific Coast by a land mass and thousands of miles of ocean. But this upstart nation was moving inexorably westward by both land and sea, and it would only be a matter of time before it would push its way to the west coast. The captains of the Boston ships returned home with enthusiastic reports on the favorable conditions in Alta California, and they encouraged others to come out and see for themselves. The Spaniards were legally forbidden to trade with foreign vessels, but trade they did, and thereby helped to seal the doom of their province as a Spanish realm. There was practical wisdom in this law, which the colonists ignored to their peril.

To begin with, the mission settlements were founded during the dying years of the Spanish empire. The men who devoted their lives to extending the faith and the Spanish coat of arms into Alta California were engaged in a lost cause without knowing it. The authority of the Spanish Crown, which had dominated the world for two and a half centuries, was then being challenged within its own dominions by its colonies and outside by the growing strength of new empires being built by England and the Netherlands.

The Spanish colonies had been designed to become self-supporting, and it was thus only a question of time before *self-support* became *independence*. One after another the colonies seceded from Spain, which was helpless to challenge the defections. In 1810, New Spain broke away from the mother country and set itself up as the Republic of Mexico. The effects of this move on the California missions were far-reaching. Channels of authority became confused as governors

The shady arcade that surrounds the patio at San Juan Capistrano outlasted the buildings it was built to serve. The pillars and arches of cut stone and hand-burned brick were impervious to rains that dissolved the adobe buildings.

followed one another in rapid succession and small-scale revolutions erupted in the province as men jockeyed for power. Supplies and funds for the colonists no longer arrived, or appeared infrequently. The missions had to support themselves entirely and also to supply the civilian and military settlers. In some instances, this sustenance was given grudgingly because the padres were reluctant to force their Indian charges to work doubly hard in order to supply the needs of the colonists.

To add to the over-all confusion, long-postponed orders to secularize the missions were finally promulgated by the Mexican government. The idea behind secularization was a simple one: after the missions had fulfilled their function of civilizing the Indians in ten years' time, they were to be replaced by another colonial institution, the pueblo. This scheme had worked well throughout the Spanish empire wherever the mission system had been introduced, and this final step was long overdue in Alta California.

Under this law, the Church was allowed to retain only the priests' garden, and the church and priests' quarters in the mission quadrangle. These facilities were transferred from the missionary order that had held them to the regular clergy who would operate them as a parish church. The remainder of the mission buildings were to be used for public services for the new pueblo. The mission crops and herds were to be administered by a commissioner in the interests of the pueblo as a whole. The land itself was divided three ways. A large block was set aside for communal pasturage and agriculture. Space was set aside for the town itself, to be formed around an open square in the manner of the Spanish town. And finally, each Indian family was to be granted a plot for a residence and sufficient land for sustenance crops.

The Disaster of Secularization

Although secularization succeeded in the other Spanish lands, its application in California proved to be disastrous. The missionaries had long opposed it on the grounds that the Indians were not ready to conduct their own affairs. Civil authorities were also reluctant to enforce it because the missions comprised nearly the entire economy of the province and the sole source of food, and they could foresee the unfortunate results that the dispersal of the mission facilities and labor force would cause within the province.

But the pressure to secularize mounted as the years passed. Two generations of Spanish-Mexican settlers had grown up in the province since its founding, and the men were beginning to face an unemployment problem. They could not own property and they faced an ugly choice of either joining the army or doing nothing. All the property in California was owned by the government and held in stewardship by the padres for the Indians. The few land grants given out by the government were to Indians or to retired soldiers as a reward of service. By 1830, only 21 pieces of property were in private hands in all of Alta California. Secularization was thus seen by some as the only means of opening the province to private ownership.

Most of the missions were abandoned for decades. Their roofs gave way first, exposing the soluble adobe walls to the rain; but at Carmel, the walls of stone still stood in 1882, 30 years after the tile roof had collapsed.

When the order finally came through in 1833, some of the missions were processed almost immediately; others were secularized over the next 16 years. Whatever its long-term benefits may have been to the settlers as a whole, the order meant the complete destruction of the mission system as a going concern. One after another, the missions were released. The buildings were divided into public and religious segments—sometimes with an actual wall built right through the patio—and the land turned over to the Indians. Unaware of the significance of their property acquisitions and incapable of using the land to advantage, the Indians were easily hoodwinked out of their property—many of them gambled away their rights—and it quickly passed into the hands of speculators.

As can be imagined, the break-up of the missions had tragic effects on the lives of the mission Indians. Dependent on the mission life, they could not return to their old ways, and most of them went to work for the new landowners, who cared nothing for their welfare and treated them as virtual slaves. At some of the missions, the padres who remained as parish priests could comfort their former charges, but with the mission discipline broken, they could no longer help the Indians to support themselves.

The mission orchards, herds, fields, and foodstocks disappeared rapidly into private hands as secularization progressed. Within only a few years, there was little left to indicate the prosperity and industry of these once-thriving concerns. After the American occupation, the property rights of the missions were reviewed by the Federal Land Commission, and some of the lands and buildings were returned to the Church by acts of Congress in the 1850's and 1860's. Most of the missions were given back the land occupied by the original quadrangle. In some instances, these structures had long since collapsed, but in others they were still usable. However, the Church often found itself encumbered with buildings too vast to use for religious functions, so the outbuildings were leased or rented to private parties, and stores, bars, and inns began to occupy the quarters where the padres once meditated. A pig farm operated at San Fernando for several years; at San Juan Capistrano, Serra's chapel was used for hay storage. Tile roofs were removed to pay debts, and to cover new haciendas or town houses and even to roof railroad stations in later years.

In time, most of the missions began to fall into disrepair. Without active parishes to keep them in top condition, the old buildings fell prey to the weather. Roofs collapsed when the reeds and timbers rotted out beneath the heavy tiles, and once the protective roofs were gone, the adobe walls returned to the earth in only a few winters. Many of the old buildings were abandoned as unsafe or unsalvageable; many were torn down.

The Rewards of Restoration

For many decades, dissolution of the missions continued, until public-spirited citizens began to take an interest in them and to propose their restoration. First to appreciate them and to promote their revival were artists who discovered their picturesque decay and recorded it in etchings, watercolors, and oils. The fine collection of Turneresque oils by Edwin Deakin at the Los Angeles County Museum and the Santa Barbara Historical Association are the best remaining examples of this work. A fine set of watercolors by Chris Jorgensen may also be viewed at the Sonoma Mission. Following on the artists' heels came photographers' wagons, and a flood of stereopticon views of the collapsing structures appeared on the market. The paintings and photographs attracted general interest in the missions and they became tourist destinations early in the 1900's. Special rail excursions were run to them, and guide books were written for the edification of travelers.

With interest growing, wealthy individuals and organized groups began to campaign for their restoration. Pioneer in this enterprise was the Landmarks Club, founded by a newspaperman named Charles Fletcher Lummis. The club raised enough money to keep several of the missions in southern California from complete collapse. Often, some of the earlier restorations were well intentioned but badly executed, usually because of inadequate information about the original form of the buildings. An early attempt to restore the stone church at San Juan Capistrano resulted in further destruction when gunpowder charges brought more of the church down in ruins. A steep shingle roof, added to the mission at Carmel, gave it an incongruous air that it wore for fifty years before funds were acquired to effect a more authentic roofline.

Some of the missions that escaped the erosion of time and weather suffered in the hands of "modernizers" who wanted to bring the shabby old buildings up to date. One padre with a passion for tongue-and-groove sheathing left his mark on three missions in the 1870's. He covered the entire façade of San Luis Obispo with wooden siding and concealed the beamed ceiling and tile floor with wood. He applied the same treatment to the interiors of San Buenaventura and San Juan Bautista, and as a fillip for the latter, he added a wooden New England steeple to the façade.

More recent restorations were accomplished with historical and scientific accuracy. Old records, drawings, and photographs were studied and archeological research done to trace foundation lines, floor patterns, and outlines of outbuildings long since departed. Noteworthy in this regard have been the buildings at La Purísima, restored by the National Park Service and the C.C.C., as well as missions San José, San Carlos Borromeo, San Juan Bautista, San Antonio de Padua, and San Juan Capistrano.

Although intrinsic interest will vary from mission to mission, today's visitors will find something worth seeing at every stop. Travelers can spend several hours absorbing La Purísima or San Antonio de Padua, pass a pleasant hour at Carmel or San Juan Capistrano missions, and take in the little that remains at San Miguel Arcángel in only ten minutes. Seven missions are national historic landmarks; two are run by the state park system. Few of the original buildings are intact, but many chapels and some quadrangles have been restored to approximate the condition of their heyday. Preservation, including expensive earthquake retrofitting, is ongoing, though hampered by lack of funds and coordinated efforts. Except for La Purísima and San Francisco Solano, all missions are governed by the Catholic church but administered by various dioceses and three different orders.

Architectural Significance of the Missions

Viewed simply as structures, the missions are interesting in their own right. Together with the Spanish ranch house, they have exerted a powerful influence over the residential and commercial architecture of California. Not too many years ago, mission-style architecture was in high favor, and an abundance of schools, libraries, courthouses, stores, universities (notably Stanford), railroad stations, theaters, and homes were built with strong mission echoes.

Architecturally, the mission buildings as a group represent a very satisfying combination of honest design and simple construction materials and methods.

The padres were not trained engineers or architects, and their building plans incorporated features that they remembered from the churches they had known in Mexico or Spain but adapted by rule of thumb and harsh necessity to the unique conditions in this outpost. As a rule, they could draw upon the services of only a

Ornamented Openings
Following an architectural custom introduced by the Moors, Spanish public buildings for centuries had been mainly ornamented around openings. The embellishments in Spain and Mexico, often lavish, were echoed faintly in decorations around doors and windows in California missions. Deep-set openings in thick walls permitted decorative shaping.

The Espadaña
An ornamental false front known as an espadaña, was a device freely used in Spain and the Netherlands, long a Spanish dominion, to make a façade seem more imposing than it would appear if its true, low roofline were revealed. Used at several of the California missions, principally San Diego, San Luis Rey, San Carlos Borromeo.

few trained artisans and experienced workmen; and they also had to create the building materials out of the soil they stood on and the trees that shaded them.

When they were able to secure a skilled designer, as at Carmel, San Juan Capistrano, San Luis Rey, or Santa Bárbara, they were able to erect buildings that faintly echoed some of the rich ornamental feeling of the more elaborate structures in Mexico, but even these are bare by comparison. In general, the padres limited their decorative touches to simple embellishment of doors, windows, belltowers, and church interiors.

In basic structure, the missions embodied some centuries-old features of Spanish architecture. Most of the buildings were built around a patio, all of them featured the covered arcades common in Spain and Mexico, and some of them carried forward the special features charted above.

To a large degree, the form of the missions was dictated by the nature of the building materials used. The low silhouette, massive pillars, and pleasing overall proportions of the buildings are largely due to the limitations of the adobe blocks of which most of them were built. Because of their heavy weight, the blocks could not be stacked too high, since they tended to topple. To be self-supporting, the walls had to be four or five feet thick to sustain their own weight and that of the tile roofs. Made of sun-dried mud, the adobes tended to dissolve in the rain. The wide eaves and roofed corridors that are such an appealing feature of the buildings served a practical function in shielding the soluble walls from rain. As further protection, all the exposed surface was plastered with lime stucco.

Decoration as an Aid to Worship

The plain façades of the California missions scarcely prepare the visitor for the richness of decorative detail that he is likely to find when he enters the church. What catches the observant eye is not the gilt, the winking ruby candles, or the figures of the saints found in all Roman Catholic churches, but the simple orna-

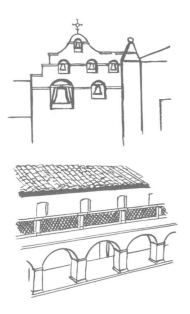

The Campanario
Of the various ways of hanging church bells,
the campanario is unique to Spain and Mexico.
Distinct from a campanile, or belltower, the campanario
was simply a wall, pierced for the bells. Sometimes the
wall would be freestanding, as at Pala; sometimes it was
an extension of the mission wall itself, as at San Gabriel,
where one replaced a campanile downed by an earthquake.

The Corredor
The arcade or corredor, long a structural fixture in Spain
and other countries rimming the sunny Mediterranean,
provided a shady outdoor hallway and a pleasant room
itself for hot weather relaxation or meditation.
A common feature of all the missions, it was usually
placed along the inner wall of the quadrangular buildings.
The arches were supported by brick or heavy adobe pillars.

mentation applied by artists' hands from another world, trained in another century, and stating their creative message in fresco, stonework, woodcarvings, and forged iron.

The padres favored the embellishment of the missions as an aid to worship, a joyful expression appropriate to the house of God. With the limited means at their disposal, and no training in art, they did remarkably well. Masons and artisans were imported from New Spain and set to work with Indian help to decorate the inside of the churches and chapels. Although the Indians had no traditions in the decorative arts beyond the simple geometrics of basket and pottery patterns, some of them quickly learned under guidance how to paint, carve, and forge.

Design elements were sometimes adapted from Indian basketry, particularly around Santa Bárbara, but they were most often copied directly from books in the mission libraries, patterns embroidered on the priests' ceremonial robes, or details carved on the altar pieces shipped in from New Spain.

Some of the mission churches vibrate with barbaric color chosen to please the Indians. Reds, greens, blues, and ochres derived from pigments found in soil, in berries, lichens, and mosses, glow on the walls and ceilings. Fresh, naive decorations flow over ceilings and along beams, twine around pillars and arches, and wreathe windows, doors, and niches.

In an effort to re-create the elegance of the cathedrals of their homeland, the padres instructed the artisans to paint imitation marble on the walls and to draw altars, niches, doors, pillars, balconies, and corridors in perspective. Samples of this illusion can best be viewed at Santa Bárbara, Santa Inés, and San Miguel.

Decoration extended to more than wall adornment. Benches, tables, chairs, pulpits, and confessionals were decorated with intricate wood carvings. Stonemasons chipped local granite into baptismal fonts. Where a forge existed, the mission Indians shaped iron bars into filigreed gates and window gratings and elaborate crosses to surmount the roof.

*The oldest mission in California, initial link in the chain
that stretched for 650 miles up the King's Highway,
Mission San Diego is a modest structure for one of such
historic importance. The plain, almost homely façade
lacks the elaborateness of some of its successors, but its
simplicity and rough-hewn character perhaps reflect
more of the spirit of the founding padres than some of the
more sophisticated structures that followed.*

San Diego de Alcalá

*First mission, founded July 16, 1769, by Fr. Serra. Named for St. Didacus
of Alcalá. Moved from Presidio Hill above Old Town to present site in 1774;
burned in Indian attack, 1775; rebuilt, 1780; destroyed by earthquake, 1803;
restored and enlarged, 1813. Present building, restoration of 1813 church,
rebuilt 1931. Secularized 1834; sold 1845; returned to Church 1862.
Located 5 miles east of Interstate 5, off Interstate 8.*

On the brow of a landscaped hill overlooking the bay of San Diego stands a tall
brick cross and not far away are rows of mounded earth that were once the walls
of an old fort. By these two symbols, the beholder of today is reminded that here
the Cross and the Sword, working together in the interests of the Spanish Crown,
founded California, the last outpost of the global empire. For it was on this hill,
now graced with a park, that a handful of dedicated Spaniards planted the first
permanent settlement under conditions of agonizing hardship.

Plans for the settlement had been carefully worked out months before in
Mexico City. A large expedition was formed under Governor Portolá and
Father Serra to establish three missions to hold the northern frontier against
Russian encroachment. Two of the missions were to be established at the major
ports previously explored by Spanish vessels, San Diego and Monterey, and
the third was to be located halfway between.

The port of San Diego had been known to the Spaniards for 200 years, ever
since it had been discovered and mapped by Juan Rodríguez Cabrillo in 1542.
Recognized as "the best to be found in the whole South Seas," the port was
selected as the rendezvous for twin expeditions, one by land, the other by sea,
which set out from Baja California in the summer of 1769.

The packets *San Carlos* and *San Antonio* reached San Diego before the land
expeditions. Both ships were in a tragic state because of the devastating inroads
of scurvy, from which sixty of the ninety crewmen had died. When the land
parties arrived, they found the wretched survivors of the sea voyages camped
at the mouth of the San Diego River where it emptied into the bay. Most of those
still alive were suffering from scurvy, and the camp was a virtual hospital.

In spite of the sorry state of the colony, Governor Portolá decided to continue
the expedition northward, and he set out with a small party to seek the harbor
of Monterey. Father Serra remained in San Diego and ordered a brushwood

chapel erected on the hill where the monument now stands, and there on July 16, 1769 he formally dedicated the first of the missions.

The mission got off to a slow start. At first, the Native Americans came only to accept gifts, or to make off with unguarded items. They were fascinated by fabrics, although they had no use for them, and supposedly removed sheets from bedridden invalids and attempted to cut the sails from the *San Carlos*. Fortunately, the natives would not touch Spanish food, believing it to be the cause of the sickness in the colony, or the settlement might have died from hunger.

Once they had become accustomed to the Spaniards' presence, the Indians became insolent. They jeered the padres and ridiculed the soldiers, mimicking the firing of the guns, which the soldiers discharged into the air. At length, their insolence degenerated into hostility, and a party attacked the weakened colony with bows and arrows. Unfamiliar with the deadly power of firearms, the Indians showed no fear when the soldiers returned the sally with a volley from their muskets, but they soon learned the fatal difference between their simple weapons and those of the Spaniards. Two Spaniards died, three were wounded, and at least three Indians perished. The Indians later brought their wounded to be treated by the Spanish doctor, who cured them of their injuries. Although they no longer challenged the mission soldiers, they were still in no mood to accept conversion.

One native boy braved the unknown and paid frequent visits to the padres. They favored him with gifts and tried to learn his language so they could teach him Spanish and thus make contact with the tribe. This took months, but at last the boy mastered a little Spanish and Father Serra persuaded him to induce an Indian father to have his baby baptized. At length, a father appeared before the delighted padre and offered his child for baptism. Father Serra gathered the community for the important event, but just as he was about to baptize the child, another Indian snatched it away and ran off to the village. The incident grieved Father Serra so much that long afterward his eyes filled with tears whenever he recalled the unhappy event.

The sight of white sails rounding the tip of Point Loma brought rejoicing to the sick and half-starved colony at San Diego. For months they had waited for the return of the supply ship, and if it had not appeared in answer to the padres' prayers, the entire expedition would have been abandoned.

The Ship! The Ship!

When Portolá returned from his expedition to Monterey, six months later, he found the little mission in pitiful condition. An additional nineteen men had died, and supplies were running low. The community had only a few rickety tule buildings within a stockade. No improvements had been possible because of the debilitated condition of the men. The Governor decided that the mission would have to be abandoned unless relief could be secured. He told Father Serra that if supplies did not come by the feast of St. Joseph (March 19) the expedition would have to return to New Spain.

This decision was like an arrow in Father Serra's heart. He prayed incessantly for the safe and swift return of the relief ship, *San Antonio*, which had been dispatched to San Blas seven months before. The anxious padre resolved heroically to remain alone with Father Crespí, if necessary, and leave the result to God.

On a dark night in 1775, a horde of Indians attacked the mission, burned the buildings, and killed three Spaniards, including Fr. Jayme, first martyr in Alta California. The raid delayed the founding of other missions until more troops were available; but because it failed, it also discouraged the Indians from trying to expel the foreigners.

If it were not for sketches such as this one, rendered in 1853 by an army engineer with a railroad survey party, there would have been no record of the form of San Diego's now-famous belltower, which collapsed long before professional photographers and artists recorded the mission in the next decade. The drawing also shows an enclosed front portico.

But on the evening of the set day, the sails of a ship were sighted. Although it disappeared from view, its arrival was considered a miracle, and Portolá agreed to wait a few more days. The ship proved to be the *San Antonio*, which was on its way to Monterey but had lost an anchor and doubled back to San Diego, arriving there four days after it had first been sighted.

The shipload of supplies relieved the crisis, and within a month the expedition was able to continue to the realization of its second objective, the founding of a mission at Monterey. Portolá led a land party northward and Serra sailed to the port in the *San Antonio*.

The Indians' Desperate Revolt

In August 1774, the mission was moved from its site on Presidio Hill to a new location six miles up the river. The original site had proved to have disadvantages. The Indians did not get along well with the garrison and there was not enough land to support the growing number of neophytes.

Buildings of logs, palisade-style and roofed with thatch, were soon completed at the new site, and the padres continued their slow conversion of the natives. They labored under a severe handicap, however, which later had fatal consequences. Unlike most of the California missions, San Diego lacked the water and soil to support field crops in sufficient quantity to feed the neophytes. As a result, the Indians were permitted to stay in their villages and only come to the mission to work or attend services. Under such loose discipline, the Indians were Christians in name only, and many were subject to reversion to their old ways.

Some of the Indians began to see that sooner or later the padres would win over all the tribes, so they resolved to kill them and and destroy the mission. Plans were laid for a massive attack on the mission that was the most ambitious and best organized of any of the native forays. Messengers secretly went from village to village enlisting support for the raid, and on the appointed night in November 1776, an army of 800 armed natives fell upon the sleeping community. They looted the sacristy and storerooms and set fire to the tinder-dry buildings. Half of the Indian force had been detailed to attack the presidio, but on their way they saw the flames and concluded that the fire would arouse the presidio, so they turned back and joined the others in the assault on the mission.

Father Luis Jayme, a blacksmith, and a carpenter were killed and two soldiers wounded. Father Jayme rushed out into the melee, calling, "Love God, my children!" But he was seized and dragged to the river, where he was clubbed and shot full of arrows. The courageous padre thus became the first martyr of the California missions.

When the battle was over, a runner was sent to secure help from the presidio garrison, which, it developed, had slept soundly through the whole affair. The padres moved back to the presidio and remained there for several months.

The attack changed the complexion of the mission situation. For fear of further attacks, the Governor refused to permit the founding of additional missions without adequate military protection. Comments Professor Charles E. Chapman, "Latter-day historians have been altogether too prone to regard the hostility to the Spaniards on the part of the California Indians as a matter of

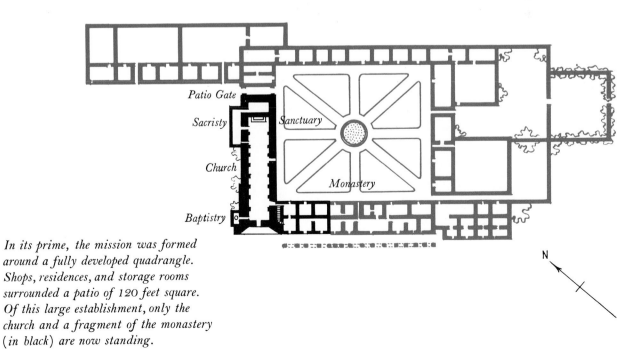

In its prime, the mission was formed around a fully developed quadrangle. Shops, residences, and storage rooms surrounded a patio of 120 feet square. Of this large establishment, only the church and a fragment of the monastery (in black) are now standing.

small consequence, since no disaster in fact ever happened. . . . On the other hand the San Diego plot involved untold thousands of Indians, being virtually a national uprising, and owing to the distance from New Spain and the extreme difficulty of maintaining communications a victory for the Indians would have ended Spanish settlement in Alta California." As it turned out, the failure of the Indians strengthened the Spaniards' position, because "the Indians felt from this time forth that it was impossible to throw out their conquerors."

The burned-out mission was not rebuilt for nearly eight months. When it was finally reconstructed, it was carried through to a full quadrangle of major size. Over a period of years (1807–1816), the padres designed and erected a dam six miles upriver and brought the water to the mission through cement flumes, built at great effort by the Indians through the almost impenetrable gorge. Chunks of this dam, now almost silted to the brim, are still standing.

In 1813, the adobe church that is almost the trademark of San Diego, was dedicated. After secularization, the mission declined rapidly and its immense ranchos were passed into private hands. The old buildings were left to decay. For a twelve-year period they were occupied by units of the United States Army, which kept them from disintegrating, but when the soldiers departed, the mission gradually disappeared. At the time of its restoration in 1931, only the façade was still standing.

After secularization, the buildings were sold to private parties and even the mission church fell into disrepair. For twelve years (1850–1862), the church was occupied on and off by the U.S. Army, which built a second story inside and quartered horses on the ground level. Note the enclosed portico in front and the missing campanario, which had collapsed.

By 1892, half of the church had caved in. The roof tiles had long since departed to cover the homes of Old Town and most of the quadrangle had gone back to the soil. Unoccupied since the army decamped, the property had not been maintained. BELOW. *The mission dam, built 6 miles up the river in 1816, outlasted the mission that it served by several decades. Its stored water was brought to the mission by miles of aqueduct. It stood unbreached until a flood burst it open. As late as 1930, when this photograph was taken, a large segment still stood. Even now, fragments can still be viewed.*

The simple sanctuary shown above was reconstructed in a more richly decorative style in 1970. A carved reredos *now stands behind the altar, its colors, including hand-painted motifs, replicating those used during the mission period.*

Striking feature of the mission is the handsome campanario that rises above the mission gardens. The bells that hang in the five niches were scattered to the four winds during the decades of neglect, and were only re-assembled after diligent search. Largest bell is the 1,200-pound Mater Dolorosa, cast in San Diego in 1894 from five bells of 1796 sent to the mission by the Viceroy.

*In the century-old cemetery, paper flowers blow in the
wind, respectful tributes placed by the Indians.*

Santa Ysabel

In the mountains 60 miles east of San Diego Mission, a white stuccoed church
stands on the site of an asistencia founded by the padres in 1818 in the waning
days of the mission era.

The sub-mission was established to serve a group of 250 neophytes who lived
in the Santa Ysabel Valley and who found it difficult to reach the San Diego
Mission for divine services. Although the padres from the mission visited them
periodically, the fathers felt that the Indians needed a branch mission, and they
petitioned the Governor in 1816 for permission to found one. Unenthusiastic
about the proposal, the Governor refused to grant the needed authority; so the
padres took matters in their own hands and erected a temporary chapel in 1818.
It was soon followed by permanent buildings of adobe that included a chapel,
granary, and houses. By 1822, more than 450 neophytes were attached to the
asistencia.

After secularization, Santa Ysabel was quickly plundered. The lands were
bought up by large landowners and the chapel was permitted to weather into
"indistinguishable heaps of earth." The Indians carried on as best they could.
A brush ramada served as a church whenever a visiting priest reached the site
or when the village chief recited the services. Only the two bells, bought by the
Indians themselves for six burro loads of barley and wheat, remained for several
years, hanging from a crude framework, until they vanished in 1926.

The present structure was dedicated in 1924, and other buildings were erected
in later years. It is now served by the Sons of the Sacred Heart.

*Standing on the site of the first adobe church, the stuccoed Santa Ysabel chapel
is designed with the simple dignity of the mission style. Dedicated in 1924,
it was built with funds contributed from a personal legacy by Fr. Edmond La
Pointe, a Canadian-born missionary priest who served this mountain area for
29 years and is buried alongside the church he created.*

SAN DIEGO DE ALCALÁ **81**

San Carlos Borromeo de Carmelo

*Second mission, founded June 3, 1770, by Fr. Junípero Serra at Presidio of
Monterey; moved to Carmel following year. Named for St. Charles Borromeo,
a Cardinal of the 16th century. Present church (the seventh) begun 1793
under Fr. Lasuén, dedicated 1797. Headquarters of mission chain 1770–1803.
Secularized 1834, returned 1859. Restoration 1884, 1924, 1936.
Located just south of city of Carmel, near State Highway 1.*

Most beautiful of the California missions, San Carlos Borromeo exerts a romantic
spell over all who visit it. The rough-hewn church reflects the design of a
master-mason, interpreted to crude perfection by Indian apprentices. In its
setting against sea and river, its fair gardens, the unequal towers through which
the cliff swallows sweep past the full-skirted bells, the star window "that seems
to have been blown out of shape in some wintry wind, and all its lines hardened
again in the sunshine of the long, long summer," the solid competence of its
vaulted ceiling—in all these things it tells the viewer that here stands the work
of men with the mind and heart to design with integrity and warmth.

The viewer wonders what Father Serra would have thought of the building
had he lived to see it. Serra had planned for a stone church and had ordered the
quarrying of stone for it in 1781. It is possible that he even sketched out the
design. A few days before his death he told Father Palóu, "When the stone
church is built you may place me where you will"; and when the church was
actually completed 16 years later, it was built around the earlier church in which
Serra was buried and it thus encompassed his remains.

This is the seventh in a series of churches that stretches back to 1771 when the
first crude shelter of logs was erected at Carmel. Prior to that, services had
been held at the presidio of Monterey, where the mission had been founded the
preceding year in a joyful dedication, celebrated with the firing of muskets and
cannon that so frightened the Indians that they went into hiding.

The establishment at Monterey soon proved inadequate. Conditions were not
suitable for crops, there were few Indians living around the bay, and the mission

*With its rough sandstone walls, Moorish tower,
unique windows, and its beautiful setting against the
sea and the mountains, Carmel Mission is the romantic
gem of the California chain. The striking star window has
been a frequent source of speculation, some viewers
concluding that it should have been placed on its side as a
rectangle rather than balanced on one point as a star.*

French voyager La Pérouse anchored in Monterey Bay in 1786 amid spouting whales and visited the mission, where Fr. Lasuén received his party "like lords of a parish when they make their first appearance upon their estate. The president of the missions received us at the door of the church illuminated as on the grandest festivals."

was too close to the presidial garrison for the good of the neophytes. Serra resolved to find a more suitable site, and he traveled over the hills seeking a better location. He found his ideal site in the beautiful Carmel Valley on a hillside overlooking a fertile plain and "two gunshots" (2,400–2,800 feet) from the sea. He put men to work cutting timber for buildings and left five soldiers for their protection. But it was six months before the wooden chapel, a dwelling, storehouses, soldiers' quarters and a corral were finished and surrounded by a palisade.

Mission San Carlos Borromeo del Rio Carmelo became Serra's headquarters as Father-President of the entire chain. Although he was seldom there, spending a good deal of his time making the rounds of the burgeoning mission settlements spread out over 500 miles, he was equally at home to governors and Indians. He lived in a tiny cell about a hundred yards from the church. It was frugally furnished with a cot of boards, a single blanket, a table and chair, a chest, a candlestick, and a gourd.

Father Serra was small of stature (5 feet 2 inches) and never robust, but he had an iron constitution and walked thousands of miles in his lifetime in the pursuit of his noble calling. After his arrival in New Spain in 1749, he walked the entire distance from Vera Cruz to Mexico City. En route he suffered an injury to his leg caused by an insect bite that left him with a painful handicap from which he suffered all the rest of his life.

At the age of nearly 71, worn out from the exactions of his duties and suffering from a tubercular infection, he called his dear friend Father Palóu to him "to assist him to die." This Father Palóu did, staying with him and tenderly performing the last rites. Death came quietly on the afternoon of August 28, 1784. The sad news spread rapidly and mourners streamed to the adobe church at the mission. The booming of a General's salute from a bark in Monterey Bay was answered by the presidio's guns and the tolling of the mission bells. The beloved padre was interred in the sanctuary near the altar and next to his lifelong friend, Fr. Crespí. Within a few years, the adobe church in which he was buried was replaced by the present stately one of stone, built on the same site.

Following Serra's death, Father Palóu shouldered the responsibilities of the Father-Presidency for a brief interval and then turned the office over to the man who was destined to contribute almost as much to the missions as Serra himself, Father Fermín Francisco de Lasuén. An able successor, Lasuén carried forward the missions that Serra had founded and added an equal number himself. Like Serra, he considered Carmel as his headquarters and he based his operations here for the next 18 years.

Lasuén made an excellent impression on the first foreign visitors to stop in Carmel. French navigator La Pérouse (1786) and the English captain, Vancouver (1792 and 1793), published astute and generally complimentary observations about the missions after they returned to Europe. The drawings accompanying their reports are among the earliest sketches of mission life extant.

In 1791 a master mason, Manuel Ruíz, was imported to design and build the Royal Chapel at Monterey and the stone church at the mission. After some

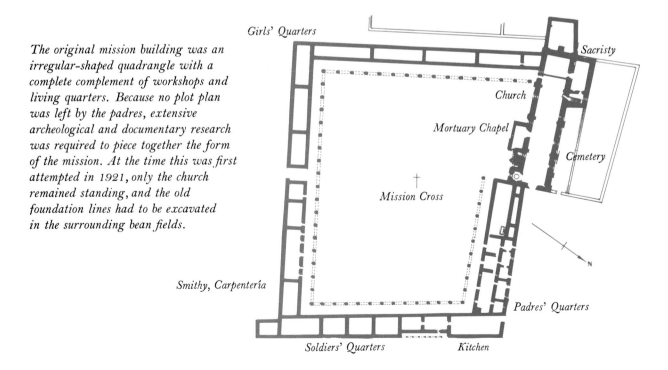

The original mission building was an irregular-shaped quadrangle with a complete complement of workshops and living quarters. Because no plot plan was left by the padres, extensive archeological and documentary research was required to piece together the form of the mission. At the time this was first attempted in 1921, only the church remained standing, and the old foundation lines had to be excavated in the surrounding bean fields.

Girls' Quarters

Sacristy

Church

Mortuary Chapel

Cemetery

Mission Cross

Smithy, Carpentería

Padres' Quarters

Soldiers' Quarters   Kitchen

SAN CARLOS BORROMEO DE CARMELO **85**

Drawing made in 1792 by the artist with the British expedition under
Capt. George Vancouver shows: 1. Site of present church. 2. Cross in courtyard,
still standing. 3. Present sacristy. 4. Sixth church. 5. Tile kiln.
6. Cattle stockade. 7. Indian brush huts.

delay, the cornerstone was laid at Carmel in 1793, and the building was dedicated four years later with a grand fiesta.

Father Lasuén died in 1803 and was buried alongside his illustrious predecessor in the sanctuary of the great stone church. His successor transferred the seat of mission authority to Santa Bárbara, where it remained for several years.

In November 1818 two vessels hove in sight approaching Monterey. They were recognized as those of Bouchard, the pirate. Four hundred of his freebooters landed, set the torch to Monterey and the presidio, and destroyed $5,000 worth of supplies. The Governor and a 25-man defense force retreated toward Salinas. The mission was evacuated; but if Bouchard's men came near the mission, no one will ever know. It was unharmed.

After secularization, the mission passed out of the padres' hands, and the Indians were left to shift for themselves. The land was sold right up to the walls of the church—in fact it later became necessary to buy a small strip in order to enter the front door without trespassing. The neglected roof beams rotted and gave way under the weight of the tiles, and the gaunt stone walls stood roofless for 30 years. Services were held monthly in the sacristy, which somehow survived the general collapse.

In 1882, the resident pastor in Monterey, Fr. Angelo Casanova, decided to open the tombs in the littered sanctuary to quiet rumors that Serra's body had been removed, a persistent legend that had even managed to make the staid pages of the *Saturday Evening Post* that year. Accordingly, the graves were opened, the remains viewed and identified, and the tombs were then re-sealed.

Two years later, Fr. Casanova conducted a successful campaign to repair the church in time for ceremonies to honor the centennial of Father Serra's death. Money was subscribed and a shingle roof was built over the church. Unfortunately, the steep pitch of the roof was not in harmony with the original design, and it drew well-merited criticism for years—for that matter, for the full half century that it remained in place. Oddly enough, this awkward roof is permanently enshrined in the rotunda of the Capitol in Washington D.C., where a statue of Father Serra stands as one of the two representatives of California. The statue depicts Serra with a cross in one hand and a miniature of the Carmel church in the other—a miniature with the inappropriate roof.

Restoration of the mission to its present state of maturity was begun in the 1930s under the technical supervision of the careful and competent Harry Downie, who rebuilt most of it only after a long and painstaking research into physical and written records. The church today is thus one of the most authentic restorations in the entire mission chain. It is honored with the classification of *basilica* because of its historic importance and its connection with the work of Father Junípero Serra, who is currently a candidate for canonization.

Idyllic view of mission, drawn in 1826 by the artist with the British scientific expedition under Capt. William Beechey, shows wide-spread mission at its peak.

*Not many years after its secularization, Carmel Mission
began to deteriorate rapidly. The lands had been sold to the
walls of the church itself, the Indians had gone, and the
church was left to the mercy of vandals and relic hunters.
In 1851 the roof fell in, covering the sanctuary with
debris. Windblown sand drifted in through open doors
and windows, covering the floor and giving haven to
grasses and weeds high enough to be cut by a sickle.
A visitor in 1861 reported, "hundreds (literally) of
squirrels scampered around their holes in the old walls;
cattle had free access to all parts; and thousands of birds,
apparently, lived in nooks in the old deserted walls."
ABOVE. Eventually, funds were raised to build a shingle
roof over the exposed church in 1884. Although the new
roof protected the building from collapse for 52 years,
it marred its appearance with an ungainly roofline.*

Even after the mission had fallen into ruin, services were occasionally held in the sacristy, which was undamaged. In this painting, Fr. Casanova, pastor from 1870 to 1893, is depicted leading a group of Indian worshippers into the sacristy for a baptism. In the background, the catenary arches of stone stand revealed, a unique feature of Mission Carmel.

Carved in stone in the wall of a courtyard shrine are the coats of arms of the brother Orders of the Dominicans and Franciscans, which often appear together in Franciscan missions, along with statues of the founders of the Orders, St. Dominic and St. Francis. The two saints were close friends in life, and their two orders have always maintained close ties.

Restored after a thoroughgoing structural overhaul, the beautiful church approximates its original form, revealing ample evidence of the skill and talent of its original designer. The first reredos was destroyed when the roof collapsed; the present (third), built in 1957, is adapted from one at Mission Dolores.

*In the mortuary chapel stands the treasured statue of the
Virgin that traveled with Serra to the founding of the
San Diego Mission and later to the dedication
of the mission at Monterey. The beautiful statue has
Spanish features of an olive cast.*

*In the busy round of their daily obligations, the padres
still took time to read; and several of the missions had
extensive libraries. Re-created to represent the original
library of 1,500 volumes, this one is stocked with
leather-bound volumes on theology and practical matters,
such as agriculture, architecture, and medicine.*

*Although the tombstone says Old Gabriel
was 151 years old when he died,
he was actually much younger—
a modest 140 years of age. An error in
reading the birth register resulted in the
mistake on the stone. Old Gabe was
baptized by Fr. Serra in 1780 when
he was then 30 years old; he died in
Salinas in 1890. In the course of his
long life, he had five wives.
Gabriel's remains were transferred to
his home mission in 1963 on
San Carlos Day.*

TO
The Memory of
OLD GABRIEL
Who died
March 14, 1890
Aged 151 years.

Gabriel was Baptized by the
Rev. Fra Junipero Serra, the
First Missionary of California

R.I.P

Fr Junípero Serra

Carmel Mission was the headquarters for the little padre from Mallorca, Fr. Junípero Serra, whose energy, zeal, and devotion planted the mission chain that led to the founding of California. During 15 years of service, he founded nine of the 21 missions and inspired such devotion among his followers that many considered him a saint, a feeling not shared by California's Native Americans. In recognition of his achievements, his birthplace in Petra (above) was made into a museum and deeded to the city of San Francisco. Although he associated with governors and prelates, as well as his native charges, he lived an ascetic life, sleeping on a bed of boards in a sparse cell (left), now restored at the mission.

RIGHT. *The elaborate sarcophagus by sculptor Jo Mora depicts a recumbent Fr. Serra in the grieving presence of the three other padres who are buried with him under the sanctuary floor in the church. At his head stands Fr. Crespí, his lifelong friend.*

For nearly a century, the remains of Fr. Serra and his compatriots lay almost forgotten in the weed-grown sanctuary of the mission. To quiet rumors that Serra's body had been spirited away and buried elsewhere, the padre's remains were examined in 1856 and again in 1882 (above) in the presence of witnesses, including cadets from St. Patrick's School in San Francisco in resplendent uniforms, dignitaries from political and religious walks of life, and a few mission Indians. Serra's remains were satisfactorily identified and then returned to slumber until 1943 when they were once more disturbed in connection with canonization proceedings launched at that time and still in process today. This ancient procedure takes decades, even centuries, of painstaking research into the life and accomplishments of a candidate. At one stage, evidence of his achievements is gathered under courtroom procedures for referral to Rome for final evaluation.
RIGHT. Lay historian, Dr. Herbert E. Bolton, offers testimony before a tribunal of church authorities as part of the 1950 investigations. LEFT. Reliquary found in Serra's coffin when his remains were exhumed.

The Royal Chapel standing today was under construction when the artist with the Vancouver expedition made this sketch in 1792 of the Monterey presidio.

La Capilla Reál

Standing on busy Church Street in Monterey is an ornate church with a carved stone façade that has a strong resemblance to Mission Carmel. The similarity is no coincidence. The two were designed by the same architect, Manuel Ruíz, built of the same kind of stone, and completed in the same year.

The history of the Royal Chapel (La Capilla Reál) is linked closely with that of the mission. Serra founded San Carlos Mission at the Monterey presidio in 1770 and used a storeroom as a temporary church until the mission was moved to Carmel Valley the following year. The storeroom continued to serve as the presidio chapel until a new church of stone and adobe was built in 1775. It was replaced by the present building, erected on the same site in 1794.

For many years, the Royal Chapel served as the key church in the political life of the province. The only church in the capital, it was attended by provincial and foreign dignitaries and was the setting for many important political ceremonies. Since it did not have a chaplain in attendance, it was served by padres from the mission until 1840 when it became a parish church.

In the rear garden of the present church is a fragment of the ancient oak tree under which the Vizcaíno party said Mass in 1602 and Father Serra dedicated Mission San Carlos Borromeo de Monterey 168 years later.

With all its ornateness, the church is the handiwork of Mexican and Indian craftsmen, whose naive renderings of Mexican decorative motifs are rare examples of primitive art. Especially noteworthy is the figure of the Virgin of Guadalupe, carved in chalk rock at the top of the façade. The only presidio chapel remaining in California, it has been in use since 1794.

To the traveler, remote San Antonio de Padua is one of the most interesting of the missions. Faithfully restored in 1949 to an authentic approximation of its original state, the mission captures some of the atmosphere of its heyday. The elegant campanario of burned brick stands unique among the bell-walls of the mission chain. Behind it is a barrel vault that leads into the church itself.

San Antonio de Padua

*Third mission, founded July 14, 1771, by Fr. Junípero Serra. Named for
St. Anthony. Mission moved to present site in 1773. Adobe church completed
1782; present building begun 1810, completed 1813. Secularized 1834.
Offered for sale in 1845, but there were no takers. Mission abandoned
1882–1928. Restored: 1903–07, 1948–49. Off U.S. Highway 101, 27
miles northwest of Bradley, 23 miles southwest of King City.*

Though located off the beaten path in the midst of a military reservation criss-crossed with tank tracks, Mission San Antonio de Padua offers more rewards to the traveler of today than any other mission, except perhaps La Purísima. Almost completely restored, it spreads out in grand style like a miniature city in the midst of an oak-studded valley. The traveler coming upon it senses the spaciousness that characterized all the missions in their heyday.

Nearly all of the story of San Antonio is a glad one of acceptance, prosperity, and good will. In its prime, the mission was the home of thirteen hundred Indians, who worked at a score of handicrafts, produced bountiful crops, and herded some 17,000 livestock.

San Antonio was the third mission in the California chain to be founded. Another mission—San Buenaventura—had been officially designated as number three when the Alta California expedition was launched, but because of unsettled conditions in the area where it was due to be established, its founding was postponed, and San Antonio took its place as the next mission to follow the first two, San Diego and Monterey.

Serra lost no time in establishing the new mission. He had just moved the Monterey Mission to Carmel, and while workmen were erecting the stockades, he impatiently set out with two padres, some sailors, and neophytes to found the new one at a spot in the Santa Lucia Mountains that had caught Portolá's eye when he had passed through the area two years before. After a laborious trek of twenty-five leagues, Serra's party reached the site, a pleasant basin well wooded with live oaks, alders, and willows, which they called Los Robles (the oaks), and they pitched camp near a stream that Father Serra christened Rio de San Antonio.

The little mule train had hardly been unburdened and a bell hung from a stout oak, before Father Serra in a burst of enthusiasm suddenly rang the bell and shouted, "Oh ye gentiles! Come, come to the holy Church!"

This outburst amazed the company, and they reminded him that there was as yet no church, nor was there even an Indian in sight.

But the zealous padre pleaded, "Let me give vent to my heart which desires that this bell might be heard all over the world!"

In a few days a large cross was raised and blessed in the conventional manner, and Mass was celebrated under a brushwood shelter, in honor of St. Anthony of Padua. This first service was an auspicious beginning, for Father Serra's quick eye caught sight of a young, bronze-skinned figure peering at them from a distance, doubtless attracted by the bells. At the first opportunity Father Serra went over to him and gave him several little gifts.

This move had the desired effect, for that very day the Indians came in droves to meet the kind strangers and receive handouts of glass beads and other trinkets which they prized so highly. In return, they brought gifts of acorns, pine-nuts, and wild seeds they had harvested. The strangers' language they could not understand, but they did recognize Father Serra's gentle courtesy, which touched their hearts. He stayed with the new mission for 15 days and then returned to Carmel, leaving two competent padres in charge.

One of the padres was Father Buenaventura Sitjar, who remained at San Antonio for 37 years and was the guiding hand responsible for many improvements. He tapped the San Antonio River about three miles above the mission, and impounded the water by means of dams, then brought it by long aqueducts to the mission grounds where it was stored in reservoirs. Water turned the gristmill; it supplied the mill-race, and the fountain, even a bathing pool. Much of this initial water system is still visible, including the original retaining walls of a reservoir constructed in the early days of the mission.

Father Sitjar also completed a valuable grammar and a 400-page vocabulary of the Mutsun language, spoken by the Indians of the San Antonio valley. Through these books Father Sitjar was able to prepare catechisms in the language of the neophytes and thus attain his goal of conveying to the Indians full understanding of the Christian life.

With secularization the church and the work centers fell into ruin, but what was worse, the Indians, who had been content under the protection of the padres, were mistreated and then forced back into the mountains to exist on seeds and game. Deprived of its parish, the mission was abandoned for 46 years, and the buildings, including the church, were abandoned. Being remote from the routes of travel, they were brazenly plundered of all usable construction materials.

Restoration Was a Formidable Task

In time, a group of public-spirited citizens became aware of the missions' plight, and banding together to restore them, they formed the California Historic Landmarks League under the leadership of the Honorable Joseph R. Knowland. Teamed with other civic and history-minded organizations, the League campaigned for funds. Knowland stumped the state, proclaiming: "The

Before the dedication of the site, Fr. Serra could not contain his exuberance, and he rang the bell and called out, "Oh ye gentiles! Come, come to the holy Church!"

conviction comes strong on one that in no civilized country in the world save our own, would such despoliation grow unhindered—with no hand to stay it. No Californian can view these picturesque ruins and fail to become an enthusiastic advocate of mission restoration!"

Selecting San Antonio because it was "the largest and most picturesque of the remaining missions of Northern California" the League began work on it in 1903. To arouse interest in the project, they held annual meetings at the mission on St. Anthony's Day, June 13, where they joined with the local residents in the celebrations.

Restoration was a formidable task because of the extent of the ruins, the perpetual lack of funds, and the quirks of nature. Heavy rains (22 inches!) in 1904–05 washed out some of the work put up the previous summer, and the repairs were in turn toppled by the earthquake of 1906. In 1907, lumber for the roof could not be delivered because of the muddy roads. Despite these reverses, the restoration of the church was completed in 1907, and it stood until 1948 when the thoroughgoing restoration was effected with the help of funds from the Hearst Foundation and the Franciscans of California. The buildings were stripped to the ground, all but the church, and painstakingly rebuilt from scratch. Although old materials and methods were used wherever possible, the new structures were liberally strengthened with steel and concrete.

Because of the careful work done in the last restoration, the mission as it now stands is an accurate replica of the 1813 original. Parts of the mission compound are reserved for the use of the Franciscans, but most of the grounds and all of the exhibits and museums are open to the public, which is welcomed.

By the time this photograph was taken in the 1890's, the mission had been vacant for nearly a decade. Tiles, timbers, and hardware had been appropriated by ranchers; squatters occupied some of the crumbling quarters. All the religious objects had been scattered, some retained by the Indians. Fence around the mission was built to keep cattle out of the building.

Wooden head, one of two figureheads from a colonial frigate, now at the mission. By legend, the heads are said to have been brought to the mission by sailors as a thank offering after a stormy and perilous voyage.

*Interest in restoring the mission began
to grow in early 1900's. Beginning in
1903 celebration of Saint Anthony's
Day was resumed and carried on in the
ruins for several years.* ABOVE. *Buggies
wait outside the church in 1903.*
BELOW. *The services are celebrated in
the fallen sanctuary. Indian musicians
accompany the service with the typical
instruments of mission days: drum,
violin, and flute. The drum shown
here is on display in the museum.*

*First restoration was started in 1903
by the California Historic Landmarks
League and the Native Sons under the
direction of Senator Joseph R. Knowland.
The building was almost a total wreck,
as the photo shows. Roof beams had
rotted, spilling tile onto the ground,
and the exposed adobe walls had melted
into mounds of soil. Rebuilding
progressed slowly, hampered by heavy
rains, and work was still in progress
when the earthquake of 1906 struck,
knocking down much of the new
construction. Most of the new adobes
visible in the large photograph opposite
fell in the quake. Restoration was
finished in 1907.*

*When the mission was being restored, descendants of
Indians who had once worked on the old structure used
some of the same construction techniques as the
original builders. As the wall grew, posts were temporarily
cemented into the wall itself to support the catwalks.
When the wall was finished, these posts were
withdrawn, and the openings filled with adobe, or
in some instances they were sawed off and left in place.
The hoist for raising loads of adobe to the men
working on top shows signs of maritime rigging. Often,
sailors were employed in the mission construction,
and they applied their knowledge of ship's rigging to
the handling of loads.*

The earlier restoration gave way in time, and the mission had to be rebuilt
all over again. The shingle roof put over the church in 1903–07 disintegrated
and had to be replaced. For lack of funds, the restorers were unable to rebuild
the quadrangle, and it was left to collapse. Although the church was reactivated
in 1928 to serve the local parish, the buildings were still in ruinous condition.
When restoration was recommenced in 1948 with a grant from the
Hearst Foundation, there was little left of the quadrangle except the single row
of arches made of burned brick, impervious to the elements. The old building
was completely cleared off the land, and the structure rebuilt from the
ground up. The Franciscan Fathers finished the quadrangle.

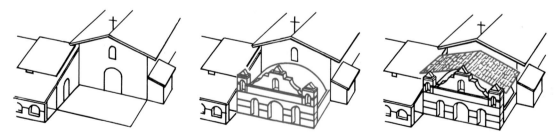

Evidence turned up in the last restoration indicated that the original façade of
San Antonio was probably as plain as San Miguel or Santa Inés.
The campanario was added at an unknown date to embellish the façade.
Rainwater later weakened the barrel vault behind the campanario and an
ungainly shed roof was erected to shield it from the elements. This roof was
still in place in 1948.

*Restoration of the quadrangle was a painstaking
performance. Bulldozers cleared away the mounds of
dissolved adobe until the original floor tiles and
foundation stones were revealed. Then, workmen swept off
the exposed tiles with brooms and whisks until the lines
of the original building were clear. In the photograph,
some of the pattern of the old structure can be seen in the
differing surfaces of the soil. New adobes were made from
the great mounds of powdered wall pushed aside by
the bulldozers.*

To support its Indian population, the mission raised and processed wheat in abundance. The wheat was threshed in the stone-covered area shown below left. The Indians heaped grain on the stones and drove wild horses through the mound, grinding it to bits in a very short time. The conversion of wheat to flour required an elaborate waterworks to operate the mill. A system of reservoirs and flumes brought the water from a dam 3 miles up the river, channeled it down an open millrace past the tanning vats and into the mill house just visible at the top left of the photograph. There, the water spun the apparatus diagrammed below and then flowed into irrigation ditches.

Museum display dramatizes devices used by the padres to teach music to the
Indians. Painted on the wall are a sample of the two-color, two-shape musical
notations that the Indians could read and a diagram of the hand signals
used to teach the scales.

San Gabriel Arcángel

*Fourth mission, founded September 8, 1771, by Frs. Pedro Cambón and Angel
Somera. Named for the Archangel Gabriel. Mission moved to present site
by Lasuén in 1775. Present church begun 1791; completed 1805; damaged by
earthquake 1812; repaired 1828; damaged by earthquake 1987. Secularized 1834;
restored to Catholic Church in 1859. Located on Mission Drive in San Gabriel,
9 miles east of downtown Los Angeles.*

San Gabriel Mission is distinctive, both in its structure and in the story it has
to tell.

Architecturally, the mission church is unlike any of its sister churches: the
side wall is the real façade; the Moorish appearance of its capped buttresses and
long narrow windows, found in no other missions, may be traced directly to the
Cathedral of Cordova, Spain. It was at Alcarazegos, bishopric of Cordova, that
Father Antonio Cruzado, in charge of the building of a great portion of the
original church, was born and reared.

Assignment to missionary work at San Gabriel was perhaps more demanding
than at any other mission. Sitting astride three well-traveled trails—two from
Mexico to Alta California, and one, at a later period, from the East Coast of
the United States to California—it was a wayside stop for the weary but honorable, the riffraff from Mexico and the East, and the missionary and colonizing
parties from Mexico en route to Alta California. The mission was continually
overrun by the military, whose behavior was a constant trial to the mission
fathers. It was this element, more than any other, that was largely responsible
for the mission's constant trouble with the Indians.

Economically, Mission San Gabriel, although it suffered hardships in its early
years, was not only prosperous in its own right, but was the spiritual and
cultural center of vast ranches engaged in cattle-raising and agricultural activities.

San Gabriel was founded on September 8, 1771, by Fathers Cambón and
Somera on a site (approximately nine miles east of the heart of present-day
Los Angeles) previously selected by Father-President Serra. Coming from

*Simplicity of form and material combine to give this
much-photographed stairway its charm. The chipped plaster
reveals a blend of building materials, hardburned brick on
top of stone. This combination is used throughout the
structure, the stonework stopping at the base of the
windows where the bricks take over, presumably to stiffen
it against earthquake shock.*

San Diego, the padres found the designated site, which was near a river known to the soldier-guard as the Santa Ana, but was named by its discoverers as the Rio de los Temblores. It was so-named because at this site on the day of its discovery four severe earthquakes were felt.

As the founding expedition of padres and soldiers with their pack mules now approached the river, they were surrounded by a large band of yelling natives. Fearing an attack, and perhaps hoping to pacify the Indian tribe, one of the friars unfurled a large banner with a painting of the Virgin on one side of it. At the sight of this image the natives threw down their bows and arrows. Furthermore, two Native American chieftains placed their bead necklaces at the feet of the "Beautiful Queen." At this display of confidence, natives from all of the nearby rancherías gathered seeds, which they placed before the painting, while gazing at it in wonder.

This painting, whose influence on the natives was thought by the Spaniards to be nothing less than miraculous, is now some 300 years old and is still venerated and on view in the mission sanctuary.

In spite of this encouraging incident, the padres decided the nearby land was unsuitable for a mission. They pressed farther on, to San Miguel Valley, so named by Portolá the year before, when he camped there on his way north from San Diego in search of the port of Monterey. On a hill near the source of the

The American, Jedediah Smith, and his party stopped at the mission in 1826 in violation of a Mexican law that forbade foreigners from entering the province.
The starved and tattered men were courteously received by the padres and allowed to remain for the ten days it took to get legal clearance.

*Alfred Robinson, an American trader, visited the mission and sketched it on a
Sunday in 1828. He was impressed by the "imposing ceremony, glittering
ornaments, and illuminated walls" and by the Indian musicians. After the
services, the Indians devoted themselves to a fiesta, some of them gambling away
"clothes, beads, baubles of all kinds."*

stream of the same name, they raised a large cross and celebrated the first mass
in a brush-wood hut.

The Indians willingly helped in the work of building, carrying timbers for
the temporary chapel and other necessary structures. The walls were made of
willow poles, and tules covered the rafters to form the roof. A stockade of poles
sharpened at the top enclosed the buildings in case the Indians changed their
minds and decided to attack.

Unfortunately, the misconduct of one of the soldiers soon after the founding
of the mission destroyed the Indians' confidence in the missionaries, delayed
conversions, and created a lasting hatred for the military. The story is briefly
this: A soldier assaulted the wife of the Indian chief. To avenge this wrong, the
chief, with a large band of natives, charged the culprit in an attempt to kill him,
and was himself killed in the skirmish. The corporal of the soldier-guard cut off
the head of the chief and impaled it on a pole to warn against further attacks.

A few days after the fracas, tribesmen came to beg for the head of their
chief. No further attacks were made, but it was a long time before the natives
allowed themselves to be seen at the mission.

Unaware of the soldiers' culpability in this bloody incident, the Governor increased the guard by assigning soldiers previously slated for Mission San Buenaventura and thus forced postponement of the founding of the latter mission for
several years. This regrettable occurrence was only one of a long series of similar wrongs committed by the military against Native Americans at San Gabriel.

Meanwhile, the Fathers Cambón and Somera, both too ill to continue their work, were replaced by the Fathers Paterna and Crusado. The gentleness and understanding of these two missionaries gradually regained the confidence of the natives, so that in time, a few children were presented for baptism. The first to be offered was the son of the slain Indian chief.

When the Fathers Palóu and Lasuén passed through San Gabriel in 1772, the mission still boasted only the first crude buildings and stockade. Spring floods had ruined the first crops. Lasuén recommended moving to a better site, but it was not until 1775 that the move was made.

It was the new site that Anza visited on his second journey from Mexico to Alta California at the end of 1775. He found the mission well able to feed his entire party of colonists and soldiers, the main part of which he left at the mission to recuperate from the exhausting journey from Sonora, Mexico, while he and Rivera, accompanied by Father Font and 17 soldiers, hastened to San Diego to help put down an Indian uprising.

Father Paterna, who left with the Anza party when it resumed its journey north, was replaced by Father Sánchez in February, 1776. It was the Fathers Cruzado and Sánchez, working together for nearly thirty years, who made San Gabriel the heart of agricultural development in that area.

San Gabriel grew so prosperous that it became known as "The Queen of the Missions." Because of its situation in a fertile valley with adequate timber, fine pasturage, and plenty of water for irrigation, it was soon producing abundant crops of corn and beans and building up great herds of cattle.

San Gabriel became famous for its fine wines. Soap-making and tallow-rendering were important industries at the mission. The Indians became skilled also at the crafts of weaving and leather-work.

In 1779, a new church, built of stone and concrete up to the windows and of brick from there on up, was started. A vaulted concrete roof, subsequently cracked by earthquakes, was replaced in 1803 by a flat tile roof. It was not until 1805 that this splendid church was completed. The two faithful padres, Cruzado and Sánchez, who had spent 26 years building it, did not live to enjoy it. Both died that year.

It was Father José Zalvidea who carried on the mission's work for the next 20 years. After the 1812 earthquake, which greatly damaged the monastery and toppled the church tower, which at that time was at the front of the church, Zalvidea and the other padres moved into the granary, which they converted into a temporary chapel. In 1828, the church was completely restored. The new bell-tower was erected at the far end of the side wall. Three rows of arched openings held the bells.

Great strides were made by Zalvidea in crop yield. Although a succession of padres worked under him, for 20 years Zalvidea *was* the mission. A man of great physical strength, a fanatic in religion, a born leader, he worked himself far harder than those who worked for him. It was under his direction that the church at the Pueblo of Los Angeles, "The Church of our Lady of the Angels," was completed. Another contribution was his hospital for the Indians.

When this drawing was made by Henry Miller in 1856, the outbuildings were
being used as a "haunt of some notorious cattle thieves." The church was still
well preserved, but everything else was "dilapidated or totally in ruins."
The cactus hedges, planted to protect the orchards, were full of ripe fruit.
Miller stayed long enough to watch a bull and bear fight, and buy the
bear's skin for $3.

Secularization hit hard at San Gabriel. Father Esténaga, then in charge, sadly turned over all of the mission's vast wealth to the secular administrator. When, in 1843, the mission properties were returned to the Franciscans, nothing was left at San Gabriel but ruined buildings and half-starved Indians.

Pio Pico somehow possessed himself of all the mission properties, and just before his death he gave the mission buildings and immediate surroundings to two Americans in payment of a debt. This deal was later declared illegal. But during this troublesome period after Esténaga left, the church, itself, was never completely deserted. The Indians remaining on the land and the church were cared for by successive Franciscan padres until 1852.

When President Buchanan restored the deserted property to the Catholic Church in 1859, it was used for a parish church until 1908, when it became the property of the Claretian Fathers. Asistencia Mission, a subsidiary built by San Gabriel's Franciscan Fathers between 1830-1834, stands on Barton Street in Redlands.

Architecturally, Mission San Gabriel differs from most of the others in the California chain. The capped buttresses and the long narrow windows are found in no other missions. Sometimes described as "fortress style," it has many elements that can be traced directly to Spain. One of the most persuasive theories of origin comes from the architectural authority Rexford Newcomb, who relates this building to the cathedral of Cordova, where the padre who designed San Gabriel received his early training.

The cathedral, formerly a Mosque, sketched at left, had capped buttresses, arched shell decorations above the doors, and long, narrow windows. The roof of San Gabriel was originally a low stone vault.

The plain entrance to the church was once graced by a bell-wall that toppled in the earthquake of 1812. The campanario was rebuilt at the other end of the church. No one knows exactly what the original looked like, but Rexford Newcomb deduced the design (above right) reprinted with his permission from his book on the architecture of the California missions.

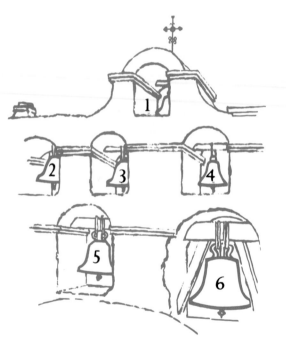

KEY TO THE BELLS OF SAN GABRIEL:

1. *Sold to the Plaza Church by San Gabriel, this bell hung there for a century until its return to the mission in 1931. Cast in 1828 in Medford, Mass., by Holbrook.*

2. *Though undated, this was probably cast in 1795 in Mexico City by Paul Ruelas and is thus one of the oldest in California. Its Latin inscription reads:* AVE MARIA PURÍSIMA. S. FRANco. PAULA RUELAS ME FECIT. *(Hail Mary Most Pure. St. Francis. Paul Ruelas Made Me.) It is tuned to B-natural.*

3. *Another Holbrook bell of 1828 vintage, doubtless traded to the mission for hides and tallow. Founder of the Massachusetts firm, Major G. H. Holbrook, learned the craft from Paul Revere.*

4. *One of the original set, removed from the mission in the 1870's — the bell was said to have been blown into a passing buckboard by a high wind—it rang on the ranch of "Lucky" Baldwin until the 1930's, when it was finally returned to its mission home.*

5. *Another Ruelas bell of 1795 casting is of heavy Mexican styling. One of "two swinging bells given to the mission by the King at the request of Fr. Serra."*

6. *This large bell has rung the Angelus over the countryside for over a century. Its clear tone could be heard in the Pueblo of Los Angeles, 8 miles away. Weighing at least a ton, it hangs from a crown-shaped top, symbol of a royal bell. Dated: 1830.*

JOHN S. WEIR

*Immaculately preserved church glows with strong colors—
barn red, gold, and forest green dominate. Light through
the green glass windows gives the room an almost
under-water luminescence. A tongue-and-groove,
painted ceiling conceals the original beams.*

Side bracing for the ceiling cross-beams reveals the traces of an inappropriate Victorian-style ceiling support with scroll-sawn arches, installed in the last century and modified in the 1930's.

One of the remarkable set of Indian paintings of the Stations of the Cross displayed in the museum. The only authentic Indian paintings in the mission chain, they were painted by an Indian at San Fernando. The set was exhibited at the World's Columbian Exposition in Chicago in 1893, then became part of a Los Angeles Chamber of Commerce exhibit, and was eventually given to the padres at San Gabriel.

Mission San Gabriel was noted for its vineyards and its wine production. The mission had the oldest (1771) and at one time the largest winery in California, with three wine presses and eight stills for making brandy. The old winery is preserved as a museum. After the mission period came to an end, the vineyards were neglected or sold. Some of the vines were trained on trellises, and open-air taverns operated under the leafy shade, such as the one in this photograph taken in 1900.

*To grind bumper crops of grain, a waterpowered flour mill was built in 1810
near the present city of San Marino. Damaged by the 1812 earthquake and
abandoned, it later became a private dwelling, here being painted in 1897 by
the wife of sculptor Gutzon Borglum, who is watching over her shoulder.*

*In 1818–22 the padres of San Gabriel donated 7 barrels of brandy to help
establish a chapel for the young pueblo of Los Angeles, 8 miles away.
The Church of Our Lady of the Angels still stands in downtown Los Angeles.*

San Luis Obispo de Tolosa

The fifth mission, founded September 1, 1772, by Fr. Junípero Serra.
Named for Saint Louis, Bishop of Toulouse. Present building built 1792–94;
vestibule added in 1820, torn down in 1877, restored 1933.
Building modernized in 1876 with wooden siding; restored to original form
in 1934. Located at corner of Monterey and Chorro Streets in downtown
San Luis Obispo, a busy city on U.S. Highway 101.

Portolá's half-starved expedition, returning to San Diego from its vain search for Monterey in December 1769, came upon a spacious marshy valley, well trampled and full of holes. Puzzled by the torn-up soil, the men soon saw the reason: troops of bears kept the surface pawed up, searching for their favorite food, the juicy roots of young tules.

The famished men rejoiced at this providential encounter, for it seemed to offer an end to their short rations. But they underestimated the ferocity of the beasts, and when they attempted to kill one, they were lucky that none of them was killed or maimed before the grizzly was finally dispatched. They ate the meat with relish, and in honor of the occasion, they named the place La Cañada de los Osos (Valley of the Bears).

Thus, when the missions at Carmel and San Antonio were themselves near starvation in 1772, this Valley of the Bears was remembered. A hunting party was sent down to kill grizzlies and send the meat back to relieve the missions. The hunters stayed three months, living on bear meat and seeds. According to the story, this must have been history's record bear hunt, because the men are said to have loaded the pack-mules with nine-thousand pounds of salted and jerked bear meat! In addition, they sent back twenty-five loads of edible seeds, secured from the friendly Indians in exchange for meat. The Indians had been impressed by the ease with which the Spaniard's firearms could bring to earth their traditional enemies, the bears, which their swiftest arrows could only wound.

While the hunters were away, Father Serra learned that two ships had reached San Diego with much-needed supplies. He decided to go to San Diego himself

Simple, almost stark façade was restored to its original
form in the 1930's. The combination of belfry and
vestibule is unique among California missions. Bells in
belfry were recast in 1878 from originals made in
Peru in 1818.

*Bear hunt in 1772, which netted 9,000 pounds of meat,
saved Carmel and San Antonio de Padua colonies
from starvation.*

and persuade the ship captains to proceed north to Monterey, even against the stormy weather which had held them back. He also planned to establish the fifth mission near the Valley of the Bears, where the Indians had been cordial, while on his way south.

Accordingly, with soldiers, muleteers, and a string of pack-animals loaded with church goods and farm implements for the new mission, Serra reached the valley, and selected a low hill near "a stream of the finest water" where he celebrated the first Mass in a shelter of boughs and named the new mission for St. Louis, bishop of Toulouse.

Eager to continue the journey, Serra departed the very next day, leaving behind Father José Cavaller, five soldiers and two neophytes to erect the first buildings. For their sustenance they were left fifty pounds of flour, some chocolate, three pecks of wheat for sowing, and a box of brown sugar to trade to the savages for seeds. This was very little, but the men survived with the help of the friendly Indians, who supplemented their meager food supply.

There was no native village near the valley, but attracted by the building going on, Indians came from afar, out of curiosity. Soon many were persuaded to bring their children to be baptized, and a colony slowly grew up around the mission. These Indians were friendly and helpful, but they were deliberate about accepting the mission way of life. They had ample food and were not particularly impressed by the gifts offered to them by the padres. Not all of the Indians in the area were cordial to the missionaries. In the rugged country to the south lived tribes of volatile disposition, who caused trouble several times in the first decades of the mission's existence. The first flare-up occurred on a November night in 1776. A watchman saw a sudden burst of flame back of the padres' quarters. It spread quickly as he roused all the residents and together they finally put out the fire, but only after it had consumed all the log buildings except the church and granary.

The blaze had been started by flaming arrows shot by enemies of the mission neophytes, natives who lived in a village 10 leagues distant. Two of the leaders were caught and sent to Monterey as prisoners, but similar attacks followed. The mission buildings were vulnerable to fire damage because of their dry tule thatch, and the padres were forced to devise protection from the harassment. Recalling the tiled roofs in their native Spain, they began experimental manufacture of curved tiles in 1790. Their first tiles (of which a few specimens remain) were about 22 inches long and tapered from 12 to 20 inches across. The clay was worked in pits under the tread of animal hoofs. Then when it had "fermented," squares of clay of the right thickness were patted over curved wooden forms, well sanded to keep the clay from adhering. The edges were trimmed, the clay dried in the sun and then baked in a kiln.

These roofing tiles, said to be the first made in California, were quickly copied in all the other missions as new ones were built. The tiles were a great advance over the thatch commonly used to cover mission structures. In addition to offering protection from fire raids, the waterproof surface kept the interiors dry in winter and shielded the adobe walls from rain.

In time, the mission developed into a prosperous institution, noted for its locally-produced wines, olive oil, fruits, and vegetables. Principal architect of the mission's prosperity was Father Luis Antonio Martínez, who served for

Tule roof of first mission was fired in 1776 by flaming arrows shot by hostile Indians. Two more attacks in following years caused padres to make first tile roof.

thirty-four years. Martínez was a portly, jovial friar, whose hospitality, generosity and humor quickly won him fame. He was also a keen trader, and he carefully supervised all the mission activities and financial affairs. However, he was equally frank and critical, and his quick temper often got him into trouble with the Governor, with the final result that he was arrested on a flimsy charge and banished in 1830, much to the sorrow of the Indians.

Toward the end of his long career, Father Martínez realized that secularization was going to come soon, so he let the mission property get into disrepair. As he foresaw, the mission was secularized five years after his banishment. At that time, the property was valued at $70,000, but within a few years its value dwindled almost to nothing. Indian bands drove off the livestock, the buildings and facilities were allowed to deteriorate, and by 1845 when all of the property except the church itself was put up for public sale, it brought only $510.

During the Mexican War, it was the scene of a farcical skirmish between Frémont and a handful of women and children. Learning that the mission was being held by a band of Mexican insurrectionists, Frémont surrounded the building in the dead of night with his forces, only to find that it was occupied solely by non-combatants. Frémont later sat in judgment here on the treason trial of a Don Pico, who was charged with conspiring against the United States government. He was found guilty and condemned to death; but his sentence was reversed a few days later, and he was released, much to his relief and the rejoicing of his many friends.

In 1859, what was left of the mission was returned to the Church by the government. In 1868 the buildings were remodeled to look like a parish church, the mellowed adobes being encased in white-painted siding. This sad disguise it wore until 1934 when it was removed and the building restored to its former simple grace and dignity.

*One of the first sketches of the mission, by H. M. Miller
in 1847, shows the original church front with its
belfry-like façade. Damaged by earthquakes in 1832 and
1868, it was taken down in 1880 and not rebuilt until
1934. The mission floor was at ground level in
the 1840's, but when the street was cut through a few
years later, the building became 10 feet above the street.*

Described in the novel Ramona *is a
lively scene attributed to the eccentric
Father Martínez. To entertain a
Mexican general and his bride,
the padre "caused to be driven past the
corridors for their inspection, all the
poultry belonging to the Mission.
The procession took an hour to pass. . . .
It would be safe to say that a droller
sight never was seen, and never will be
on the Pacific Coast or any other."*

Because of their favored locations, several of the missions became the nuclei for flourishing cities and towns after California entered the Union. San Luis Obispo was one of eight missions from which towns sprang. By 1875, hotels and markets were already in evidence across from the mission.

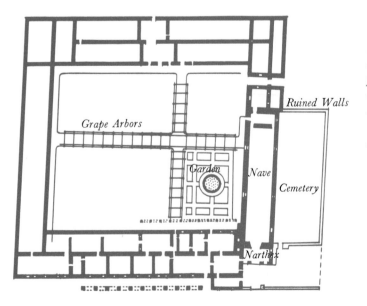

Little remains of the original structure that once surrounded the traditional patio. The church occupied the north side of the square, priests' house the east, and shops and storehouses the west. Behind were tanning vats, a reservoir, and a grist mill. The patio was divided into four unequal areas by grape arbors. A garden filled the northeast quarter.

After the American occupation, the town acquired settled, bucolic air and was well on its way to becoming prosperous settlement by the 1890's. At the head of the tree-shaded street can be seen the incongruous steeple added to the mission in 186.

Up until the late 1870's, the church façade remained more or less unchanged.
The belfry-vestibule was damaged by two earthquakes, and a few years
after the second one (1868), roof tiles were removed to relieve strain on the
structure. Finally, the whole front part was taken down in 1880
and a New England steeple added. At the same time, the whole face
of the mission was boarded over.

*Once more restored to its original appearance, with the steeple and the
sheathing removed, the façade has a rugged grace, especially when viewed
from the south. Unique among mission corridors, the colonnade outside the old
priests' quarters has square openings and round pillars. The floor of the
colonnade was once level with the ground but is now above the street.*

When the interior was modernized in 1876, the beamed ceiling was covered with tongue-and-groove sheathing, the altar was painted white, new side altars added where none had been before, and the mezcla floor covered with wood, as shown in this 1885 photograph. The wooden coverings remained in place until 1920 when a fire in the sacristy exposed the original structural members for the first time in decades. Fortunately, the covering protected the original ceiling from the fire, and it received only minor damage.

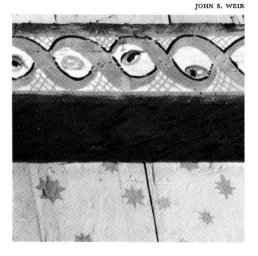

Restoration of the interior to its 1794 state was done in 1947. The beamed ceiling with its colorful floral designs resembling eyes (above) was revealed for the first time in decades. The reredos (right) was repainted in its original quaint style, side niches were uncovered, and the mezcla flooring restored.

San Francisco de Asís

Sixth mission, founded June 29, 1776, by Fr. Francisco Palóu. Named for St. Francis of Assisi, founder of the Franciscan Order. Present building begun April 25, 1782, dedicated April 3, 1791. Secularized 1834, mission lands sold 1845; properties returned by Presidential Proclamation in 1857. Located in San Francisco on Dolores Street, between 16th and 17th Streets, 3 blocks south of Market Street. On 49-mile historic drive.

"If St. Francis desires a mission, let him show us his harbor and he shall have one," said Inspector-General Gálvez to Father Serra when they were working out their original plans for the establishment of the first three missions in Alta California. Serra had lamented that there was no mission planned to honor the founder of his order, and Gálvez had facetiously offered this challenge.

At the time that Gálvez and Serra were making plans, a San Francisco Bay was known to exist, but it was not the great port that today bears the name of the saint. It was a small harbor to the north, now known as Drakes Bay, which had been named for St. Francis by a Spanish explorer in 1597. It had earlier been given another name by Sir Francis Drake, who had careened his ship there 16 years before the Spaniards found the harbor, but the Spanish grandly chose to ignore it.

The Bahía de San Francisco had not been explored since it had been named 170 years before Gálvez and Serra conferred, and Gálvez was justifiably skeptical that it could easily be re-located or would provide a suitable site for a mission.

However, providence contrived to shift the name southward to the great bay that it now identifies, but which at that time was not known to exist. Because of its narrow entrance, it had escaped the scrutiny of passing vessels and no overland explorers had chanced upon it. Its presence was thus an overwhelming surprise to the Portolá party when they came upon it while looking for Monterey Bay. Having over-shot the latter because they did not recognize it, they had continued northward and stumbled upon the tremendous bay spread out before their eyes. They did not recognize it as a bay and considered it an arm of the

The little church of Mission Dolores looks much the same as it did when it was completed in 1791, 15 years after the founding of the mission. The original bells, one cast in 1792, two in 1797, still hang from rawhide thongs. They are rung during Holy Week.

"On Sunday, when the service is ended," wrote the Russian von Kotzebue in 1816, "the Indians gather and dance. Half of the men adorn themselves with feathers and girdles ornamented with feathers and with bits of shell, or they paint their bodies with regular lines of black, red, and white. The men dance six or eight together, all making the same movements, all armed with spears."

sea that they would have to get around to reach the true San Francisco Bay farther north. It took two subsequent explorations to reveal the true extent of the port, which was finally seen to be large enough to "hold all the ships of Spain."

When the importance of the great bay was finally recognized, it absorbed the name from the northern harbor, and plans were rapidly prepared to secure it against foreign colonizing or attack. The Viceroy ordered that two mission settlements be established there, one with a presidio to protect the strategic port. In order to effect a stable settlement, plans called for planting a colony of married families; and a large overland party was organized and placed under the command of Lt. Col. Juan Bautista de Anza, a pathfinder who had already explored a route from northern Mexico to Monterey.

In one of the incredible feats of Western history, Anza led the party of 240 settlers and 1,000 head of cattle across the desert, over the mountains, and up the valleys of California with the loss of only one person, a mother who died in childbirth. Anza arrived at Monterey with 244 individuals, several children having been born en route, and a substantial portion of the livestock intact. Taking a smaller party with him, he continued to San Francisco where he selected a site for the presidio and one for the mission. For the latter, he chose a spot on the bank of a rivulet which he named Arroyo de los Dolores because it was the feast day of Our Lady of Sorrows. The name Dolores soon became attached to the nearby lake and eventually to the mission itself.

Anza returned to Carmel, pausing en route to select a site for the second San Francisco-area mission, Santa Clara. He turned the whole party of emigrants over to Lieutenant Moraga and headed home to Mexico. Moraga assembled a large number of the Anza colonists, who left Monterey for San Francisco on June 17, 1776 to establish the presidio and the mission. The rest of the Anza party stayed in Monterey, there to await orders for settling Santa Clara.

When the company arrived at its destination, a large group set up camp at the presidio site and a small number pitched their tents beside the small lake into which the Dolores Creek emptied. There, on June 29, just five days before the Americans in faraway Philadelphia signed the Declaration of Independence, Father Palóu had a brushwood shelter constructed and offered up the first Mass.

Seven weeks later, the *San Carlos* sailed into the bay, loaded with supplies for the presidio and the mission. With work well under way at the presidio, a detachment was sent to the mission site to aid in erecting a chapel, and by October 9, a wooden church plastered with mud and roofed with tules was ready.

The finished church was adorned as elaborately as possible with cloths and draperies, including banners and pennants from the ship. The dedication ceremonies ended with the ringing of bells, booming of cannon, and rattle of musketry. Even firecrackers and ship's rockets were set off to mark the occasion. "The day had been a joyful one for all," wrote Palóu, "Only the savages did not enjoy themselves on this happy day!"

When this sketch was made in 1826 by an artist with a British expedition under William Beechey, the mission was in an unhappy state. Illness had reduced the Indian population to 230 from 1,800 in five years; many of the neophytes were at the hospital mission in San Rafael. Note the shed at left of church, which then enclosed the baptistry and mortuary chapel.

By 1850 most of the Indians were gone and the mission had lost much of its influence. The rambunctious Fortyniners changed the district to a lively neighborhood where horse racing and bull-and-bear fights took place on former mission lands, and bars, dance halls, and casinos flourished.

Indeed the noise so frightened the Indians that they were not seen for several days. Nor did it help when soon after, natives from the village of San Mateo, mortal enemies of those in San Francisco, attacked them and burned one of their largest villages. Again San Francisco Native Americans scattered in fright, escaping across the bay in tule rafts.

For weeks their visits to the mission were rare; they only appeared when they came to the lagoon to hunt ducks. When they did come, they resorted to thievery and other annoyances. On being punished, they disappeared again for three months. Thus it was almost a year after the founding before the first three Indians were baptized.

The problem of runaways always plagued Mission Dolores. Even when the mission numbered over 4,000 converts in its records, the neophytes would still run away, attracted to their carefree friends across the bay. Their favorite hide-outs were on the opposite shore (Contra Costa), where it was difficult and dangerous to locate them. Even twenty years after the mission's founding, fourteen native neophytes sent to search for runaways were attacked and half of them were killed.

Mission life was none too attractive to the natives living in the area. The severe climate took its toll. Chilling fogs and blustery sea winds sweeping down on the mission were no help in treating measles and other foreign epidemics that struck the natives with devastating force. After the opening of the hospital mission at San Rafael in 1817, hundreds of the Dolores Indians were transferred there to recuperate in the sunshine.

The mission began to decline soon after secularization. It was a sleepy, isolated community when the Gold Rush struck it like a cyclone. Because of its remoteness from the center of town, the neighborhood became a center for high jinks, and people flocked to the area to enjoy the horse racing, gambling, and tavern life that erupted here. In time, the area was swallowed in the advancing expansion of the city, and respectabiity took over.

The beautiful church that is such a familiar landmark to San Franciscans was begun in April 1782 when Father Palóu decided to move the mission to a more favorable site. It was dedicated in 1791 and has suffered little change since. The large quadrangle, of which it was once a corner, disappeared piece by piece over the years, but the church has remained untouched. Missed by the earthquakes of 1906 and 1989, and spared from the misguided hands of "restorers," it has been carefully preserved, strengthened when necessary, and faithfully kept in its original state.

Connected with the city by two plank roads, the remote Mission District was a popular place for an outing. "On fine days, especially on Sundays, the roads to the Mission show a continual succession, passing to and fro, of all manner of equestrians and pedestrians, and elegant open carriages filled with ladies and holiday folk," reported a writer in 1854.

After secularization, portions of the mission quadrangle were sold or leased to business firms. Even after the mission properties were returned to the Church, space in the vast adobe was leased for private use. In 1865, when this photograph was taken, rooms were occupied by a print shop and the famous Mansion House, a tavern noted throughout the city for an exhilarating milk punch.

When the site for the mission was selected in 1776, a spot was chosen alongside a stream which the exploring party named Arroyo de los Dolores (Stream of the Sorrows) in honor of the Friday before Palm Sunday. The name Dolores has ever since been attached to the mission. The first mission, dedicated here in October, 1776, was a log-and-thatch structure built at the foot of present-day Camp St. In 1782, a short distance away, the cornerstone was laid for the present building, which was completed nine years later. The small lake into which Dolores Creek emptied was later filled, graded, and eventually covered with houses. When the 1906 quake struck, buildings on the filled area were severely damaged.

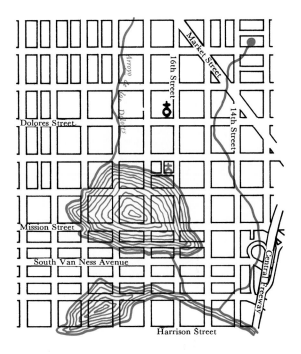

By 1876, *the fast-growing city had overtaken the old mission. Dolores Street
had been graded, cutting off a portion of the already-compressed cemetery and
forcing construction of a retaining wall in front of the mission. The chapel had
been sheathed with wood to protect it from rain; the big storage wing of the
original quadrangle had been razed to permit the extension of 16th Street;
and part of the old convento wing had been torn down to leave room for the
big new church alongside. As the population of the Mission District had
expanded following the Gold Rush, the little chapel had become too small to
serve the parish, and the large Victorian church was built to take over as the
parish center. It was dedicated in 1876 on the hundredth anniversary
of the mission's founding.*

When the great earthquake of 1906 struck at 5:12 a. m. on April 18, it set the church bells ringing all through the city. Mission Dolores, which had already withstood several severe quakes, came through unscathed. A few tiles shook off the roof, the tomb of Governor Argüello slid off its pedestal and some of the statuary toppled, shearing arms and wingtips. Damage by the fire that followed the quake stopped just short of the mission. The raging holocaust of the second day was halted across the street by heroic effort.

RIGHT. *The modern church next door did not fare so well. Built in 1876, it was in the process of being enlarged when the quake hit. The structure was so weakened by the shocks that it had to be dismantled a few weeks later.*

A temporary wooden church, built in back of the mission chapel, served the parish until a new masonry building was built several years later.

The ruined parish church was not replaced until 12 years after the quake. Begun in 1913, the stone mission-style structure was delayed in construction by World War I and was not completed until 1918, when it was dedicated on Christmas.

THE CHANGELESS CHAPEL

1791. Chapel built, occupies southeast corner of quadrangle. Shed on left for baptistry and mortuary chapel. Convento connects with storehouse on right.

1861. Chapel has lost the small side chapels on the left. Portion of convento remodeled to two stories in height, used as a seminary and priests' quarters.

1876. Chapel unchanged, but storage wing razed for opening of 16th St. Convento cut in half to give room for new church, dedicated on mission's centennial.

1906. Chapel unchanged, but convento removed to give room for addition of new wing to big stone church. Addition never finished because of earthquake.

1918. Chapel unchanged, but big church damaged by quake of 1906 replaced 1918 by church begun in 1913. In interim, wood church behind mission served parish.

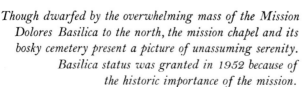

1926. Chapel unchanged, but parish church remodeled for sesquicentennial of mission founding. Architectural style influenced by designs used at San Diego Exposition of 1915.

Though dwarfed by the overwhelming mass of the Mission Dolores Basilica to the north, the mission chapel and its bosky cemetery present a picture of unassuming serenity. Basilica status was granted in 1952 because of the historic importance of the mission.

JOHN S. WEIR

The long, narrow (22x140 feet) chapel has changed little since the days when the Indians knelt on its tile floors. The baroque reredos behind the altar and statues on side altars are fine examples of Mexican ecclesiastical decoration of the early 1800's. Against the right wall is a large scene painted on canvas stretched on a frame. Used in mission days, this Mexican painting was placed in front of the altar on Holy Thursday.

The tall candlestick made by a native craftsman receives the Paschal candle, kept burning from Easter Sunday to Ascension Thursday. The quaint iron seat is called a bishop's chair.

Decorative panel covers opening in arch in front of the sanctuary. Mission Indians painted the red acanthus leaf design and symbol for Jesus on plastered matting set in place over the opening. (Symbol IHS stands for Greek letters Iota eta sigma, a contraction of the Greek name for Jesus.) Red, gray, and white chevron pattern on arch was painted on canvas applied in restoration of 1890. Close inspection reveals ghost image of numerals and handwriting on the canvas over which paint was applied.

SAN FRANCISCO DE ASÍS **151**

San Juan Capistrano

*The seventh mission, founded November 1, 1776, by Fr. Junípero Serra.
Previously established by Fr. Fermín Lasuén October 30, 1775, then abandoned. Named for St. John of Capistrano, Italy, a 14th century theologian
and inquisitor. Stone church begun 1796; completed 1806; destroyed by earthquake 1812. Mission secularized 1833, sold 1845, returned to Catholic Church 1865;
preservation started after 1987 earthquake. In San Juan Capistrano off Interstate 5.*

The mellowed ruins of San Juan Capistrano tell a story of mixed achievement and
disaster. The wide-spreading adobe structure reveals the existence of a once-
large and thriving establishment; and, looming above the low buildings, the
massive remains of a great church stand as a monument to a brief but glorious
chapter in early California history. The broken ivy-covered walls of the church
are all that remain of a once-magnificent structure that took nearly a decade to
build, was used for only a brief six years, and collapsed in one minute in a violent
earthquake in 1812.

The first glory of the mission has departed, but an afterglow of charm lingers
in the colorful remains. Nature has thrust fingers of ivy and ropes of rose vines
over the old stones gathered and fitted into place by the Indians. White doves
splash in the mossy fountains, flowers brighten the paths, and in summer the
famous swallows add their high-pitched chatter.

In its prime, the mission was one of the most prosperous in the chain, but in
the beginning, there was little to foretell the ultimate success of the venture.

Capistrano was really founded twice. In 1775, Father Lasuén set up a cross and
dedicated the ground. A crowd of Indians curiously watched the rites and willingly helped to haul timber for the construction of a temporary chapel and other
buildings. The work went on for eight days, but was suddenly stopped when
news arrived of an Indian attack at the San Diego Mission. The bells were
hastily buried and the small party hurried to San Diego where they took shelter
in the presidio.

When peace was assured, a second founding party under Father Serra journeyed to the site a year later. They found the cross still in place that had been

*White doves stroll on the rim of the Moorish-style fountain
in the plaza garden in front of the mission. Built in the
1920's, the fountain is faithful to the design and spirit of
the mission.*

erected the year before. They dug up the bells, hung them from a tree, and recited the service on November 1, 1776.

In another year, the first little chapel was built, a modest structure that is still in use today. Considered the oldest church in California, it is called "Father Serra's Church" because it is one of two still standing where it is known that he said Mass (the other is Mission Dolores).

Once established, the mission prospered almost from the start. The beautiful valley was fertile, pleasant, and blessed with a moderate climate. Outlying fields yielded abundant harvests of grains, vegetables, and fruit, and livestock flourished on the open range. In due time, storehouses, shops, and barracks for the soldiers were built around a large patio. The enclosed square was capacious enough to hold all the neophytes and their belongings in case of trouble. The patio was irregular in shape, each side being a different length, because the padres paced off the measurements instead of using surveyor's instruments.

The Tragedy of the Great Stone Church

By 1796 the little adobe church had become outgrown by the large number of neophytes in attendance and work was begun on a much larger stone sanctuary. An expert stonemason from Mexico was put in charge of construction. Most of the work was done by the Indians, who carried the stones from a quarry six miles northeast of the mission. Heavy boulders were hauled in squeaking carretas, large stones were dragged with chains, and smaller ones were carried by the neophytes. Even women and children carried stones in nets on their backs. For endless days they formed two lines to the rock-filled creek beds, going empty-handed and coming back laden.

Nine long years were consumed in building this cathedral-like church. When it was finished it stood as the most magnificent church of all the California missions, 180 feet long and 40 feet wide. Designed in the form of a cross, it had a vaulted ceiling surmounted by seven domes. The main entrance was crowned by a massive belltower 120 feet tall that could be seen for ten miles. Its four bells,

The yellowish sandstone for the great church was carried by the Indians in a never-ending procession from a quarry six miles away.

cast in 1796 and 1804, could be heard from an even greater distance.

Completion of the great church in 1806 was celebrated with all possible pomp and ceremony. All the civil, military, and religious dignitaries in California attended the blessing of the great church and the two-day fiesta that followed.

This most elaborate and beautiful of all the mission churches stood for only six years. At the end of an early morning service in December in 1812, just as the bells began to ring for the next Mass, a tremendous rumble and jangle of discord from the tower warned of an earthquake. The vault split open and the walls swayed back and forth, dumping the massive concrete ceiling on the kneeling congregation. Only the faithful who obeyed the father's frantic beckoning and fled to the sanctuary were saved. Forty bodies were dug out of the rubble. The two boys who had been ringing the bells in the tower were killed, although the bells were not damaged by the collapsing masonry.

The sanctuary was left virtually intact, and many fine wooden statues escaped destruction, as well as the old stone baptismal font with its carved wooden cover, some candlesticks, vestments, and pictures.

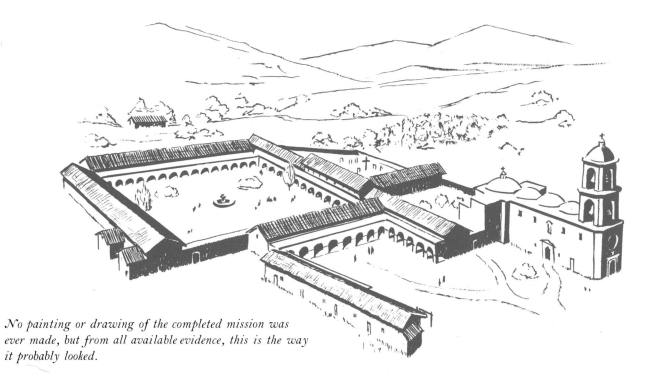

No painting or drawing of the completed mission was ever made, but from all available evidence, this is the way it probably looked.

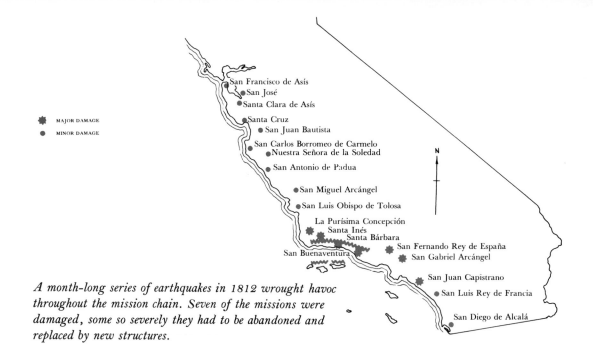

MAJOR DAMAGE

MINOR DAMAGE

San Francisco de Asís
San José
Santa Clara de Asís
Santa Cruz
San Juan Bautista
San Carlos Borromeo de Carmelo
Nuestra Señora de la Soledad
San Antonio de Padua
San Miguel Arcángel
San Luis Obispo de Tolosa
La Purísima Concepción
Santa Inés
Santa Bárbara
San Buenaventura
San Fernando Rey de España
San Gabriel Arcángel
San Juan Capistrano
San Luis Rey de Francia
San Diego de Alcalá

N

A month-long series of earthquakes in 1812 wrought havoc throughout the mission chain. Seven of the missions were damaged, some so severely they had to be abandoned and replaced by new structures.

The mission recovered from the tragedy and went on about its business. It was unthinkable to raise the elaborate church again, so the padres moved back into Serra's Church, and further construction was limited to utilitarian needs.

At the time of the earthquake, the neophyte population stood at 1,361 and it remained around a thousand for 14 more years before it began slowly to decline. The mission fields yielded bumper crops, reaching a peak in 1818 of 14,562 bushels. Twenty-thousand head of cattle and sheep roamed over the mission's eight ranchos.

Capistrano conducted a thriving trade in hides and tallow. As described in *Two Years Before the Mast*, the hides were flung from the top of the cliffs to the beach exposed at low tide, 280 feet below, where they were picked up and carried to the boats. Dana wrote in 1839: "Down this height we pitched the hides, throwing them as far out into the air as we could; and as they were all large, stiff, and doubled like the cover of a book, the wind took them, and swayed them about, plunging and rising in the air, like a kite when it has broken its string."

The mission's prosperity came to an end soon after secularization, and for a decade the mission was embroiled in a complicated political turmoil involving the Indians and the mission properties. The Indians were "emancipated" in 1833, but were subject to the control of civil administrators whose salaries were paid out of the Indian's toil. Half free, half subject, the Indians suffered the loss of their property, crops, and livestock. By 1844, only a handful were left.

Plundered of tiles and timber, buildings deteriorated rapidly. A "restoration" in the 1860s destroyed more than it restored, but the next attempt in the 1890s by the Landmarks Club saved the Serra Church from disintegration. A major restoration was begun in the 1920s by Father St. John O'Sullivan, who, over the years, laid out gardens and patiently repaired buildings. The latest, and most ambitious, preservation project was started by Monsignor Paul M. Martin after the 1987 Whittier earthquake.

Earliest (1850) sketch of the ruins of the stone church shows that more of the structure survived the quake than is now standing. Two domes above the transept and a full dome and lantern above the sanctuary came through intact.

By 1876, when this photograph was taken, the extra domes and lantern shown in the sketch above had long since disappeared. They had been blown to rubble with gunpowder in the 1860's by misguided restorers in a futile attempt to rebuild the church.

The vast quadrangle covered a great deal of ground, as this plot plan shows. Ranged around a patio nearly an acre in extent, the building housed storage rooms for barley, wheat, hides, and other provisions; shops for making candles, soap, shoes, hats, blankets, and harness; living and dining facilities for the padres; and of course the church and chapel. A wing to the south housed soldiers, a jail, and next to it, a powder magazine. The presently restored portions (in black) comprise only a fraction of the original plant. Irregular form of the quadrangle and its offshoots attributed to the padres' pacing off the measurements instead of using surveyor's instruments.

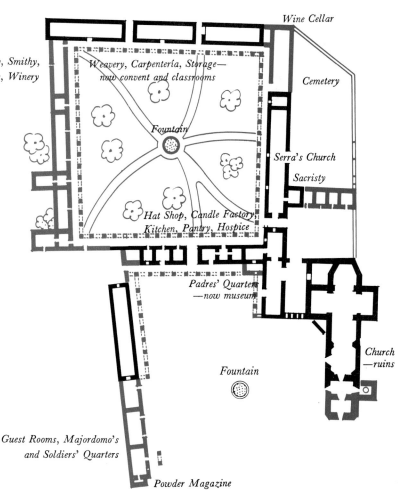

Wine Cellar

Soap Factory, Smithy, Olive Press, Winery

Weavery, Carpentería, Storage— now convent and classrooms

Cemetery

Fountain

Serra's Church

Sacristy

Hat Shop, Candle Factory, Kitchen, Pantry, Hospice

Padres' Quarters —now museum

Church —ruins

Fountain

Guest Rooms, Majordomo's and Soldiers' Quarters

Powder Magazine

After secularization, tiles were removed legally and illegally from the
buildings and arcades to roof the homes of the new pueblo. Once the walls were
exposed without protection of the tile overhang, they slowly dissolved. As this
1897 view of the inner patio shows, not much was left of the big rambling
building. Fortunately, the roof over what is now known as the Serra Chapel
(left) had been kept in repair, because it had been leased for several years for
hay storage, and the roof that kept the hay dry also kept the walls intact.

The four bells that hang in the low
campanario have been as widely
celebrated in song and story as the
mission's famous swallows. Tales tell
of their ringing by themselves at
tragic or romantic climaxes in love
affairs. The bells fell with the tower
in 1812 and were hung in this wall
the following year. Somewhat hoarse
and cracked in voice, they still toll
with mellowed authority. The largest
one is unique because it is inscribed
with the names of the padres at the
mission when the bell was cast. The
two large bells were cast in 1796,
the others in 1804. The bells have
always been rung by ropes attached to
their clappers, as shown in this
early photograph of bell-ringer
Don Ramon Argüello II.

*For more than a century, the picturesque ruins of San Juan Capistrano have
attracted artists, photographers, and tourists. In 1900, pioneer
photographer A. C. Vroman (seated in chair) posed with a Pasadena camera
club for a collective self-portrait. In 1912, the Inyo Good Road Club in
a quartet of Studebakers stopped in front of the ruined church on their way
around the state to propagandize the need for good roads.*

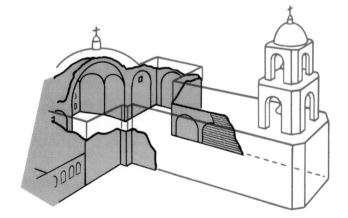

Except for normal deterioration, the ruins of the stone church changed little in more than a century, as a comparison of the photograph above, taken in the 1860s, with the one at left shows. The mission chapel served as parish church after the 1812 earthquake.

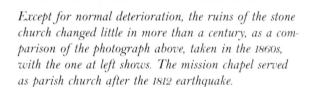

White doves wheel and strut where 40 Indians were crushed in the collapse of the great stone church in 1812. As shown in the sketch above, the standing masonry comprises only a small fragment of the original church, which in its day was the largest and most elaborate in the mission chain. The arch of the sanctuary rises five stories in height. Adobes, filling in the arches on the right, were installed in an unsuccessful attempt to restore the stone church.

SAN JUAN CAPISTRANO **161**

*Subject of story, poetry, and song, the swallows of Capistrano
(Las Golondrinas) are the best-known feature of the mission.
By legend, these birds drop from the sky in the early morning
of St. Joseph's Day each spring to rebuild their mud nests
for the annual brood. Some of the birds arrive before the
set day, many come afterwards, but the bulk usually arrives
on the traditional day. Sometimes, they are delayed
for days or weeks because of storms along the 2,000-mile
route from their wintering grounds. The birds are cliff
swallows (petrochelidon pyrrhonota), not to be confused
with their fork-tailed cousins, the barn swallows.
The restless birds are constantly on the wing,
swooping and diving for air-borne insects. They build
their gourd-like nests of saliva and mud, plastering
them against the broken arches. They also frequent Carmel Mission.*

JOHN S. WEIR

*The stone-work facings are more
elaborate than at any other mission.
Work of a master-mason brought from
Culiacán for the purpose, the carved
arches, doorways, capitals, and keystones
reveal the elegant touch of a sure hand.
The classic form of the broken
stonework suggests the haunting
grandeur of a Roman ruin.*

The crude designs on the ceiling above the nave, painted when the chapel was restored in 1922, contrast sharply with the sophistication of the gilded reredos.

Simple, childlike Indian decorations on the Serra Chapel wall are painted in the bright primary colors that were popular with the natives.

The baroque reredos brings a golden radiance to the old adobe chapel, named for Fr. Serra who said Mass here. Far more elaborate than any altarpiece used in mission days, the reredos was brought from Barcelona in 1906 to grace a new cathedral in Los Angeles. Never used for that purpose, it remained in storage until it was installed in this chapel in 1922–24. The piece was actually too large to fit the narrow room and had to be trimmed to size. It is thought to be at least 300 years old, and is a rich example of giltwork, a form of decoration that requires a three-dimensional surface to catch the light.

*Richly ornamented façade of Santa Clara Mission church
is a modern (1929) interpretation in stucco and concrete
of the simple structure of 1825. Decorations in bold relief
follow the original designs that were painted on the
façade in false perspective. Cross of 1777, sheathed in a
protective covering of redwood, stands facing the church.
In belltower, one of the original King's bells still tolls.*

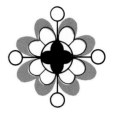

Santa Clara de Asís

Eighth mission, founded January 12, 1777, by Fr. Junípero Serra. Named for St. Claire of Assisi, founder of the order of nuns called the Poor Clares. First and second churches of logs built 1777 and 1779 by banks of Guadalupe River; third, 1784; fourth church, 1818–19. Fifth and present church built 1825; remodeled 1861, 1887; burned 1926; replaced 1929. Secularized 1836; transferred from Franciscans to Jesuits, 1851. Located in Santa Clara, on The Alameda.

Santa Clara was the second of the San Francisco missions to be founded in obedience to the Viceroy's order to plant two settlements near the great port to hold it against enemy occupation or attack. The first, Mission Dolores, had been established in 1776 and all was in readiness for the founding of the second mission, but the authorization was delayed because of an Indian uprising at San Luis Obispo.

After a wait of two months, the approval was granted, and parties from both San Francisco and Monterey set out for the new site, which had been chosen by Juan Bautista de Anza at the same time as the one in San Francisco. The site was about forty miles southeast of Mission Dolores, on the bank of a stream which Anza had named Rio de Nuestra Señora de Guadalupe.

Lieutenant Moraga, Father Tomás de la Peña, and some soldiers and their families left San Francisco on January 5, 1777, and headed for the Guadalupe River. A few miles upstream from the bay shore, they discovered a copiously flowing creek, near which on January 12 they planted the cross and made an arbor to serve as a temporary church.

Laying out the usual square with space for a church, dwellings, granary and guardhouse, they awaited the arrival of Father José Murguía, who was to come from Monterey with church goods, cattle, and necessary tools. He arrived in two weeks, and soon the buildings were well under way.

The natives nearby were friendly, but tempted by greed for the soldiers' goods. Their first mistake was to kill some of the mules. A runner carried this news to the presidio in San Francisco, which sent a detachment at once. On their way to the mission the soldiers saw the natives in their village, feasting on the meat of the mules. On attempted capture, the Indians hid in the brush and shot volleys of arrows at the soldiers who retaliated, killing three culprits and capturing some of the leaders. They took the ringleaders to the mission

Just before the Gold Rush upset the Spanish Arcadia that was California,
life at Mission Santa Clara was an easy-going affair, as depicted by painter
Andrew P. Hill. Perpetually on horseback, the Californios *rode about,*
dressed in finery about twenty years behind the times. Indians walked or
rode in ox-drawn carretas. The adobe church and priests' quarters,
secularized in 1836, served as parish church.

and flogged them, but despite the harsh punishment, the natives soon resumed their thievery. To them, it was only a fascinating game to see how much they could steal without being caught.

In May, an epidemic struck, and many of the Native American children died. Perhaps because of this sad circumstance, the mission fathers were able to baptize about fifty children, and the mission began its work in earnest.

The mission buildings were menaced by a series of floods and had to be moved several times in the ensuing years. In 1781 the cornerstone was laid for a fine new adobe church (the third), designed by Father Murguía. It was said to have been the most imposing structure in California when it was completed. Serra was present with Crespí, his assistant, to bless the cross and the cornerstone in an impressive and solemn rite.

The church was rightly called Father Murguía's church, because he put his very heart into it. He worked with the neophytes to mold the adobes, turn and dry them, and lay them with precision to build the most beautiful church he could imagine. He looked forward eagerly to its dedication, but he died four days before Serra arrived from Carmel to officiate at its consecration. In less than four months, Father Serra himself was to follow Murguía in death.

The cornerstone of this church was recovered by accident in 1911 when excavation for a gas main exposed the long-forgotten stone. Among the artifacts contained in it, now in the museum of the University of Santa Clara, were small crucifixes and Spanish coins, which symbolized the treasury of the Church.

Padres with outstanding virtues served at the mission. Besides Father Murguía, the builder, two padres of stature were beloved at this mission, and for quite different reasons.

Father Magín de Catalá, like Serra, was a model of sincerity and piety. He too loved the native children, and they returned his love with gratitude and reverence. He was known as The Prophet because of his uncanny ability to foretell events, such as the coming of the Americans and the discovery of gold. In 1830, he is recorded as having said in a sermon: "At the place now called Yerba Buena there shall one day arise a great and populous city. The city will flourish and its inhabitants will become rich and powerful, and when at the height of its prosperity, it will perish by earthquake and fire."

By contrast, his associate Father José Viadér, was a man of immense physical stature and warmth of heart to match. A story is told of him that one night a husky young Indian named Marcelo with two companions, dissatisfied for some reason, attacked the padre as he strolled along the arched passages. To their intense discomfort, the three soon found themselves soundly thrashed by the padre, who promptly forgave them but gave them a severe lecture on conduct. Won over completely, Marcelo became one of the padre's best friends.

Although the mission prospered, for many years it was hampered by an uncomfortable relationship with the Pueblo of San José that was founded the same year as Santa Clara. The settlers' cattle mingled with those belonging to the mission Indians and there were disputes over the rights to the water in the Guadalupe River. In time, the irritations were settled, but only after several years of friction.

Father Catalá helped alleviate the situation by linking the two communities closer in spirit with a four-mile Alameda. Two hundred Indians planted three rows of black willows to border this two-way road, which provided the worldly residents of the pueblo with a direct route to salvation at the mission. In the

In 1839, heavy rains weakened the campanile and it was replaced by one of wood. By 1855, the church was showing signs of wear and tear. The tile roof was widened in 1861 to give added protection to adobe walls. Note supporting posts. In 1885, the walls of adobe were taken down, replaced by wood framing, and moved out to the line of posts. Old adobes, stacked on ground, sprouted wild flowers in the spring, the seeds having been captive in the walls for 60 years.

Grandiose plan for Santa Clara College, published in a county atlas in 1870,
shows hopeful scheme for building a classic-styled campus around the old adobe
mission. When transferred from Franciscans to the Jesuits in 1851,
mission became nucleus of new college, and adobe buildings were encased in
wood, shaped in imitation of masonry as was the fashion of the day.
1. Mission quadrangle recognizable under wooden disguise. 2. Adobe church
widened (1861), graced with twin-towered façade, covered with shingle roof.
3. Adobe wall (still standing) remnant of wing that was razed in anticipation
of extension of Lexington St. that never went through. 4. Quadrangle made
two-story. Other college buildings, real and imaginary: 5. Science building
(1836–1929). 6. Playhouse (1870–1963) moved in 1910 to site of building
No. 7 which was never built. 8. Projected classroom monstrosity,
never built. 9. Cross of 1777.

heyday of the mission, The Alameda was often a kaleidoscope of color, with groups of people gaily attired in silks and satins, mounted on their finest horses, repairing to the mission on Sundays.

Many of the willows were later replaced by other varieties of trees, and the center row was cut down when the road was widened. A few of the ancient trees were still standing along The Alameda a few years ago.

Santa Clara Mission was one of the last to be subjected to secularization. The blow fell in 1836, and the Indians' lands and chattels were quickly dispersed to the winds. After the American occupation, the lands were partly returned to the Church, which turned them over to the Jesuit Order for use as the seat of a college. Classes began in 1851 and the college was chartered by the state four years later. It is now the University of Santa Clara.

Earthquakes and fires beset the mission at intervals during its existence. Several mission churches succumbed to one or the other of these disasters, which also brought severe damage to the three bells, two of which were given by the King of Spain in 1799.

In 1926 a fire began in a tower of the remodeled mission church, and the jangling of bells awoke faculty and students, who dashed out into the plaza in their nightwear. As sirens screamed, priests and students fought to save the church and its precious relics. The church was consumed and one bell was melted and the other cracked by the heat. But one of the King's big bells, dated 1798, survived without damage, and it now hangs in the restored church (rebuilt in 1929).

At 7 o'clock one morning in 1926, the old church (left) that had stood for more than a century burst into flame. Started possibly by faulty electrical insulation (eroded by bat guano) in the south tower, the flames engulfed the roof in 20 minutes and soon reduced the building to ashes. Only portions of the adobe walls incorporated in the building were standing after the fire. The two King's bells fell with the towers. One (1799) shattered when struck by water from the firehoses and was later recast. A replacement was sent by King Alphonse XIII of Spain in 1929, and it now hangs in the modern belltower. The other bell (1798) survived the fire and was promptly hung on a temporary scaffold so it could ring out the All Souls' bell, as it had since 1799 without interruption. The building was replaced three years later.

The interior of the present-day mission church retains some of the original atmosphere of the 1825 church, but obscured under embellishments of a garish Victorian cast. Some of the original statues, most notably a magnificent crucifix above a side altar, were saved from the fire. The reredos and its statues were restored to match the original, and the ceiling above the sanctuary was repainted to simulate the Dávila design.

In few of the California missions were the decorations designed or painted by professional artists; most were the work of talented amateurs. The ceiling of Santa Clara, one of the few exceptions, was designed and executed by Agustín Dávila, who was imported from Mexico for this assignment. Under his direction, neophytes applied the bright mineral colors, mixed with cactus juice, to the rough-hewn redwood ceiling slabs. The interpretation of the Trinity as three men is a quaint Mexican conceit, no longer permitted in ecclesiastical decoration. The painted ceiling was retouched in the successive remodelings of the church, and was still fresh and colorful when it was consumed in the fire of 1926. A copy of it now adorns the restored church.

San Buenaventura

Ninth mission, founded March 31, 1782, by Fr. Junípero Serra, his last. Named for St. Bonaventure. First church damaged by earthquakes of 1812; reconstructed in 1816. Mission secularized 1836; parish church 1842–43; rented by Gov. Pico 1845 and sold following year; returned to Church in 1862. Located in city of Ventura, just east of U.S. Highway 101.

From the first it had been the plan to found a third mission (after those at San Diego and Monterey) to be named for San Buenaventura "in order that he defend it." But the founding was postponed for twelve years, for one reason or another, often because of troubles at other missions which required so many guards that military escort could not be spared for the new mission.

At last a large cavalcade set out from San Gabriel in March, 1782, for the site of the new mission. Included were eight soldiers and their families, officials, muleteers, cattle, and pack animals loaded with church goods, furnishings, and tools for tilling the soil. Governor Neve himself, in full regalia, rode at the end of the procession with his own guard of ten Monterey soldiers.

The mission was to be located at an Indian town of 500 souls, which Father Crespí had named La Asunción de Nuestra Señora, one of many villages of the Chumash Indian tribes, who were friendly, inventive, artistic and industrious.

The Channel of Santa Barbara, wrote Palóu, was "so densely populated with heathen that right on the road, which runs close along the shore, there are twenty-one large towns, and it is necessary to pass through them in the middle of some and on the edge of others and past others about a gunshot off." He estimated that no fewer than twenty thousand Indians lived in those towns.

The founding company wove its way through these villages, finding the natives friendly and courteous. On arriving at the proposed site, Father Serra inspected the territory carefully, though he had already done so before, and selected a suitable spot. On Easter Sunday morning they took possession with a Mass and a fervent sermon by the Father-President, and Father Pedro Cambón

The creamy façade of the mission church, decorated with red trim, has changed little since it was rebuilt after the severe quake of 1812. Heavy buttress at the left was installed then. Triangular line above the door suggests possibility that church once had a lower roofline, but structural analysis has proven that this was never so.

sang the responses. Then they set about building a chapel, a dwelling and a stockade.

Local Indians gladly helped with this work, for payment in beads and other trifles, and construction proceeded. But while they were curious about the new-comers, the Indians were slow to give up the joys of freedom for confinement behind mission walls.

These intelligent Indians had homes built igloo-style with doors and holes for windows. They slept on beds rather than the ground, on mattresses made of reeds. However, the men often slept in nearby caves as a matter of defense, to be sheltered in case of night attack.

The Chumash were renowned for the large canoes they built and rowed expertly in the channel no matter what the weather. They made frequent trips to the Channel Islands, where other Indians of the same tribe lived. The canoes, which could carry eight or ten men easily, had graceful lines, were made of well-joined pine boards caulked with natural pitch. The workmanship is considered remarkable, because these natives had no knowledge of iron and steel and used only tools of flint.

The Indians were also noted for fine basketry. They wove the reeds so dexterously that the baskets were water-proof. But with all their accomplishments, the natives were thievish, the Spaniards reported, and they stole everything they could get their hands on.

The first mission church burned down within ten years, and a new large one of stone was begun. It was dedicated in 1809 after fifteen years of hard work. This church had been in use only three years when the violent earthquake of 1812 rocked the earth all along the coast and brought several missions down in ruins. San Buenaventura's damage was severe, and the padres feared that the ground and even the mission itself might be swept into the sea, which was not far away. But repairs were completed in a year or more, including reinforcement of the church by the addition of an immense buttress.

In 1818 a courier galloped up with the distressing news that the pirate Bouchard had been sighted offshore. Father José Señan hastily assembled his valuables: the sacred vessels, the vestments, the statues, the paintings, the silver. He buried some and rushed others to a nearby cave. Then with an anxious eye seaward he filled baskets with food and mustered his charges and livestock

Wrote a diarist in 1769, "The handiness and ability of the Indians was at its best in the construction of their canoes. They handle these with skill, and in them three or four men go out to sea to fish, as they will hold eight or ten men. They use long double-bladed paddles and row with indescribable agility and swiftness."

*When sketched in 1829 by Alfred Robinson during a visit, the mission was still
a going concern. He noted an abundance of fruits and vegetables: "apples,
pears, peaches, pomegranates, tunas or prickly pears, and grapes." Some of the
Indian brush huts were still standing, the little chapel of St. Michael had not
yet been washed away in a flood (1832), and Serra's cross still stood on top
of the hill behind the mission.*

up into the hills, where they camped out for a month, building a small chapel for
temporary worship, while Bouchard passed by.

They had hardly returned and put the treasures back in place when more
trouble came. Another Indian tribe, the Mojaves, came to trade. The soldiers
forbade this, and locked up the newcomers overnight. In the morning a brawl
resulted in twelve deaths and lasting bitterness on the part of the Mojaves,
who ever after did all they could to thwart the work of the padres.

But the general story of this mission is one of prosperity and abundance.
Blessed with excellent climate, good soil, and a cleverly devised irrigation
system planned by the ingenious padres, the well-watered mission gardens
flourished luxuriantly.

Not only the expected fruits, grains and produce were plentiful, but also quantities of exotic crops usually grown only in the torrid zone, such as bananas, coconuts, figs and sugar cane.

Whaling ships often dropped anchor here, where corn was said to be harvested within a few feet of the shore. In 1793 the English visitor, Captain George Vancouver, was favored with such a load of green vegetables and fruits for his men that twenty loaded pack mules were required to carry the produce to his ship anchored at Santa Barbara.

In 1845 the mission lands were dispersed, and the church became a parish church by order of Garcia Diego, first bishop of California. The mission survived secularization and other transitions, even its engulfing by a modern town which all but smothered it, and the unfortunate efforts to modernize the old building.

About 1893 a craze for improvement resulted in the resident priest's tearing down all the outer buildings and invading even the church with dubious changes. He lengthened the windows to give more light, then filled the holes with stained glass in dark colors. He covered the Indians' original decorations with mediocre modern designs, and removed entirely a beautiful canopied pulpit of exquisite woodwork, which originally hung from the wall. Fortunately he missed the heavy side door with its unusual arch and simple Moorish design.

And someone must have hidden from him the two wooden bells, carved out of two-foot blocks of wood and used during Holy Week when the usual metal bells are silent. These are now part of a collection of relics in the mission museum which was built in 1929.

Happily, the heavy hand of the "improver" no longer shows. Restoration completed in 1957 has returned the church to approximately its original form.

Mission San Buenaventura was noted for the bountiful production of fruits and vegetables. Sailing vessels stopped here to replenish their food lockers with fresh produce.

*By the 1850's, when these drawings were made, the
mission was mostly in private hands. The buildings
showed little change in the interval between Powell's
sketch of 1850 and Miller's of 1856. Wrote Miller,
"I found it to be quite a village of about 70 to 80 houses,
inhabited principally by natives and Mexicans.
The Church is in tolerable good preservation, in which
officiates a French priest. The mission orchard is still in
fine condition, planted with several hundred large
pear trees. I tasted here the first native wine raised on the
mission, which, although not clarified, tasted excellent but
was very strong."*

By 1875, most of the mission properties had been returned by the courts, and the church was used as a parish sanctuary for the small town of San Buenaventura. The cemetery to the left of the church is now covered by a school.

Side door to the church is graced with a Moorish decoration that the Indians interpreted as a map of the mission domain. To them, the two curved lines above the door represented the two rivers that pass on both sides of the mission, symbolized by the cross. The upper line represented the hills that rise behind the mission.

The quadrangle was still standing as late as 1875 when
this photograph was taken from the hill behind the
mission. The low adobe walls show signs of having been
built at various times and with varying standards of
quality. The windowless wing in the foreground was
doubtless used for storage.

Last Indian choir at San Buenaventura, photographed in 1860, had drums, violins, triangle, and a flute cleverly improvised from a gun barrel.

When Fr. Rubio, the modernizer, was in charge of the mission (1878–1895), the town experienced a railroad boom, and he "improved" the old mission to match the spirit of the times. Following a pattern he had used at San Luis Obispo and San Juan Bautista, he covered the beamed ceiling and the tile floors with wood, whitewashed the walls, and replaced the windows with gloomy stained glass. All these unfortunate changes were swept away in 1957 when the church was authentically restored to its original form, as at the right.

Santa Bárbara

Tenth mission, founded December 4, 1786, rededicated December 16, 1786 by
Fr. Fermín Lasuén. Named for St. Barbara. Third church of 1794 destroyed
by earthquake, 1812. Present church begun 1815, completed 1820 with only
one tower; second tower added 1831, fell 1832, rebuilt 1833. Damaged by
earthquake, 1925; façade rebuilt 1950. Secularized 1834, sold 1846, returned
1865. Located in city of Santa Barbara at end of Laguna St.

To Father Serra belonged the dream but to Father Lasuén fell the honor of the actual founding of Mission Santa Bárbara. The dream envisioned three channel missions, protected by a presidio, to bridge the gap between San Luis Obispo and San Gabriel.

The first of the channel missions had been dedicated March 31, 1782, at San Buenaventura, and Father Serra pressed Governor Neve to authorize the founding of the other two. Unfortunately, the Governor was opposed to expansion of the mission system because he felt that it gave too much economic power to the padres, and he was able to block further foundings while he remained in office.

Father Serra, however, was at first unaware of the extent of the Governor's opposition. When the Governor selected a site for the presidio at Santa Bárbara, Serra accompanied the expedition under the impression that the presidio site would encompass the mission, as at Monterey. He did not know that the Governor had already persuaded the Viceroy to withhold funds for a separate mission at Santa Bárbara.

When a suitable site for the presidio was located, Father Serra presided over the religious ceremonies of the presidio founding. He blessed the land, planted the cross, and said the first Mass. On the following day the soldiers began construction of the fort. A chapel, dwellings for the officers, married soldiers, and the chaplain, barracks, and a warehouse were planned.

Under the impression that the Governor would soon authorize the founding of the mission at a nearby location, Father Serra kept busy preparing three leather-bound registers for the anticipated mission. After three weeks of anxious waiting

The gentle light of dawn washes the classic façade
of Mission Santa Bárbara, reflected in the tranquil
fountain. Early worshippers gather in ones and twos,
as they have for well over a century, at the Queen of
the California missions.

When he sketched Santa Bárbara from the sea in 1829, Alfred Robinson noted
that the effect was striking and beautiful; but when he landed, he found
the houses of the town "in not very good condition." He stopped at the
"neat little mission" and heard musicians rehearsing "some very fine airs
and lively dancing tunes."

he was informed by the Governor that the mission would not be approved until after the presidio was completed. Father Serra sadly departed for his headquarters at Carmel to resume his duties as Father-President. He visited the presidio twice in the following year, but he died a month after receiving word from a new Governor that Mission Santa Bárbara could at last be founded.

Thus, it was Father Fermín Francisco de Lasuén, Serra's successor, who carried out the dream. He chose a commanding site overlooking the presidio, the oak-dotted valley, and the blue sea with the Channel Islands looming in the distance. Called Tanayan by the "first families," the Indians, and El Pedregoso by the Spaniards, the name in both languages had the same meaning: "Rocky Mound." Lasuén selected this place because of its close proximity to water resources.

Although an unofficial dedication of the site, which was about a mile and a half northeast of the presidio, took place on December 4, 1786, the formal dedication, attended by the new Governor, Pedro Fages, was held on December 16.

The first mission buildings started in the following spring, at the end of the rainy season, were formed of logs, topped by beams covered with reeds, which in turn were covered with mud and thatch. In time, an adobe wing was added, a dormitory, kitchen, and storeroom, until the traditional quadrangle was complete. Some 250 neat Indian houses, plastered, whitewashed, and having doors and

*As late as 1880, when this photograph was taken, some of the outlying buildings
were still standing, including several of the Indian dwellings.*

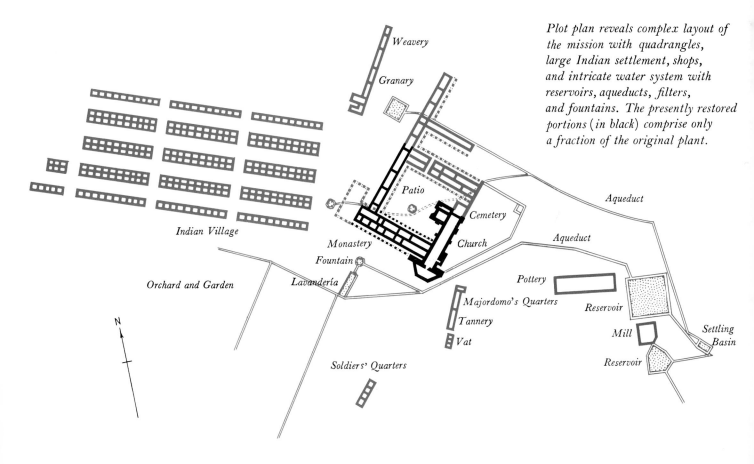

*Plot plan reveals complex layout of
the mission with quadrangles,
large Indian settlement, shops,
and intricate water system with
reservoirs, aqueducts, filters,
and fountains. The presently restored
portions (in black) comprise only
a fraction of the original plant.*

Weavery

Granary

Indian Village

Orchard and Garden

Patio

Cemetery

Monastery

Church

Fountain

Aqueduct

Aqueduct

Lavandería

Pottery

Majordomo's Quarters

Reservoir

N

Tannery

Mill

Settling
Basin

Vat

Reservoir

Soldiers' Quarters

movable windows, were placed back to back in rows to the left of the mission. A tannery, a pottery, and warehouses were added, and a water system was completed which was so remarkable that parts of it are still used by the water company of the city of Santa Barbara.

A creek two miles above the mission was dammed, and the water conducted by stone aqueduct, following the contour of the hills, to a storage basin near the church. This aqueduct was so well constructed that parts of it are still in excellent condition.

The mission's beautiful Moorish fountain, built in 1808, is shaded by huge pepper trees, and its overflow runs into a stone laundry basin, where Indian women knelt and soaped their families' garments, beating them with paddles and rinsing them in the clear, cold water.

As converts began to come in new structures were added. Three churches, each larger than its predecessor, were constructed before the disastrous earthquake of 1812 almost destroyed the last one. It was repaired and used for several years while a great new church of stone was being built around it. This church, essentially the one that is still standing today, was dedicated in September 1820 after five years of construction. The colorful dedication celebration was attended by Governor Sola and other political and ecclesiastical dignitaries.

In 1925 another earthquake damaged the towers and façade as well as a wing of the living quarters. All of California came to the aid of one of its most beautiful churches: costs of restoration totalled nearly $400,000. Nor was that all. No earthquake was responsible for the next damage, but cracks appeared again in the façade in 1950. Chemical disintegration of the concrete used in the 1925 repairs had so weakened the front of the church that it had to be dismantled and rebuilt again with steel-reinforced concrete. The stone facing, however, retains the contours, dimensions, and appearance of the original.

The only California mission with two similar towers, it has been a noble landmark from the day of its completion. No wonder it is called the Queen of the Missions.

"They are musicians whom it cost me twelve years of labor to teach," wrote Fr. Durán of his orchestra, noted for its polished performances.

The tile roof that is such a familiar feature of the monastery wing today made its reappearance in 1888 after an absence of some 30 years (see sketch on page 192). Dormer windows that once lighted the upper story disappeared from across the front when the tiles were reapplied. The back half of the roof facing the cloister was not tiled until 39 years later.

SANTA BÁRBARA **191**

The mission suffered serious damage in the earthquake
of 1925 that reduced some of Santa Barbara to rubble.
One of the towers had to be torn down and completely
rebuilt; the second story of monastery wing was nearly
destroyed. Repairs took two years.

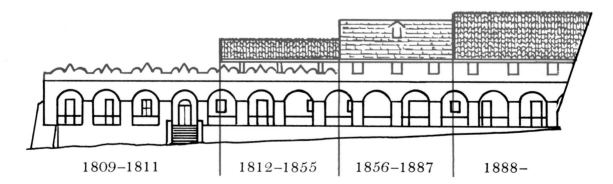

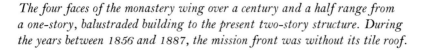

1809–1811   1812–1855   1856–1887   1888–

The four faces of the monastery wing over a century and a half range from
a one-story, balustraded building to the present two-story structure. During
the years between 1856 and 1887, the mission front was without its tile roof.

JOHN S. WEIR

The classic façade, built over an earlier facing,
was copied from a book on architecture by Vitruvius,
a first-century Roman. This widely republished book was a
model for a great deal of architecture throughout Europe;
and the Spanish edition, published in Madrid in 1787,
was in the library of the mission when the new façade
was designed. Originally, statues of Faith, Hope, and
Charity stood on the bases marked "A" in the sketch at
left. A fourth statue, of Santa Bárbara, was added in 1927.

SANTA BÁRBARA **193**

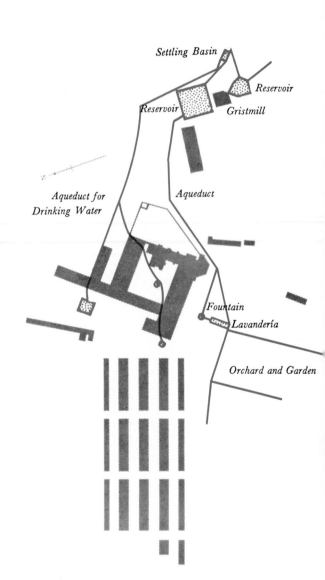

Settling Basin

Reservoir

Reservoir

Gristmill

Aqueduct for
Drinking Water

Aqueduct

Fountain

Lavandería

Orchard and Garden

The most complete water system at any of the missions,
the network of dams, reservoirs, and aqueducts at Santa
Bárbara was well engineered. Water supply came from a
dam in Pedragoso Creek that is still standing
(photo above), whence it was conducted by a stone
aqueduct two miles to a storage reservoir and from there
to a 110-foot-square reservoir that is still in use today
as part of the city water system. From the second
reservoir, the water ran through aqueducts to the ornate
fountain, gardens, and orchards. Overflow from the
fountain in front of the monastery was led to a stone
lavandería where the Indian women dipped garments
into the water, pulled them onto the heavy rolled rim,
and soaped and paddled them after the manner of women
in Spanish-speaking countries. Another aqueduct led
drinking water from the first reservoir to a settling tank
and from there through an aqueduct that arched over the
road and ran to the rear of the mission.

*Fragments of the rock walls of the abandoned gristmill still stand northeast of
the church. Water flowing downhill from the reservoir above powered the
mill that ground the mission grain.*

SANTA BÁRBARA **195**

MARTIN LITTON

To accommodate the needs of the seminary for theological students for the Franciscan priesthood, Mission Santa Bárbara has been expanded in recent years until it covers several times the area of the original structure that Ford etched in 1883. Most of the new construction has followed the foundation lines of the old quadrangles and has been kept in harmony with the original building. A modification of the campanario at San Diego Mission stands at the corner of the novitiate chapel. Most of the new construction was erected in 1956–58 through the generosity of the Max C. Fleischman Foundation.

Roman doorway leading from the church to the cemetery is decorated with a macabre touch: two genuine skulls and crossbones embedded in mortar and one (under the Moorish window) carved in stone, a decorative device not uncommon in Mexican churches. The cemetery itself, as the photographs on the opposite page show, has not always been the neatly groomed place that it is today. In the early 1880's (below left), it was neglected and weed-grown; but it had been greatly improved by 1890 when the upper photograph was taken. Pattern of paths worked out then is still maintained. Within this cemetery lie the remains of 4,000 Indians. For several years in the 1880's, access to the area was sealed off to prevent clandestine burials.

The big church has changed little since it was built in 1820. The original canvas
reredos, statues, and paintings were still in use when this photograph was taken
in 1898. The only changes had been an application of wainscoting along the
walls to cover the scribblings of visitors, a wooden ceiling in place of the
original plastered one, and fenced-in side altars. The arches and pilasters were
decorated with imitation marble.

The appearance of the interior today is very close to that
of the original. The striking winged-lightning ornaments
from which the light fixtures hang are direct copies of the
design pictured above in the Vitruvius book on architecture.

JOHN S. WEIR

La Purísima Concepción

Eleventh mission, founded December 8, 1787, by Fr. Fermín Lasuén. Named "The Immaculate Conception of Mary the Most Pure." First buildings begun in 1788, completed 1791, destroyed in earthquake of 1812. Mission moved to new site, buildings erected 1815–18. Secularized 1834, sold in 1845, returned to Church 1874 but sold because of dilapidated state. State acquired property 1935, restoration 1935–37, 1941. Located 5 miles east of Lompoc.

Stretched-out mission buildings differ from form of others
in chain because of absence of quadrangle. Ditch in
foreground carried excess water to fields.

On December 8, 1787, almost exactly a year after the founding of Santa Bárbara, came the dedication of the site for Mission La Purísima, about equally distant from San Luis Obispo and Santa Bárbara.

Conditions augured well for a successful outpost. The land chosen for this mission site was situated in a rich and fertile valley, the Indians were friendly and intelligent, and the padres eager and energetic.

Construction of the necessary buildings was delayed, however, until the end of the rainy season. In March, 1788, soldiers and workmen were sent up from the presidio in Santa Bárbara.

Early in April, the Father-President, Lasuén, arrived with two padres to take charge, and in four months they had baptized a total of seventy-five neophytes.

Within three years the mission was flourishing. The padres and their charges, working together in the fields, reaped ever-increasing crops and tended the growing herds. The Indians were happy in their new abode, according to records, and so were the padres as they heard the neophytes sing and pray. At this time Father Mariano Payéras began his nineteen-year service at this mission. Four of these years he served as Father-President, during which Purísima was the seat of government for all of the missions.

The first buildings, hastily erected, rapidly went to ruin. In a few years it became necessary to start new facilities, built of adobe and roofed with tile. These were completed in 1802.

A long period of unusual prosperity followed the rebuilding of the mission. By 1804 the population numbered 1,522, and in 1810, the number of livestock reported numbered over 20,000. But this mission, which began with promise, and flourished for twenty-four years, was doomed to a series of misfortunes.

Earthquake and sudden disaster! On the morning of December 21, 1812, (twenty-five years after the founding of La Purísima) the serenity of the community with its fine church and many mission buildings, was shattered. A tremendous shock, lasting four minutes, badly damaged the walls of the church. The second quake, one half-hour later, felled most of the buildings. Then like a wicked after-thought the hillside back of the mission opened in a great crack, to let torrents of water flood the site, bringing complete devastation. Adobe, tiles, tools, stock and stores all disintegrated or floated on a sea of horror.

Lesser men than these frontier missionaries would have been defeated by this disaster. For there were a thousand-odd homeless neophytes to shelter, feed, and clothe. When it was all over, the courageous padres, realizing that a new building site was necessary, found a promising spot four miles northeast, on the other side of the river, in the "Valley of the Watercress."

After temporary shelters were erected, construction of a new and finer mission was begun. Under the vigorous direction of Father Payéras, the natives worked hard to complete the new set of buildings. As with other missions, nearly everything was made with materials at hand: adobe, clay, rawhide, timber, and tules.

Earthquake resistance was built into the new structures. The southwest wall of the residence building was buttressed with stone and the walls were 4½ feet thick.

Soon after the twenty-fifth anniversary of its founding, the mission buildings and 100 adobe Indian dwellings were collapsed by violent earthquakes, followed by torrential rains.

*Abandoned soon after secularization, the buildings were plundered of tiles
and timber, the walls were washed out by runoff from the hills, and only the
monastery remained standing. Over the years, this last building served as a
private residence, then, at the time of this drawing, as a sheep ranch,
and finally as a stable until it collapsed.*

Water for irrigation and domestic use was brought from springs in the hills,
three miles away, by an elaborate arrangement of open aqueduct, clay pipes,
reservoirs, and dams.

A ten-year period of marked prosperity followed, during which La Purísima
became entirely self-supporting. The herds, counted in the tens of thousands,
were famous. Construction of utility buildings included large warehouses for
storing hides and tallow, a mill, a blacksmith's shop, bakeries, carpenter shops,
pottery shops, and weaving rooms. Soap and tallow vats were added. To care
for the sick, there was even a small hospital.

Between 1816 and 1818, setbacks occurred. During a drought in the winter
of 1816–17, hundreds of sheep died for lack of feed. Again, in 1818, fire destroyed
nearly all the neophytes' homes.

Further misfortune befell the mission. The death of the beloved padre, Father
Payéras, in 1823, left La Purísima without his exceptional guidance in temporal
as well as spiritual matters. New troubles had been brewing two years before
his death. Since 1821, when Mexico declared her independence from Spain, the
missions had received no supplies and the soldiers no pay. The Indian population
had begun to decline and on those neophytes remaining fell the thankless burden

JOHN S. WEIR

of supporting the soldiers, whose petty acts of cruelty toward them further aggravated conditions.

The inevitable revolt of the natives came, in 1824, at Mission Santa Inés, after a neophyte corporal from La Purísima was flogged by a guard attached to that mission. The Indians, finally aroused to action, began an affray with bows and arrows, attacking the soldiers, who crouched in a building behind the church and returned fire on their assailants. The skirmish resulted in the death of two Indians and great destruction at the mission.

When the news reached La Purísima, the Indians there, aided by rebels from Santa Inés, seized possession of the entire mission. Using their knowledge of construction, they fortified the grounds by building stockades, cutting loopholes in the church walls and mounting two old cannons heretofore used only for celebration of feast days. They held the mission for nearly a month.

Justified as this rebellion may have been, it was soon ended when news reached the Governor. Soldiers sent down from Monterey pounded away with their heaviest weapons at the walls which fortified the rebels. A detachment of cavalry circled around to the rear to cut off retreat.

The battle was ended in less than three hours. Untrained in accurate use of the cannons, the Indians' shots went wild. With retreat cut off, the frightened rebels sent an arbitrator to intercede for them. Father Rodriguez, who had elected to protect the soldiers' families, stepped out with a flag of truce and offer of surrender.

Thus the battle was over. Sixteen Indians were dead and many wounded; one soldier died and three were wounded. To the soldiers went the booty: the two old cannons, sixteen muskets, six cutlasses, a hundred and fifty lances, and countless bows and arrows.

Subsequent punishment of the ringleaders of the revolt saddened the padres. Seven Indians were condemned to death and eighteen others sentenced to various terms of imprisonment. The Governor defended the penalties exacted by the military as necessary to prevent future revolt.

Soon after the end of these hostilities secularization came, and Mission Purísima relapsed into ruin. In 1844, only two hundred Indians remained at the mission, which the next year was sold with all its lands and treasures to Don Juan Temple of Los Angeles for $1,100.

The crumbling remnants of the mission complex were rescued in the 1930's by the National Park Service and the C.C.C. When restoration began in 1934, only fragments of the walls and a few lonely pillars were still standing. The National Park Service assigned a staff of historians, archeologists, engineers, and architects to dig out the facts about the mission's original structure, and after nearly a year of study, they developed the plans from which C.C.C. Company 1951 rebuilt the entire mission, using original tools and methods wherever possible. When completed, the mission was turned over to the state to administer as a Historic Park. The most completely reconstructed of the missions, it was considered one of finest historic restorations of its day.

As restored, the structure at the right captures the feeling of the original, with its amateurish masonry, rough-plastered surfaces, and exposed beams lashed with rawhide.

The linear layout of the mission is most clearly apparent from the air. All of the missions except La Purísima were built in the form of a quadrangle, principally as a means of defense and of keeping the Indians confined. No one knows why the padres here departed from the traditional square, but they may have believed the Indians were no longer a potential menace or they may have felt that a line of buildings would be less vulnerable to earthquake damage than a square and easier to evacuate without panic during a quake. As the plot plan indicates, the mission was organized in three main units: a church; a building for workshops and storage; and a residence building where the padres lived, guests were quartered, and meals were served. At its peak, more than a thousand Indians lived and worked at this mission.

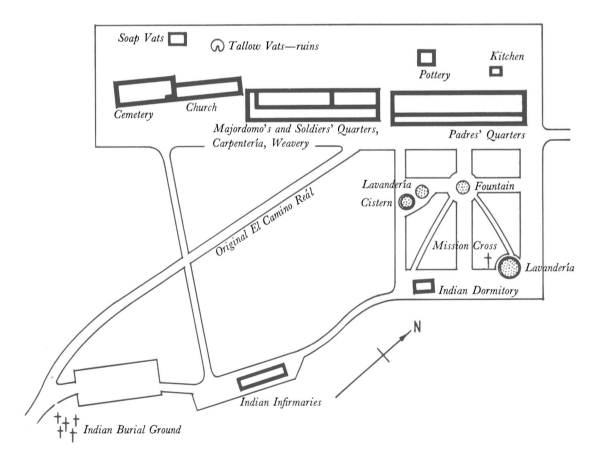

Soap Vats

Tallow Vats—ruins

Pottery

Kitchen

Cemetery

Church

Majordomo's and Soldiers' Quarters,
Carpentería, Weavery

Padres' Quarters

Original El Camino Reál

Lavandería
Cistern

Fountain

Mission Cross

Lavandería

Indian Dormitory

N

Indian Infirmaries

Indian Burial Ground

JOHN S. WEIR

La Purísima offers the visitor an unparalleled opportunity to see how the Indians practiced the mission crafts. One of their most important activities was the processing of hides, which together with tallow, were the coinage of the mission economy. Trading ships from New England loaded up with hides and bags of tallow, which they secured by trading manufactured goods to the missions. In mission days, fresh hides were scraped clean of meat to keep the valuable skins from being destroyed by flies. The scraped hides were then hung on racks or pegged to the ground to dry, as in the sketch. When dry, the unwieldy "Yankee banknotes" were stiff as boards, ready to be tamped into the holds of trading vessels.

RIGHT. The large whipsaw, poised in its kerf, serves to remind the viewer that the missions were built with tools not unlike those in the carpenter's chest of today. Actually, all the basic hand tools now in use were familiar to the artisans of mission days. With this rig for ripsawing beams, the man on the ground pulled the saw down on its cutting stroke and his partner upstairs merely pulled the saw back up to its starting position. In actuality, in installations of this type the lower man usually stood in a pit and the other at ground level. This permitted the heavy logs to be rolled into place without hoisting.

JOHN S. WEIR

*Like all the missions, La Purísima had a highly
developed water system designed to provide an ample supply
for cooking, washing, craft work, and irrigation.
Water was brought by a series of flumes and clay pipes to
fountains and lavanderías (laundries), where the
constantly overflowing basin kept it clean and clear.
The storage reservoir above was reclaimed from the
junk-filled ruin below.*

*La Purísima's simple campanario was copied after the one
at neighboring Santa Inés, in the absence of drawings or
descriptions of the original structure. Even the
bell-ringer's platform was adapted to the restored mission.
The tower has two rolling bells and one stationary one.*

LA PURÍSIMA CONCEPCIÓN **213**

Restoration of an olive-crusher, a device
derived by the Spaniards from their
arrastra, or ore-crusher. Ripe olives
were dumped into the mill and crushed by
the large wheel that rolled over them,
powered by a patient burro hitched to
the long cross-arm. The oil crushed
from the olives was left to settle,
to separate the oil from the water,
and then drawn off. It was used for
cooking and for sanctuary lamps.

Tallow was in demand for manufacture
of soap and candles and for trading
with foreign ships. Fat from slaughtered
steers was cooked over low heat in these
great vessels, many of them from
whaling ships, where they were used for
rendering whale oil. As the fat melted,
it was allowed to clear and was then
drawn off and stored in large skin bags.

Without candles, the dank, small-
windowed adobe buildings would have
been dark indeed. Tapers were needed
constantly and in good supply. This
rotating candle-dipper was able to
produce them in quantity. Strings
attached to cross-arms were dipped into
a metal container filled with molten
tallow, kept fluid by a gentle fire
underneath. An extra bag of tallow was
kept at hand to replenish the supply as
it was consumed.

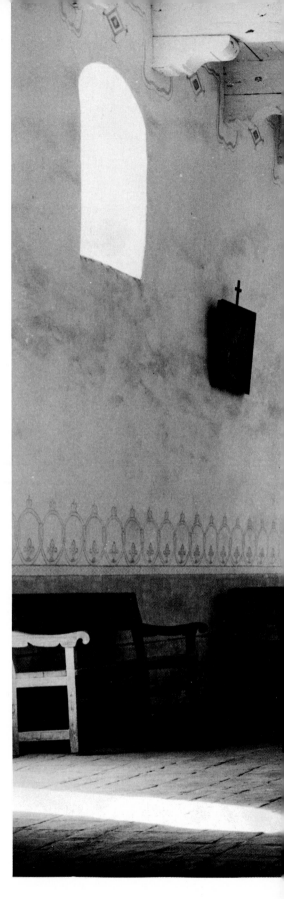

*Restoration catches the straightforward simplicity of the
mission atmosphere, with sparse furnishings copied from
other missions, rough-textured walls and floors,
and crude, stenciled wall decorations. The large church
duplicates a smaller chapel in the monastery building.
The original church was undermined by hillside runoff and
was abandoned, its adobes used for other structures and
its altar moved into one end of the monastery. True to
the common practice in Spanish and Mexican churches,
and in the missions as well, there are no benches in this
church. The congregation sat or knelt on the floor
throughout the services; men on one side, women on the
other, the two separated by a line down the center,
represented here by a subtle change in the tile pattern.*

Santa Cruz

Twelfth mission, founded August 28, 1791, by Fr. Fermín Lasuén. Named for the Sacred Cross. Church begun 1793, completed 1794; quadrangle finished, 1795. Nearby pueblo of Branciforte established July 1797, combined with mission 1841. Mission secularized 1834. Bell tower collapsed 1840, remainder downed by quake, 1857. Frame church, 1858–1889. Present church, 1889. Mission replica built 1931. Location: Emmet and School Sts., Santa Cruz.

On a beautiful site overlooking the city of Santa Cruz, an aging adobe building and a modern replica of a mission church stand as the sole reminders of the ill-starred mission that struggled here against odds to achieve its goals.

Mission Santa Cruz started auspiciously. When founded in 1791, it seemed to have everything in its favor: a commanding site, good climate, fertile soil, and Indians amenable to conversion. Within six years, the quadrangle was completed, with workshops and a two-story granary. Millstones made at Carmel ground the mission's own corn and wheat into fine flour, and the prospects looked good for a serene and productive future.

Then came the first of a series of misfortunes—the founding of an unsavory pueblo across the river. Although Spanish law forbade the location of a pueblo within a league of a mission, the Governor notified the padres that one was to be founded nearby to be named Branciforte in honor of the Viceroy, and the padres would be expected to help support it. The padres protested vigorously, but to no avail.

When the first colonists arrived for the pueblo, the worst fears of the padres were realized. Instead of upright, God-fearing men, there were nine vagabonds and criminals with their families, seventeen in all, sick, destitute, indolent, and immoral. More of the same type arrived later. The settlers encroached on mission lands and usurped the Indians' pasturage. When the padres complained, the Governor defended the settlers by saying that the mission Indians were dying out anyway and soon there would be no further need for the mission itself.

The padres were forced to use stern measures to keep the ruffians of Branci-

Small replica of the mission church, built in 1931 as a memorial chapel, is about one-third the size of the original, which was razed in 1858 after extensive earthquake damage. Façade of the little chapel follows closely the early sketches of church built in 1794. Museum wing, left, contains beautiful vestments.

When Henry Miller sketched the mission in 1856, he wrote, "In the upper town stands the courthouse and a large hotel together with the mission building and a number of ancient adobe houses, occupied principally by natives, which however are unoccupied at present." The hotel he referred to was the two-story Golden Eagle Hotel, a former mission building. The mission church, diagonally across the quadrangle from it, was already without its belltower when the sketch was made and collapsed completely the next year.

forte away from the mission and the Indians separated from the Brancifortians. It was probably the restraint put upon the mission Indians that led to the murder of one of the padres, a large and fearless man who was found dead in bed, presumably from natural causes, for a cursory investigation revealed nothing more ominous. But two years later, suspicions were aroused, and after an autopsy (the first in California's medical history), seven neophytes were charged with murder. They pleaded excessive cruelty on the part of the padre as their defense, but the Governor could find no evidence to support their stand, and he sentenced them to a severe flogging.

Misfortune struck again in 1818 when pirate Hyppolite de Bouchard appeared offshore. He had already terrorized Monterey, capturing the presidio and setting

Rascally settlers at Branciforte, ordered to remove mission supplies for safe-keeping when pirate raid threatened in 1818, helped themselves with pleasure and returned little of the goods they "saved."

fire to the buildings, and it was feared that he might attempt a landing on the northern shore of Monterey Bay. The Governor ordered the padre in charge, Ramon Olbés, to pack up all valuables at the mission, send them inland, and flee to Mission Soledad for safety. Obeying the command, the padre left word with officials at Branciforte to carry out the Governor's orders, and hurried away from Mission Hill with his frightened neophytes.

Bouchard did not land at Santa Cruz—but conditions at the mission could have been little worse if he had. The Brancifortians carried out the order to remove foodstocks and supplies with unbridled enthusiasm. The party helped themselves to grain and agricultural implements and emptied the casks of wine and brandy—mainly down their own throats. Fired with spirits, the party looted the mission. When Father Olbés returned, he found it almost destitute. Enraged and despairing, he immediately put in a request to abandon the mission. However, he was dissuaded and encouraged to continue with his difficult task.

The total population at Santa Cruz reached five hundred and twenty-three at its height, the lowest of all the missions. The mission slowly declined, in inverse ratio to the temporary growth of Branciforte, which attracted settlers with a bent for smuggling hides and tallow.

Santa Cruz was among the first to be secularized. Stock was sold and land granted to individuals, and the Indians just faded away. The decrepit buildings collapsed one after another. The church tower fell in 1840. The church itself collapsed following an earthquake in 1857, and a high tide rushing upriver destroyed building materials stored nearby. A frame church, which replaced the old adobe in 1858, stood until 1889, when it in turn was replaced by the white-painted structure now standing on the square. In 1931, a small replica of the mission church was built 200 feet from the original site.

A half block away stands the restored Mission Adobe (now a state park), built in 1822 to house native neophytes. Artifacts portray their domestic life; a film recalls the sorry history of their interaction with the Spaniards.

Intimate little chapel makes no pretense at duplicating original church in size or design, but it does contain the statues, candlesticks, paintings, and the tabernacle used when the mission was active. The tiny chapel, rosy with the light from tinted windows, is used for weddings and private Masses.

Several hundred infants were baptized at this font during the life of the mission. Carved from local sandstone, the heavy piece is typical of the work of the Mexican masons and their Indian understudies who created fonts, wash basins, water coolers, and fountains for the missions. Often copied from designs in a book, these pieces have a certain clumsy elegance. This font is similar to a lavabo still in use in the Carmel Mission.

*At 3 a.m. on a chilly February morning in 1857 the old
church caved in with a resounding crash that awakened
the village. It had been weakened a month before by two
severe earthquakes. This sketch of the ruined interior,
painted the day after the collapse, is the sole record of the
interior of the mission, which was apparently similar to
Dolores in decorative treatment. Church was replaced in 1858
by a frame structure, which in turn was replaced in 1889
by the present white-painted brick church.*

Nuestra Señora de la Soledad

Thirteenth mission, founded October 9, 1791, by Fr. Fermín Lasuén. Named for
Our Lady of Solitude, one of the many designations for the Virgin.
First church of thatch-roofed adobe completed 1797, enlarged 1805, collapsed
1831. Present chapel built 1832, restored 1954. Secularized 1835, sold 1846,
returned to Church 1859. Located on side road off U.S. Highway 101,
3 miles south of town of Soledad and 1 mile west of highway.

*For almost a century, Mission Soledad was a bleak
and mournful ruin. As recently as 1954, the mission
consisted entirely of crumbled adobe walls.*

Captain Gaspár de Portolá and Father Juan Crespí, on their tiresome march in
1769 in search of the Port of Monterey, trudged north along the Salinas River
Valley. The land lay brown and sere, and the mountains bordering the valley
baked in the heat of summer. The men camped on the bank of a sluggish river,
hardly bothering to post a guard, the place looked so desolate.

A few natives approached and stared at them curiously. Father Crespí tried
to talk to one of them, and though he could understand very little of what the man
said, he caught a word that sounded like "soledad," the Spanish word for lone-
liness. When Father Serra stopped here two years later on his return to Carmel
after founding San Antonio de Padua, he visited briefly with the natives, and
when he asked an Indian woman her name, to his surprise she repeated the same

word, resembling "soledad." Thus the Indians, coincidentally named the thirteenth mission—and an appropriate name it turned out to be!

When Father Lasuén dedicated the mission to Our Lady of Solitude in 1791 and planted the cross, the solitude was all too evident. The members of the little company were the only figures to break the monotony of the silent wastes extending along the level valley.

The buildings went up slowly. In about a year a temporary church was usable, but it was six years before a large church was built. There were few natives living nearby, so conversions did not come easily.

But the little mission did prosper. The fathers tapped the Salinas River to irrigate the wide-spreading fields. Crops flourished and the mission herds multiplied and grew fat on the lush pasturage. Within nine years the neophyte population totaled 500. Horses, a thousand cattle, and several thousand sheep grazed over the plains surrounding the mission quadrangle. In five more years the population grew to 727; and the peak of prosperity was reached by 1820, when conversions totaled more than two thousand.

But there were troubles—one after another. The river, upon which the abundance of the mission crops depended, nearly erased the establishment several times. It rose in 1824, destroying the church, and again in 1828, taking out the chapel that had been built to replace the church. Before reconstruction could be completed, a third flood in 1832 presaged the end of the mission. A few years later, secularization destroyed what the floods had spared.

An epidemic—scourge of the missions—killed dozens of the Indians, and many fled in fright, doubtful of the blessings of a religion and way of life that could bring so much sorrow with it.

The rooms were damp, cold and gloomy. The missionaries assigned here were subject to attacks of rheumatism. In fact, missionaries often asked to be relieved of this assignment after a year or so, and in the brief span of the mission's life, almost thirty came and went. Father Ibañez stayed the longest, and that only because there was no one to replace him.

One of Father Ibañez' old friends, José Joaquín de Arrillaga, first Spanish governor of Alta California, died at Soledad while making a tour of the missions

When Fr. Sarría died in 1835, his loyal Indian subjects carried his body on a litter 25 miles to Mission San Antonio de Padua for burial.

Wrote J. Ross Browne of Soledad in 1849, "A more desolate place cannot well be imagined. The old church is partially in ruins, and the adobe huts built for the Indians are roofless, and the walls tumbled about in shapeless piles. Not a tree or shrub is to be seen anywhere in the vicinity. The ground is bare, like an open road, save in front of the main building where carcasses and bones of cattle are scattered about, presenting a disgusting spectacle."

in 1814 and was buried beneath the church floor. When the church was destroyed by a flood, his grave was obliterated and was only recently discovered during excavations prior to present reconstruction.

The most pathetic of Mission Soledad's losses was the death of Father Vicente Francisco de Sarría, a scholarly and amiable friar who had been Father-President and the first Comisario-Prefecto of the missions. By 1835 Father Sarría had seen the lonely outpost of Soledad dwindle in numbers of converts and in quantities of supplies and herds. The handful of faithful neophytes who lived at the mission often went hungry.

One Sunday morning in May the weary father was saying Mass when he fell before the altar. That afternoon he passed away, and a few devoted Indians made a litter and gently carried his emaciated body over the long miles to Mission Antonio de Padua for burial.

With the death of Father Sarría the mission died too. The few Indians dispersed to look for a better living elsewhere. The very roofs of the mission buildings were taken off to pay a debt to the Mexican government, and the winds sighed through the spreading window holes as each year the elements reduced more and more of the adobe to brown dust. Up until restoration began a few years ago, only a few crumbling ridges remained.

*After secularization, the mission
declined rapidly, and by 1843 it had
virtually ceased to exist. Sold by the
Governor in 1846 for $800, it served
for several years as a ranch house,
and then was abandoned. Although the
Church regained the property in 1859,
the mission was not reactivated for
90 years. At the time the photograph
on the right was taken (1885–90),
the form of the building was still
evident, but decay was already well
advanced. The sale of thousands of roof
tiles to pay debts had left the
walls unprotected.*

After a century of neglect, the restored mission is beginning to regain its original appearance, as comparison with the photograph below left attests. Now a mission of the parish of Soledad, the white chapel was restored in 1954 and the padres' wing in 1963. Originally, a church stood to the right of the padres' quarters until 1831 when it collapsed in a flood. It was in this vanished church that Gov. Arrillaga and Fr. Ibañez were buried.

When the rubble was cleared away for the restoration in 1954, all that could be utilized of the original structure was the front corner of the chapel. Tiles in the foregound covered the floor of the sanctuary; the remainder of the floor was dirt, typical of the early-stage missions. Restoration of the mission has been under the auspices of the Native Daughters of the Golden West.

NUESTRA SEÑORA DE LA SOLEDAD **229**

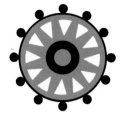

San José

Fourteenth mission, founded June 11, 1797, by Fr. Fermin Lasuén. Named for St. Joseph, Patron of the Universal Church. First church completed September 1797. Building, of which present fragment was a portion, begun 1805 and dedicated April 22, 1809; destroyed by earthquake October 21, 1868; partly restored 1916 and 1950; mission church reconstructed 1982–1985. Mission secularized 1834, sold 1846, returned to Catholic Church in 1858. Located off Interstate 680, 15 miles northeast of San Jose.

Father-President Lasuén urged the Viceroy to authorize the founding of more missions to fill the long gaps between those already established. To give impetus to his request he shrewdly suggested that the opening of these missions would cause no additional expense for military defense; in fact, by providing rest stops, such missions would save the· royal treasury the $15,000 a year then required for military escorts provided for supply caravans that stopped overnight on the lonely trails.

At last in 1795, the good news was received that the number of missions could be increased and parties should be sent to search for suitable sites. Expeditions were dispatched from Monterey, San Buenaventura, San Diego, and San Antonio in groups of seven or eight men, each accompanied by a missionary who kept a careful journal of the trip.

The area explored by the last group happened to produce the first mission. Visiting the area near San Francisco, the little party traveled northeast from Santa Clara to a point where they could see Mission Dolores as well as Yerba Buena Island. Father Antonio Danti set up a cross on a slight elevation near Alameda Creek, and the expedition returned to Santa Clara, well soaked from a rain storm.

The reports were forwarded to the Viceroy, and though haste was urged, it took two years to receive the required authority. Missionaries would be sent, wrote the Viceroy, along with goods and implements, to found five new missions. When these finally arrived, Father-President Lasuén with Sergeant Pedro Amador and a party of soldiers set out from Santa Clara on June 9, 1797. Two

An impressively authentic replica, Mission San José rises from the foundations of its original adobe brick structure, ruined by an earthquake in 1868. Completed in 1985, the restoration captures the look and feeling of the mission's period of prosperity in the 1830s. Included among its treasures from the past are the original monastic wing, wood statues and clay floor tiles unearthed by archaeologists.

days later, on Trinity Sunday, Lasuén raised and blessed the cross at the spot designated, celebrated holy Mass, and dedicated the mission in honor of the foster-father of Christ, St. Joseph.

A few days later, Sergeant Amador, two padres, and other helpers assembled materials on the site and began construction of crude shelters. Soon after these were finished, a herd of six-hundred cattle and a good-sized flock of sheep arrived from Santa Clara, and the mission was informally launched with a barbecue and fiesta.

The padres were quite aware that this was a troublesome spot. Runaway neophytes from Mission Dolores, often secreted here by their tribal brothers, caused more trouble than the presidio at San Francisco could handle. These tribes had strains of Apache and Comanche blood and were noted for their aggressive fighting spirit. The first year, only thirty-three natives were converted; but the padres kept trying, and they made slow progress, eventually converting more Indians than any other northern mission.

For twenty years, two capable padres, Fathers Buenaventura Fortuni and Narciso Durán, worked side by side, until the former was transferred to a new mission at Sonoma, leaving Father Durán in charge of the growing community. Durán was a versatile and capable leader who served three terms as Father-President of the mission chain.

One field in which he excelled was music. Although he had never had any musical training, he was an accomplished musician and he was adept at teaching others. He organized a thirty-piece band, and until real musical instruments could be obtained from Mexico, he devised practice instruments which he taught the Indians to play.

His willing pupils learned many complicated songs, chants, Masses and hymns. Indians would walk miles to hear one of the mission's concerts. Even as late as 1842, there were still on hand in the mission twenty violins, four bass viols,

Fr. Narciso Durán, pictured by French explorer Duflot de Mofras who visited the mission in 1841. The drawing shows the padre "presenting an apple to an Indian child, symbolic of his concern for the spiritual welfare of his young charges." Durán was an able and versatile padre whom the Indians revered, and who could drive a hard bargain with a ship's captain, plan a military campaign, administer complex mission enterprises, write music, and train Indians to play musical instruments and sing music creditably. He spent 27 years at the mission, and later served for three terms as Father-President.

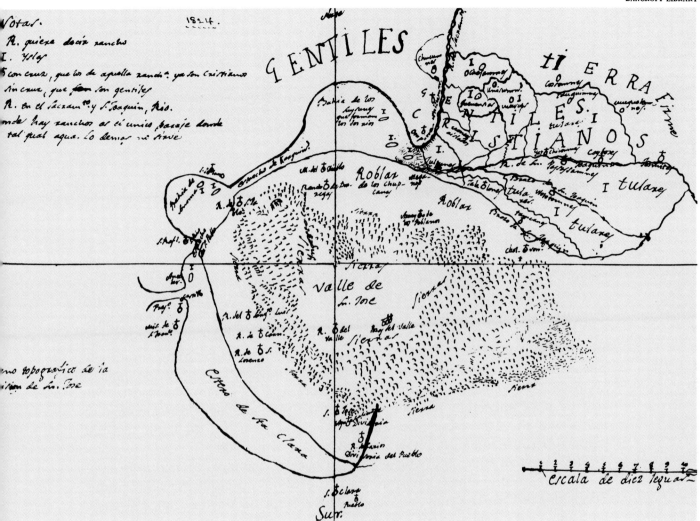

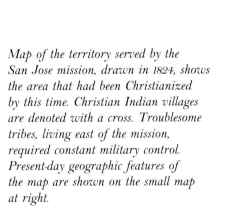

Map of the territory served by the San Jose mission, drawn in 1824, shows the area that had been Christianized by this time. Christian Indian villages are denoted with a cross. Troublesome tribes, living east of the mission, required constant military control. Present-day geographic features of the map are shown on the small map at right.

cie lo. ℈ Dios te salve Maria lle na

Se ñor es con ti go ben dí ta tu e re

Ingenious methods were needed to get Indians to read music. Durán invented a system for showing the four choir parts in two colors and two shapes for each color. He did away with a diversity of clefs and used solely the clef of F flat. The Indian musicians had little trouble reading the music, hand-lettered on parchment sheets 22x15 inches.

one contra bass, one drum, a hand organ, a book of choral music written on vellum, a great deal of music, and twenty-six band uniforms.

Throughout much of its existence, the mission served as a military base for punitive expeditions against hostile natives in the interior. One of the most serious Indian skirmishes was one in which a padre himself was almost a victim. Father Pedro de la Cueva, with a guard of three soldiers and some neophytes, went out on a sick call to a ranchería to the east. One of the neophytes, confused by a dense fog, led the party astray, and they were attacked by the natives of an unfriendly ranchería. Four of the men and all of the horses were killed, and all of the other men would have been harmed if the battle had not stopped because one of the warring natives had been killed.

The wounded survivors managed to get back to the mission, and a force of thirty-four soldiers was sent out from the San Francisco Presidio under Sergeant Luis María Peralta to search for the culprits. Aided by some settlers, they killed eleven rebels and captured many others.

Later another expedition was sent from the presidio, led by Sergeant Francisco Soto, the first Spanish child born in San Francisco. About a hundred neophytes joined Soto's force, and together they put to rout a thousand natives in the San Joaquin Valley.

One of Father Durán's favorite helpers was an intelligent Indian named Estanislao, who, to the padre's sorrow, defected to the warring tribes. Bored with the restrictions of mission living, the restless Indian led attacks on peaceful settlers, and defeated a small band under young Soto. Stanislaus County, named for him, was the scene of many of his offenses. He was finally captured by General Mariano Vallejo.

Through the years punctuated with Indian fights, the mission grew. The soil was rich, the fruit trees produced, olive trees bore well, and the herds multiplied. A large church was erected to care for the many converts, and this church with its plain undecorated fachada lasted until a destructive earthquake in 1868 brought it down. In the thirty-nine years that the mission was operating, it boasted 6,737 converts, second only to San Luis Rey in the mission chain. It was among the last to be secularized.

*After secularization, all but the church and graveyard were sold by the
last Mexican Governor and, though the sale was later invalidated, portions of the
buildings were used by renters and squatters. In the 1860s, a
Mexican tavern and hotel occupied part of the space.*

Built in 1869, a wood gothic-style church stood on the foundation of the dev-
astated mission for more than a century. Called St. Joseph, it served a Catholic
parish until 1965. Nearby, several surviving outbuildings, including the
monastery wing that presently houses a museum, remained from the former
mission complex.

The old gothic church, now known as Old St. Joseph, was removed in 1982
and carefully relocated in Burlingame. In 1985, after years of painstaking effort
by architects, archeologists, fund-raisers and volunteers, an authentic reconstruction of Mission San José was completed.

Guided by early drawings and historical accounts, the restoration was built
of authentic materials. Adobe bricks were formed in archaic sizes, and even
historic tools were used. Portions of walls and roofline are purposely uneven,
as is the tiled floor, part of it original. Beaded glass chandeliers, reflecting the
mission's opulence at its height of prosperity, are slightly mismatched, as were
their prototypes of the 1830s. The decorated nave and *reredos* behind the altar
sparkle with 23-karat gold leaf. Closer to the entrance of the sanctuary lies
the gravestone of pioneer Robert Livermore, for whom a Bay Area town was
named, which archeologists uncovered during the restoration.

Surviving fragment of the original mission of 1809, this high-ceilinged corridor serves rooms once used as padres' quarters. Its tall wooden posts were probably acquired in 1916, when the wing was altered, because they differ in style from those of other missions.

Rare old daguerreotype taken in 1852 (probably the oldest mission photo extant) conveys a real if blurred picture of the scope of the mission buildings. At the time this was taken, the parish was being served from Santa Clara; but the next year a parish priest moved into the decrepit buildings, and the old adobe was used for 15 more years before it was destroyed by an earthquake.

Victim of one of the largest quakes in California's recorded history, the mission was virtually wrecked by the tremors. The quake broke along the nearby Hayward Fault in 1868. As this crude painting (now in the Santa Clara Mission museum) shows, the walls caved in and the roof broke open. The bells that fell out of a bellcote under the eaves in 1868 hung for many years in the steeple of the wooden church and are now on display in the museum in the old monastery wing.

Old St. Joseph Church, which rested on the foundation of the ruined mission for over a century, was transported to Burlingame in 1982 to make room for the reconstruction of the mission.

One of few remaining original pieces, the baptismal font of hammered copper on a painted wooden base was used to baptize 6,500 Indians between 1797 and 1834. RIGHT: *A dazzling replica, the gilded and columned reredos of the restored mission revives the style of prosperous times in the 1830s.*

R. VALENTINE ATKINSON

San Juan Bautista

Fifteenth mission, founded June 24, 1797, by Fr. Fermín Lasuén. Named for
John the Baptist. First church completed 1798; second and present church
begun 1803, dedicated 1812. Damaged by earthquake of 1906.
Restoration 1949–50, financed by Hearst Foundation. Secularized 1835,
ground returned to Church in 1859. Located in town of San Juan Bautista,
4 miles south of U.S. Highway 101, 17 miles north of Salinas.

To visit Mission San Juan Bautista today is to step back into the California of
150 years ago, for the mellowed old building stands in the company of a well-
preserved cluster of houses and shops that date from the last days of the mission
period.

San Juan Bautista was founded by the energetic Father Lasuén in that busy
summer of 1797 that saw four new missions get under way. The Father-President
selected the site only 13 days after founding Mission San José and dedicated the
new mission to John the Baptist on June 24.

The mission grew phenomenally at first, materially as well as spiritually. The
Indians were so friendly and cooperative that within six months records show
that not only was an adobe church built but also a granary, barracks, a monastery,
and some adobe houses.

With this astonishing growth a major consideration was a church large enough
to hold all the neophytes. The fathers were pondering whether to enlarge the
church or build a new one, when a series of earthquakes lasting twenty days
jolted the area and partially solved the problem for them. A portion of the church
fell, and in rebuilding it, the padres enlarged and added to it.

But with more and more neophytes coming into the mission fold, it was
realized that even larger quarters would be needed, so an elaborate new church
was designed. On June 13, 1803 the governor and other dignitaries were invited
to attend the ceremony of laying the cornerstone. During the colorful festivities a
bottle containing the story of the dedication was sealed and inserted into the
cornerstone, and it is doubtless there to this day.

As bright as the day it was painted in 1818 by the
Boston sailor, Doak, and his Indian helpers, the golden
reredos has almost a theatrical air with its open niches with
scarlet backdrops that frame the statues of the saints.

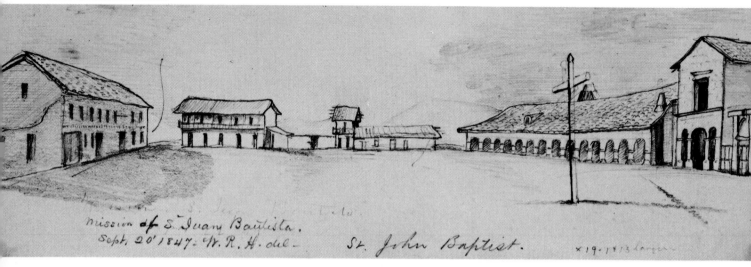

mission of S. Iuan Bautista.
Sept. 20' 1847. W. R. H. del.   *St. John Baptist.*

When W. R. Hutton, the future designer of the Holland Tunnel, spent the night here in 1847, he noted that he liked the beef brochette but he and his companions did not "like fleas, much." (Other travelers of the day reported that the fleas "came in armies to glut their appetites on human blood.") Some of the buildings that Hutton sketched are still standing, as comparison with the plan on page 249 reveals.

This church was destined to be even larger than was first planned. While it was under construction, an extraordinary padre named Father Felipe del Arroyo de la Cuesta arrived in 1808. With boundless enthusiasm and energy, he first tackled the church problem, convincing the builders that a more capacious building should be erected. Accordingly, plans were changed, and instead of the customary long narrow nave with a center aisle, a huge dignified edifice grew, with three aisles and a capacity of over a thousand worshippers.

But before the building was finished, the padres had second thoughts about the safety of the large structure in the event of an earthquake. Fearful that the open-arched walls that separated the side aisles from the nave might not support the heavy roof in a temblor, they closed in the arches, all except the first pair, which they left open to form a transept. The great three-aisled church thus became one-aisled like all the rest.

Without knowing it, the padres had erected the church on the edge of California's most destructive earthquake fault, the San Andreas. Although earthquake damage right on a fault is often less than that farther away, the site did make the church vulnerable, and the padres were wiser than they ever knew in planning for earthquake resistance. The means they took to secure the structure against damage are now considered of doubtful value, but the major buildings have survived almost 200 years of San Andreas' antics. The 1812 quake that damaged half the missions in the province did not affect San Juan Bautista because it erupted along a different fault. But when the famous shocker of 1906 struck, it toppled walls of the church and some of the outbuildings. The walls that fell had been weakened previously by groundwater that soaked the bottom courses of adobes, and the softened bricks quickly gave way. Walls standing on dry ground, however, came through the quake with little damage. After the quake, the building was strengthened with steel and concrete and heavy cross-bracing and, as a consequence, it is safer now than it ever was.

The church was dedicated in June 1812 and has been in almost continuous use ever since. The colorful reredos, added six years after the consecration, is as bright as it was the day it was finished. It was painted by a stranded sailor from Boston, Thomas Doak, who was the first Anglo-American resident in the province. The job had previously been assigned to a Mexican artist, but when he demanded seventy-five cents a day, frugal Father Arroyo chose instead to give the work to Doak, who was willing to work for room and board. Doak was certainly no artist, but he mixed strong and durable colors that glow today as brightly as they did when he applied them.

Perhaps Father Arroyo's greatest contribution to his times was his skill in linguistics. He could preach to the Indians in any of seven Indian dialects, as the congregation required. In later years when rheumatism stiffened his weary bones and confined him to a chair, he compiled a scholarly index of Indian phrases, vocabularies and other valuable works. He delighted in having beside him the Indian children whom he liked to give names from the classics, such as Plato and Cicero.

Teamed with this learned and affable padre was Father Estévan Tápis who had retired to the mission after serving nine years as Father-President. Father Tápis was beloved by the Indians, and especially won their hearts through music. Like Father Durán at Mission San José, he had a prodigious talent for music. His Indian boys choir was renowned, and he devised the system, soon in general use, of using colored notes for the different voices to follow. Examples still exist

The colorful reredos and altar were painted in 1818 by the first American settler in California, Thomas Doak, a sailor from Boston, who received meals in return for the murals.

Celebration of Judas Day by the mission Indians was one of the most popular events on the church calendar. Judas, the betrayer of Christ, was hanged in effigy, beaten with sticks, and set afire. When fireworks were available from trading vessels, they were stuffed into the straw figure, making his demise a spectacular climax to the day's festivities.

in the mission museum of the large parchment sheets on which he painstakingly painted the five music lines with large square notes in red, yellow, black and white (outlined with black) so each singer could learn to read the most complicated part without error.

So thoroughly did he ground his pupils in the art of singing that even forty years later, Indian choirs still sang the music he had adapted for them. They even asked the father who served the mission at that time to lock them up on Saturday night lest they succumb to a second love, whiskey, which would incapacitate them for singing at service next day.

No story of the mission would be complete without mention of its famous hurdy-gurdy, whose termite-ridden remains are displayed in the mission museum. This wondrous instrument is supposed to have been brought to California by Captain Vancouver in 1792, given to Mission Carmel, and passed along to San Juan Bautista in 1829. However, the instrument in the museum does not match the description of the Vancouver organ and the tunes punched into its tin cylinders were not known at the time Vancouver left England on his long voyage. According to one theory, the hand-organ that he left at Carmel is now at a seminary in Benicia—but where the one at San Juan Bautista came from is still a mystery.

Whatever its source, the hand-cranked music box was very popular with the Indians, who loved to grind out its rollicking tunes at every opportunity.

Although hardly appropriate to the sedate cloisters of the mission, the Indians' favorite tunes were the sprightly "Go to the Devil," "Lady Campbell's Reel," and "A College Hornpipe."

Of the many stories concerning this barrel organ, one of the best shows its almost hypnotic power over the innocent natives. A tribe of warring Tulare Indians swooped down on the mission one day, and the neophytes ran for cover. Fortunately the padre kept his wits. He lugged out the hand-organ and began cranking. The neophytes caught on and began to sing with the music at the top of their voices, with the result that their foes were so entranced that they lay down their weapons and demanded more music, even asking to stay so they could enjoy it all the time.

A town grew up around the mission, as early as 1814—a town now so proud of its pioneer heritage that it has become a shrine to the romantic past. The "city of history" ranged around the mission plaza contains buildings that form a state historical monument. The well-preserved mission, however, is not a part of the state monument, although its museum and grounds are open to the public. It is an active church that serves a predominantly Spanish-speaking parish.

To the north of the musty cemetery grounds runs a shaded portion of the original El Camino Reál, California's first road. This is one of the few known sections of the royal road that once connected the missions and later became a stageroad, and ultimately U.S. Highway 101.

By the time that artist Henry Chapman Ford visited the mission in the 1880's,
the quadrangle had been reduced to the large L that is standing today.
In back can be seen a portion of the convent later used as an orphanage.
Square openings in the corridor across the face of the mission were large
entryways to admit ox carts to the enclosed patio.

For nearly 90 years, the façade of San Juan Bautista included as one of its principal features a steeple that never really belonged there at all. When the building was completed in 1812, it did not have a belltower, although foundations were provided for a pair of them. The bells hung from a sturdy wooden crossbar until 1865, when a Fr. Rubio, newly assigned to the parish, decided that the church needed modernizing, and he installed a New England steeple as part of the up-dating. Carpenters from the East Coast were in plentiful supply, and it was a simple matter to duplicate a New England belfry, however incompatible it might be with Spanish colonial design. The wooden steeple stood unchanged until 1915 when it was decapitated by a storm. The pointed roof was never replaced; but in another spurt of modernization, in 1929, the tower was remodeled to give it more mission flavor and its wooden siding was plastered. This version stood until 1949 when it was torn down and the building returned to its original form.

JOHN S. WEIR

MISSION SAN JUAN BAUTISTA
1803

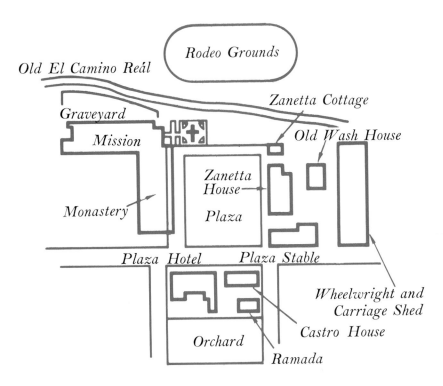

Rodeo Grounds

Old El Camino Reál

Zanetta Cottage

Graveyard

Old Wash House

Mission

Zanetta House

Monastery

Plaza

Plaza Hotel

Plaza Stable

Wheelwright and Carriage Shed

Castro House

Orchard

Ramada

To stroll around the Plaza of San Juan Bautista is to step back into the California of 150 years ago.
The carefully preserved buildings are dominated by the bold façade of the mission, which stretches across the western side. All but the mission are operated as a state historical monument. The Plaza Hotel was originally the mission barracks, increased to two stories in 1858.
The Zanetta House was built in 1868 from adobes salvaged from the dormitory for the mission girls that formerly stood on the south side of the plaza.
The Castro House, built in 1840, was the home of the Mexican administrator, Major General José Castro.
The Plaza Stable was opened by the stageline for the convenience of its passengers who stopped here.

ZANETTA HOUSE
(Plaza Hall)
1868

PLAZA STABLE
1874

CASTRO HOUSE
1840

PLAZA HOTEL
1814

Simple, massive construction of the mission is revealed
on the patio side. The bulging walls of adobe 40 feet in
height (tallest in the chain) are braced by concrete
buttresses, installed after the 1906 quake. The two-story
jail, at the left, was not affected by the quake. It was in
this jail that the Indian choir was voluntarily locked on
Saturday nights in the 1850's so they would not succumb to
the whiskey flowing in the town's saloons and be unable
to sing with clear heads and voices on Sunday.

The mission stands on the very edge of the great San Andreas earthquake fault that nearly destroyed San Francisco in 1906. In fact, bleachers for the rodeo grounds adjacent are built right on the fault scarp. When the 1906 quake struck the mission, it toppled the outer walls weakened by ground water but did not damage the inner ones. A wall also fell out in the orphanage behind the mission, nearly snuffing out the lives of the children sleeping there.

A shady pathway visible today just beyond the wall of the mission cemetery is an unchanged section of the old El Camino Reál, the long road that stretched 650 miles from San Rafael to San Diego, connecting the 21 missions.

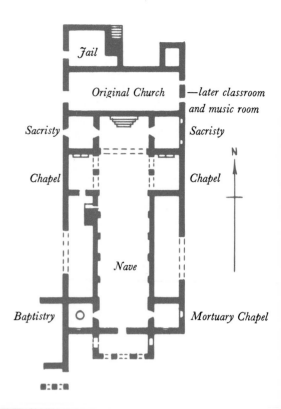

Jail

Original Church — later classroom
and music room

Sacristy   Sacristy

N

Chapel   Chapel

Nave

Baptistry   Mortuary Chapel

An 1890 photograph taken by A. C. Vroman in the old sacristy reveals a mixture of locally made objects and importations from Mexico, New England, and other faraway places—sure evidence that the mission was no stranger to the trading vessels that docked at Monterey. From Mexico came the painting of John the Baptist, the holy water vessel, and crucifix. From New England: the gilded mirror and the small chair. Locally made: the ornate carved cupboard for sacred vessels and the sturdy chair and desk. Ceremonial vestments came from Peru.

LOS ANGELES COUNTY MUSEUM

Until the restoration in 1948, the church interior was still encumbered with the woodwork applied with a lavish hand by Fr. Rubio in the 1860's. Tongue-and-groove sheathing covered the beamed ceiling; wooden flooring concealed the original mezcla (concrete) floor. As originally designed, the church was to have been the only three-aisled one in the mission chain. The full width of the building was to have been utilized, with arches separating the side bays from the nave (see plan). However, a shrinkage in the congregation and a series of earthquakes in 1800 prompted the padres to abandon this ambitious plan. They filled in all the arches except the ones on either side of the altar rail and converted the bays to other uses. The large beams that cross the nave were not in the first plan. They were installed as a precaution after the 1906 earthquake.

SAN JUAN BAUTISTA **253**

San Miguel Arcángel

Sixteenth mission, founded July 25, 1797, by Fr. Fermín Lasuén. Named for St. Michael the Archangel. Present church begun 1816; completed, 1818; decoration finished, 1821. Last mission to be secularized, 1834; properties sold 1845; returned to Church 1859. Main buildings renovated 1901 and 1928. On old U.S. Highway 101 in town of San Miguel, 9 miles north of Paso Robles, halfway between Los Angeles and San Francisco.

Driven with burning energy, Father Lasuén hurried to found the third mission in the two summer months in 1797. Mission San Miguel filled in the long gap between San Antonio and San Luis Obispo, and fulfilled such a need that a great congregation attended the service and fifteen Indian children were baptized on the day of the founding, July 25.

Building, begun at once, was aided by the willing and industrious natives. Some neophyte families from nearby San Luis Obispo and San Antonio missions came to live near the new settlement, and by their enthusiasm won the confidence of other natives. A church was quickly erected and soon a small village grew around the rectangular mission.

The mud-roofed first church was used for about a year, when it was replaced by a larger one of the same simple construction. Though the padres never got around to tiling the roof, this church lasted until 1806, when a raging fire consumed many of the buildings and their contents. All the wool, cloth, and hides that had been accumulated were lost. The two long rows of workshops and the granaries with their six thousand bushels of precious wheat were destroyed, as well as part of the church roof. The loss was a crippling one for the large settlement of more than a thousand Indians, who were dependent on the supplies. In the emergency the nearest missions contributed implements, grain, clothing and other needs to relieve the distress, and within a year the mission was again busy with all its functions.

The catastrophe led to the planning of a large new church, tile-roofed and permanent. For years Father Juan Martín kept the Indians busy making and

Although not original to the mission, the modern-fountain harmonizes with the old structure. The basin is formed of burned adobes, salvaged from the grounds, and the formation itself is a rough replica in concrete of the one at Santa Bárbara. Fountain designs were freely copied from one mission to another.

drying adobes in preparation for a big building program. Some of the adobes were even baked in ovens to speed the drying. Thus, while the new church was not "begun" until 1816, it then required only two years to erect because of the stockpile of building material assembled beforehand.

Though simple and severe on the outside, the inside of the church glows with the bright colors applied in 1820 by the Spanish artist Estévan Munras and his Indian assistants. Fortunately, the radiant hues have withstood both the course of time and the impulses of "restorers" to change or improve the originals, and the visitor of today can enjoy the embellishments in all their original purity. Artist Munras was a friend of Father Martín—they both came from the same part of Catalonia, Spain—and he agreed to decorate the interior as a favor. He based his designs on some that he found in books in the mission library and interpreted them with a rich palette. Noteworthy features of Munras' work are the simulated balconies, doors, and archways painted on the walls, the quaint octagonal wall pulpit with its crown-like sounding-board, and the elaborate reredos with its dramatic all-seeing-eye blazing above the statue of St. Michael.

With the mission firmly established, the padres turned their attention to the planning and founding of new asistencias (sub-missions) for nearby areas where the natives still "sat in darkness." One of the most sunless regions, in this respect, was the Tulare Valley, little known except for the descriptions supplied by the few Spanish pathfinders and padres who followed the first native trails.

Various expeditions were dispatched in the beginning years of the last century, and the first journey of this nature left San Miguel in November 1804, consisting of only one padre and two soldiers. Traveling eastward for three days they reached the ranchería Bubal where the Indians were friendly and even anxious for a branch mission to be founded. Another expedition returned

Artist Estévan Munras, engaged to decorate the mission interior, took his designs and stencil patterns from books and applied them from a bright palette with the help of Indian craftsmen. His name is associated today with a street and an historic adobe dwelling in Monterey.

When sketched by Powell in 1850, most of the mission was still standing.
The quadrangle behind the Church had withered away—as the faint lines of old
wall show—but the rest of it was more or less intact. To the right of the
Church stretches a line of Indian dwellings, torn down in later years to permit
passage of the highway. A few fragments are still visible today
east of the freeway.

to Bubal a few days later with a renewed hope that a mission might be founded in this inland area. The padre performed 24 baptisms and then proceeded to another village then at war with Bubal. The good father tried to reconcile the two, but the natives fled in fright when they saw the soldiers, thinking they had come to kill them. In a short skirmish, an Indian woman and two of the Spaniards' horses were killed. Hostility of the Indians compelled the padres to abandon plans for founding an asistencia; however, some of the Indians from Bubal did come to the mission to live. A few fickle ones arrived on horseback and soon left for home, driving along with them horses from the mission herds. When soldiers were sent out in pursuit, the natives concealed themselves in the tules and swamps, where they could watch the leatherjackets ride by.

The mission became a beehive of activity as the neophytes learned many trades, becoming proficient with leather, iron, wood, stone, and products of the loom. Hundreds of Indians grew crops, cared for the vineyards, and herded the thousands of animals that roamed the ranches under mission supervision.

Though the Indians were used to the climate, summers were hot and dry and the gray-robed friars suffered. Alfred Robinson reported such summer heat that even the fleas might be seen lying on the brick pavement gasping for breath.

In anticipation of the forthcoming secularization of the missions, the first Mexican Governor to be sent from Mexico, José Echeandía, issued an illegal decree in 1831 that required the missions to free any Indians who desired their liberty. A commissioner came to Mission San Miguel and made speeches to the neophytes, explaining their new rights. After listening, the Indians said they respected the Governor and the decree, but they desired no change. The commissioner then mounted a cart in the mission courtyard and pictured vividly to his audience the advantages of freedom. He asked those who wanted to remain under the padre to stand on the left; those preferring freedom to stand on the right. Nearly all went to the left, and were soon joined by the few remaining.

"The Neophytes Are Demoralized and Dispersed"

The Governor's illegal decree was not enforced, but within three years official word came through and the mission was confiscated in August 1834 and all the property distributed among the Indians. For a few years, the mission operated under a succession of administrators with decreasing success. By 1844, Father-President Durán was moved to report: "Mission San Miguel Arcángel is to-day without livestock, and the neophytes are demoralized and dispersed."

Two years later, and three days before the flag of the United States was raised in Monterey, Governor Pico sold all of the mission but the church and the priests' quarters. One of the purchasers, a William Reed, occupied one whole wing as an apartment for himself and his family of three. Although his title to the property was disputed for years, he continued to live in the mission—and thus unwittingly became the victim of one of the most atrocious murders in California history.

At that time, the deserted buildings of San Miguel were frequented by riffraff attracted by the Gold Rush who loitered here on their way between San Francisco and Los Angeles. A party of tramps stopped over one day in 1849 and chanced to hear Reed brag about some hidden wealth. They left, ostensibly to continue their journey, but instead they doubled back, and when darkness fell, they murdered Reed, his family, and six servants. They ransacked the premises, found no gold, and fled. A posse quickly caught up with them and in the ensuing fight, one of the murderers was killed, another leaped into the ocean and drowned, and the other three were taken to Santa Bárbara where they were later executed.

Although the mission properties were returned to the Church by court order in 1859, the church was not reactivated until 1878, after a lapse of 36 years. Some of the buildings were restored in the next decade and again in 1901. Finally, in 1928 it was returned to the Franciscan Order for use as a parish church and a monastery. Today, visitors will note seismic cracking from foundation to roof line; inside, water stains and cracks reach toward some of the only surviving original Indian and Spanish artwork in the mission chain—brilliantly stained balustrades and precious murals painted in the early 1820s.

Secularization struck a hard blow at San Miguel, which had no resident pastor between 1842 and 1878. Space in the rambling structure was rented for private use. In the 1860's, a tavern shared the old monastery wing with an agency for the Howe sewing machine, and the buildings were left to take care of themselves. In the lower photograph of the inner side of the mission, taken in the 1880's, the old columns show wear from the constant rubbing of cattle against their scratchy surfaces.

*Of the delightful old pulpit, an observer wrote in 1905,
"A peculiar fascination pertains to this little structure,
with its quaint sounding-board and crown-like cover,
the whole resembles a bird-nest fastened upon the right
wall." The figure of a dove, symbol of the Holy Ghost,
hangs suspended from the sounding-board.*

*Unique among the mission arcades, the colonnade has an
assortment of different sized and shaped arches.
The small Mexican bell (cast in 1800) hanging from a
beam has a hole in one side, caused by a fault in the
casting but popularly attributed to an armed patron of
the San Miguel Bar. Cannon in foreground is Spanish,
dated 1697; used by Mexicans in campaign against
Frémont in 1846.*

SAN MIGUEL ARCÁNGEL **261**

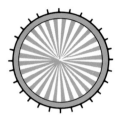

San Fernando Rey de España

Seventeenth mission, founded September 8, 1797, by Fr. Fermín Lasuén. Named for
St. Ferdinand, King of Spain (1217–1252). First church completed 1799;
replaced by new church 1800; third church completed 1806, damaged by
earthquake of 1812, restorations 1879, 1912, 1916, and 1930's, damaged
beyond repair by earthquake of 1971; exact replica dedicated 1974. Secularized
1834, sold 1846, returned to Church 1861. Located 1½ miles west of
city of San Fernando, off Interstate Hwy. 5, on Mission Blvd.

In that remarkable summer of 1797 when Father Lasuén dedicated four new missions, the gap between San Buenaventura on the coast and San Gabriel in the interior was closed with establishment of Mission San Fernando Rey de España. Although the site was supposed to be halfway between the two missions, it was actually much closer to San Gabriel; but it had many advantages.

Previous exploration had indicated that the best location for a midway mission was a spacious valley that Father Crespí had named Santa Catalina de Bononia de los Encinos (St. Catherine of Bologna's Valley of the Live Oaks). When Crespí and Portolá passed through the valley on their trip to Monterey, they had found the Indians friendly.

In addition to congenial Indians, the valley showed potential for agricultural development. The presence of four springs that flowed as though they would never run dry strongly influenced the padres' decision to settle here.

The actual site chosen for the mission was on a rancho, owned with dubious legality by Don Francisco Reyes, alcalde of the Pueblo of Los Angeles. As the property actually belonged to Mission San Gabriel, the padres had little trouble ousting Reyes, and they used his small ranch house as living quarters while the mission buildings were rising.

The first small chapel was erected within two months. Soon a granary, a storeroom, and a weaving room were erected, and in only a year a new church had to be built to care for the growing congregation.

The mission continued to mushroom and prosper. Within seven years housing had to be provided for nearly a thousand converts, a population that held steady

Massive, gravity-fed fountain is one of two that originally
graced mission grounds. The basin in the shape of a
Moorish star formed of intersecting arcs is a copy of one
in Cordova, Spain. It was moved to its present site
from an earlier location by L. C. Brand.

for almost twenty years. Soon, all the buildings were tile-roofed, and the quadrangle was surrounded by barracks, dwellings, workshops, and storerooms, and a third church was started.

The new adobe mission church was finished the next December, and its dedication ceremonies in 1806 were attended by many padres and neophytes from other missions. To the Indians the most interesting part of the program was the music. From Santa Bárbara and La Purísima came bands of Indian musicians, who brought their instruments and presented a concert of melodious songs and chants that they had learned in the mission choirs.

The mission was substantially built, but it was not strong enough to withstand the devastating earthquakes of 1812. The spasms of December 21 shook down so much of the thick-walled church that it was necessary to install thirty new beams and a burned-brick buttress to reinforce the structure. These repairs enabled the church to survive subsequent earthquakes with little damage, and the building would probably have stood intact for decades if it had not been despoiled by vandals. Over a period of time, it gradually collapsed.

After the church fell into ruin, the only building remaining from the once-extensive structure was the huge Convento that branched off the quadrangle. This large adobe, variously known as the Long Building, Monastery, Hospice, and Mission House, was for many years mistaken by travelers for the mission itself, so impressive were its dimensions. The huge building is 243 feet long and 50 feet wide, bordered for its full length by a 19-arch colonnade.

This well-preserved structure is today a fascinating period-piece. The heavy-beamed reception room is one of the most elegant of any among the missions, with its iron window grilles, decorative chandelier, irregular tile flooring, and colorful paintings. Part of the building was a hospice with bedrooms and a dining room set apart for the use of travelers, who stopped here in increasing numbers as word of the mission's hospitality spread.

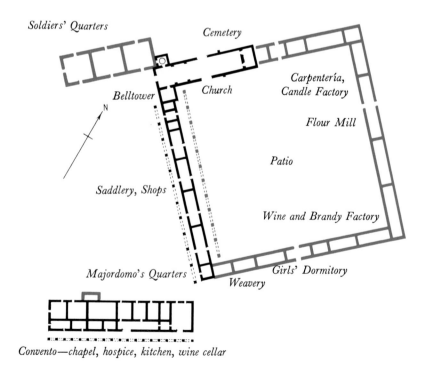

Soldiers' Quarters

Cemetery

Belltower

Church

N

Carpentería, Candle Factory

Flour Mill

Patio

Saddlery, Shops

Wine and Brandy Factory

Majordomo's Quarters

Weavery

Girls' Dormitory

Convento—chapel, hospice, kitchen, wine cellar

Fountain

Highways, streets, and parks have cut into the mission layout so that it is difficult to grasp the extent of the original institution without recourse to a plot plan. The long, Z-shaped building now standing was once part of a complete quadrangle, 295 by 315 feet. The usual complement of shops, storage rooms, and living quarters enclosed a large patio. Portions of the original structure that are restored are shown in black.

Wrote the artist Henry Chapman Ford in 1888, the long building "is at this time well preserved. The rooms are now used for the purposes of the Porter Land and Water Company and in the rear some are used as a stable. . . The church is in a sadly ruined condition, most of the tiled roof having been removed to furnish material for other buildings, thus leaving the walls to be disintegrated by the elements."

Eight years later, another writer lamented, "It is terrible to see San Fernando Mission going to ruin so fast. The great main building, with corridor fronting on the great plaza, is now desecrated by bits of harness, old wagons, grain bags, a kitchen and sleeping quarters for ranch hands, and all sorts of odds and ends. The big court in the rear, on which the church fronts, is now a farm yard, and half filled with wagons, a threshing machine and hay and grain racks. Hogs are everywhere."

Although the agricultural development did not live up to the first predictions, the mission produced a bounty of olives, fruits, nuts, dates, and field crops. Shortly after secularization, the inventory recorded 32,000 grapevines and 1,600 fruit trees in place on the mission lands.

Cattle raising was the most important industry at Mission San Fernando. At its peak in 1819, 21,000 head of livestock grazed on the mission ranchos. San Fernando conducted a flourishing trade in hides and tallow and also excelled in leatherwork. For mission use, hides were tanned and converted into shoes, sandals, saddles, and door coverings. Rawhide strips were produced in quantity for holding structural members together in the absence of spikes, which were still scarce at that time.

It was on one of the mission's far-flung ranchos that a notable event took place that assumes more importance in retrospect than it did at the time it occurred. Six years before the finding of gold at Coloma, the mission of San Fernando had its own little gold rush. A major-domo on one of the ranchos pulled up some onions to flavor his dinner and noticed flakes of shiny yellow in the soil, which proved to be gold. When the discovery became known, a small army of gold-seekers descended on the spot, and within four years the small bonanza was exhausted. The first gold flakes to be carried around the Horn were brought from San Fernando to the mint in Philadelphia by Alfred Robinson, chronicler of the mission days. The shipment was valued at $344.75, or $19 an ounce. Rumors of this gold strike persisted for years, and treasure-seekers dug up the floor of the abandoned church in their quest for gold that they falsely believed had been buried there by the padres.

In the turbulent days that followed the Mexican take-over of California, the mission became involved in the provincial power struggles. Governor Echeandía, imbued with the new liberalism in Mexico, endeavored to convince the Indians that they should be released from mission bondage, and he equipped a small army of liberated neophytes from the southern missions to fight against a rival claimant to the office of governor. San Fernando became the headquarters of this short-lived revolt that died out when he was recalled to Mexico. Later, the infamous Governor Pico made it his headquarters in 1846, abandoning it in the nick of time to Colonel Frémont of the United States Army, who occupied the building for a while.

The buildings were sold by Pico just before the American occupation, and the Indians drifted away, most of them to the Pueblo of Los Angeles. Although the structures were returned to the Church in 1861 by court action, there was little left to utilize. The church was served from Our Lady of the Angels in Los Angeles from 1847 until 1902. In the meantime, the neglected buildings fell into ruin, aided by the settlers who helped themselves to tiles, beams, and even the bells. The very nails in the church were yanked out by souvenir-hunters. The only standing building, the Long House, passed through a succession of lessees, ultimately being used as a hog farm in 1896.

This low point of sacrilege drew attention to the decrepit buildings, and soon the Landmarks Club began the difficult work of trying to restore the heap of fallen beams and crumbling walls. One August day in 1916 they arranged a colorful ceremony for San Fernando Candle Day. Some 6,000 citizens assembled at the mission and bought candles at a dollar each. Then carrying the flickering tapers high, they formed a procession and marched through the arcades.

Since that time, the mission has been undergoing gradual restoration, and though far from completely rebuilt today, it is a pleasant and fascinating place.

Rodeos were almost a daily occurrence at San Fernando, where cattle raising was a major activity. At its peak, the mission had 12,800 head on the range.

*Serene and alone, the whitewashed mission stands out
cleanly in this 1890 photograph by A. C. Vroman.
Tall Washingtonia palms tower above the fields where
grapevines once flourished and where, today, thousands of
homes now stand.*

Unattended, the chapel deteriorated over the years until little more than the walls were left when Vroman took the photograph above in the 1890's. Roof tiles had long ago been removed for use on other buildings, timbers had collapsed, and the dirt floor had been dug up by fortune seekers looking for mythical treasure. To save the old structure, the Landmarks Club put on a shingle roof in time for the mission's centennial in 1897. This roof blew off in a storm and was replaced by another in 1916, financed by the sale of thousands of candles at $1 apiece. A crowd of 6,000 donors gathered at the mission on Candle Day and, after dark, they lit the candles and promenaded through the mission.

Plain and unimposing, the chapel offered little of architectural grace to enchant the observer, but it nevertheless had an air of rugged honesty. Damaged beyond repair by an earthquake on February 9, 1971, the restored chapel pictured here was replaced by an exact replica dedicated in November of 1974.

Big, handhewn doors, graced with mission-made locks and the snakelike river-of-life pattern, once welcomed visitors to the convento. Flower patterns above the door were painted over during repairs following the 1971 earthquake, but the shell patterns and statue remain.

*The mission has a rewarding combination of painted decoration and rich
architectural detailing. The peaked arch over the door is an example
of Mudejar design, a blend of Moorish and Spanish elements. This graceful
arch lends itself to use in the 5-foot-thick adobe walls.*

San Luis Rey de Francia

Eighteenth mission, founded June 13, 1798, by Fr. Fermín Lasuén. Named for Louis IX, King of France 1215–70, canonized in 1290 because of his crusades to Egypt and the Holy Land. First adobe church 1802. Present church begun 1811, dedicated 1815. Mission abandoned 1865–92; rededicated 1893. Secularized 1833–34, sold 1846, returned to Church 1865. Located in town of San Luis Rey, 5 miles east of Oceanside, off State Highway 76.

"The largest and most populous Indian mission of both Americas," San Luis Rey flourished from the very start. Much of its growth, beauty and bounty were due to the character and energy of a single man, Father Antonio Peyri, who was its guide from the auspicious day of its founding to the melancholy time of its secularization, thirty-six years later.

It was the ninth and last mission to be founded by Father-President Lasuén, and it closed a critical gap between San Diego and San Juan Capistrano. The district was promising in prospects for conversion. When the Portolá party had passed through 20 years earlier, they had found the natives cordial. Some 40 of the most curious had visited them in the nude, their bodies colorfully smeared with paint, as was their custom when visiting or going to war. After a harangue by the chief, the Indians threw their weapons on the ground, squatted near the exploring party, and exchanged gifts of fishing nets for strings of beads. Their women and children, more timid than the men, did not come near until urged by the men; then they too received beads.

So it was that when Lasuén founded San Luis Rey in 1798, the ceremony was witnessed by "a great multitude of gentiles of both sexes and all ages" and Father Lasuén baptized 54 children. Nineteen adults also asked to be baptized but were told to wait until they had received instruction.

Acceptance by the natives continued during the entire life of the mission. During the first six months, the neophyte population increased to two hundred and fourteen, so construction of the necessary adobe buildings was accelerated. In the first month eight thousand adobe bricks were made and dried, foundations

The sure hand of a master designer reveals itself in the artfully planned façade of Mission San Luis Rey. "Gracious, dignified, and expressive," the red-trimmed structure is a remarkable example of what a talented and energetic padre could create out of the native soil with the help of Indian craftsmen who had never before used a tool.

Wrote Duhaut-Cilly in 1827, "In the still uncertain light of dawn, this edifice, of a very beautiful model, supported upon its numerous pillars, had the aspect of a palace. Instinctively I stopped my horse to gaze alone, for a few minutes, on the beauty of this sight."

were laid, and dozens of long beams were readied for building purposes.

One condition which expedited the work was an order from the Governor commanding personal labor on the part of some soldiers from the San Diego presidio. They were required to toil "without murmuring at site or work, and with implicit obedience to Father Lasuén." The good father remained at the mission six weeks to see that these orders were carried out, and to supervise the initial planting as well as building.

Father Peyri, the senior padre at the mission, brought to his post not only a genial disposition, wisdom, frugality and energy, but an exceptional talent for architecture. The mission's first year saw the completion of several buildings, which were augmented in the following months to provide adequate accommodations for the increasing Indian population. Two years later all roofs were covered with tile made in the mission's kilns, and soon the first big church was begun, a narrow structure a hundred and thirty-eight feet long and large enough to hold a thousand neophytes.

Construction activity was almost continuous throughout the life of the mission. The culmination of Father Peyri's building efforts was the noble church which now crowns the hill which in turn dominates the surrounding beautiful valley. Some critics consider this church incomplete because it had but one tower, but others point out that the composition and proportions of the existing façade are so graceful that improvement is hardly possible.

Perhaps a second tower was intended for the church and never finished. In fact some early drawings of the mission show the two towers complete, though this is no proof that the second tower was even planned. The single tower was used as a lookout. Two Indian boys were stationed there constantly so they could use flags to signal messages to workers in the fields or to announce the approach of visitors or hostile Indians.

The plan of the church was cruciform, a type of design shared only with the great stone church at Capistrano. The long nave is crossed by a transept which makes space for two side altars. At the crossing a dome was topped by an unusual octagonal lantern, the only such feature in all the mission churches. The lantern was described in 1829 as having eight columns in its design and being lighted by a hundred and forty-four panes of glass. The design of the lantern was changed in the 1890's when it was enlarged, simplified, and altered from octagonal to round.

Another unusual feature of the church is the mortuary chapel, which is entered from the nave. It is a small room with an elaborate little altar placed in a recess facing the entrance. A stairway in back of the altar once led to a small balcony that overlooked the colorful chapel. Here the relatives of the deceased could watch over the body the night before the funeral service.

Under Father Peyri's guidance, the mission developed in all directions. The main mission building expanded until it covered six acres, an extensive water system tapped the nearby river and distributed it to the mission, and most extraordinary of all, an elaborate sunken garden and lavandería were built in a little valley below the mission. Broad steps led down to a large paved area flanked by laundry terraces. Spring water flowed through the lavanderías, ran through filters, and then was channeled into the fields beyond. Exotic fruits and shrubs

When beloved Fr. Peyri left San Luis Rey after 34 years' service, the Indians followed him to the ship in San Diego and unsuccessfully begged him to return.

French visitor Duflot de Mofras generously added a second tower to San Luis Rey when he sketched it from memory in 1841, thereby supporting a theory held by some authorities that two towers were planned but never finished.

graced the sunken gardens. Long since covered with silt, the area is now being excavated and may some day be restored to its original state.

The prosperity of the mission began to decline as secularization approached. Father Peyri saw the handwriting on the wall and elected to retire before the mission was destroyed. He had gladly signed the oath of allegiance to the new government in Mexico, but as he began to understand what the future held under this regime, he asked to be relieved of his post so he could return to Spain. His request was granted and he left the mission secretly, cloaked in darkness, to avoid the pain of farewells. But when the Indians found him gone next morning, a large number rode at full speed to San Diego to beg him to return. They arrived at the harbor only in time to receive his blessing from the deck of the vessel as it sailed out of the harbor. Many of them swam toward the ship to plead with their beloved guide not to desert them. Even after he had left, the story goes, the Indians offered prayers for several years that one day he would safely return to them.

Secularization followed two years after his departure, and though the despoliation of the mission was protracted, the inevitable destruction came about. The buildings were sold in 1846, occupied for a time by units of the United States Army, and though returned to the Church in 1865, the mission was not used for religious purposes until 1893, when it was finally rededicated. In this long period of neglect, the great quadrangles collapsed and even portions of the church caved in. Reconstruction was begun in 1893 and is still going on today, so extensive were the ruins.

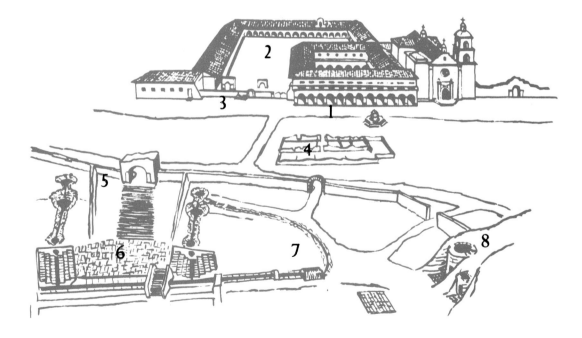

One of the most extensive missions in the chain, the buildings of San Luis Rey covered nearly
six acres and were arranged around a patio 500 feet square. In front of the mission was an elaborate
sunken garden and lavandería (laundry area), now being restored. 1. Main entrance and museum;
gift shop. 2. Monastery garden with first pepper tree in California. 3. Wall and solitary
arches are remnants of front wing, not yet restored. 4. Ruins of soldiers' barracks. 5. Ornate arch
and tiled stairway lead down to sunken garden and laundry area. 6. Lavandería received
water from springs on each side. 7. Charcoal filter purified water for drinking. 8. Lime kiln.

Kitchen tools were usually made on the spot, carved from manzanita, oak, or other hard native wood. Only the metal whisk in this line-up is an importation. It was used for whipping eggs and the ever-popular chocolate, the main confection of mission days.

Kitchens were smoky rooms suited to mass production of food. Meat was barbecued over open grills, food baked in bee-hive ovens, thick-walled enclosures that retained heat. On the counter are carrying baskets and manos and metates—hand-grinders for pulverizing flour.

Mission choirs sang Gregorian chants from large chant books, hand-illuminated by the padres and sometimes the Indians in the style of this sample, copied from a book brought to San Luis Rey from Mexico by Zacatecan friars.

*The church, where large Indian congregations once
worshipped, is cruciform in shape with a dome over the
crossing, the only dome remaining in the
California missions.*

*Gateway to the cemetery opens through a thick adobe wall
that echoes the form of the façade of the church itself.
Design on the gates was applied by Walt Disney artists
when the mission was being used as a background
for the Zorro films.*

*A lonely arch stands in the enclosed garden of San Luis
Rey, stranded survivor of an arcade that once reached
across from the church to the far wing of the quadrangle.
In time, the missing structure will be restored and the
quadrangle completed again. In the gardens grow
specimens of plants brought by the padres, including a
venerable pepper tree, the original California introduction.
The padres dried and ground the peppercorns for
seasoning.*

Water for a vast open-air laundry flowed from the mouth of the stone gargoyle, ran down the tiles, and was reclaimed for other uses. The Indian women soaked their clothes, soaped them with the crude soap shown in the photograph at the left, and beat them with wooden paddles on the stone steps.

Resembling ruins of a Roman amphitheater, the sunken gardens and lavandería (laundry) lie spread out in a hollow below the mission. Slopes once crowded with fruit trees now lie barren. Water from two springs spouted from the gargoyles and ran through two laundry areas, one on either side of the massive tile floor at the right.

282 THE CALIFORNIA MISSIONS

Indian designs painted on the walls of the chapel at Pala were plainly visible in 1897 when this photograph was taken.

San Antonio de Pala

Within a sheltering mountain valley, San Antonio de Pala stands today as the only surviving asistencia (sub-mission) of the score or more that were operated by the California missions. It is in active use as a parish church, serving the Pauma Indians as it did when it was first established by Father Peyri in 1815 as a branch of Mission San Luis Rey.

This pleasant river valley was the major grain-producing area for the mission, and Pala was established here to serve the large and cooperative Indian population that worked the fields. The asistencia rapidly grew to rival the mission in importance, and at its peak, it served more than a thousand Indians.

The thriving community was nearly destroyed by secularization and by the American occupation that followed soon afterwards. Clumsy and dishonest administration of the asistencia's affairs after secularization saw the herds, crops, and lands melt away and the Indians dispossessed. After American occupation, all the property, including the church and cemetery, reached private hands. Although litigation lasted for years, the padlocked mission was not returned to the Catholic Church until 1903 when the property was deeded to it by the Landmarks Club, which had been able to purchase it from the private owner.

The only chapel in the entire mission chain that is still being used by Indians, Pala looks today very much as it did when it was founded in 1815. A thriving asistencia, the chapel was decorated and maintained with pride by the Indians, who were very disturbed when an obtuse pastor whitewashed the walls in 1903. Fortunately, his successor restored the drawings, which were important heirlooms to the Indians.

Santa Inés

Nineteenth mission, founded September 17, 1804, by Fr. Estévan Tápis. Named for St. Agnes. Present building dedicated 1817. Served as temporary quarters for The College of Our Lady of Refuge of Sinners, first educational institution in California, 1844–1846. Mission secularized 1836, sold 1846, returned to Church, 1862. Located in town of Solvang on State Highway 150, 7 miles east of intersection with U.S. 101 at Buellton.

The last of the southern missions, and third to honor a sainted woman, Santa Inés completed the chain between San Francisco and San Diego. Dedicated September 17, 1804, by the Father-President, Father Estévan Tápis, the mission's future seemed assured. The eighteen established missions were at the height of their prosperity, ready to lend aid, if necessary. In fact, a large band of trained neophytes from other missions helped found this "hidden gem of the missions," situated in lovely Santa Ynez Valley.

The new mission, nineteenth in the chain, was favored with fertile lands, excellent for crops and grazing. Another good omen at the start was the presentation of twenty-seven Indian children for immediate baptism.

Santa Inés expanded rapidly. A building program that continued uninterrupted for the next eight years began with construction of an adobe church, completed within a year. A convento building was added as a wing, and finally other structures were erected to form the standard quadrangle.

Santa Inés became famous for its large herds of cattle and rich crops. The land sustained, in its best years, thirteen thousand animals. The craft work of the mission was known and used throughout the province.

But troubles were soon to come. The last of the buildings had barely been completed when the great earthquake of 1812 destroyed most of the church and damaged many buildings.

Rebuilding began in 1813 with construction of the new church, dedicated in 1817. Father Francisco Javier de Uría is credited with its design, as well as that of the first one. A campanario was erected beside the church and behind it, the sacristy and storage rooms.

Like the other missions, Santa Inés had an elaborate water system. This one, also designed by Father de Uría, brought water from the mountains several miles away to serve the needs of the mission and Indian village.

JOHN S. WEIR

*The mission campanario with its three ancient bells stands
bleakly silhouetted against a vivid sunrise. Third in a
sequence of belltowers—the first one collapsed in a storm
and the second was such an inappropriate structure that it
was ultimately replaced—this one was restored in 1948.*

During this period some of the construction was done by Joseph Chapman, whose name is significant only because he once served the pirate Hyppolite Bouchard. After the raider left the coast, Chapman remained in California and became "respectable." Still a young man when his career of piracy ended, he was employed as a general handyman at Santa Inés, where his skill in planting vineyards and erecting buildings proved useful. His new-found respectability is attested to in his marriage to a daughter of the Ortéga family.

Social life at Santa Inés differed in one respect from that of the other missions. Because it was off the highway it missed much of the excitement of having constant visitors. Travelers going up the coast from Santa Barbara had to brave the sometimes belligerent Canaliño tribes and either climb the rocky, treeless hills of the La Cuesta de Santa Inés, or the shorter but difficult route through Gaviota Pass, or else they had to travel the long tiresome El Camino Reál (which at that time circled around the coast) and then double back inland. It is understandable, then, why the fathers gave a sincere welcome to those who journeyed the extra miles to find the little mission in the hills. When prospective "company" was spotted coming up the long trail, one of the Indians rang the church bell as a signal. If a padre was coming he rang it one way. A different signal announced that Indians were approaching, and still another if the traveler was a white man. The signal summoned everyone to greet the visitors at the front door.

Prosperity continued at Mission Santa Inés until the Indian revolt of 1824. The trouble started when Mexico became independent from Spain. After 1821 pay for the soldiers and funds for the mission were withheld, forcing the missions to maintain the military. Support fell to the Indians, who got nothing in return but abuse. It is no wonder, then, that on Sunday, February 21, 1824, the pent-up grievances of the Indians were brought to the surface when a guard at Santa Inés flogged a neophyte corporal from Mission La Purísima. All the Indians at Santa Inés rebelled. The ensuing fight, in which bows and arrows competed with muskets, resulted in the death of two Indians and in fires that consumed much of the mission. The sacristy was partially destroyed, along with several vestments, the front wing and part of the church. When the rebels saw the roof of the church blazing they hastened to help put out the fire, for their quarrel was not with the padres but with the military.

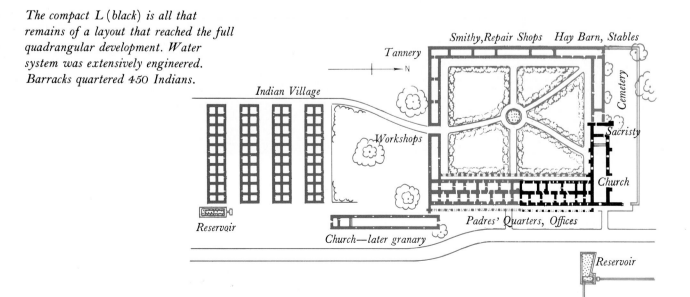

The compact L (black) is all that remains of a layout that reached the full quadrangular development. Water system was extensively engineered. Barracks quartered 450 Indians.

By 1870, the building was already showing signs of disintegration. Nineteen of the original twenty-four arches still stood, but part of the monastery wing had collapsed. Some of the walls of the old Indian barracks were still standing south of the quadrangle. Weathering of the campanario reveals the hard-burned adobes of which it was built. Note tile roof brought across the flat-roofed corridor.

On the following day military reinforcements arrived from Santa Bárbara, causing the hostiles to flee to La Purísima, where, as is recorded in the chapter on that mission, severe fighting took place.

Although order was restored at Santa Inés and reconstruction and repair were carried on between 1825 and 1832, secularization of the missions, enforced in 1834, struck hard here. In 1836 Governor Chico "granted" the mission to José Covarrubias, who rented it for $580 a year. He moved his family into one half of the building, and the padres retained the half containing the church. The "father's wall," which divided the property down the middle, was a result of a dispute between the residents of the two sections. During this period the Indians gradually fled the mission.

Although the management of the mission was restored to the fathers in 1843, its former prosperity never returned. In this year, however, the first seminary, the College of our Lady of Refuge, was established at Santa Inés. Housed first in the mission compound it was later transferred to the College Ranch. In 1846 Santa Inés was sold to Covarrubias and Carrillo for $7,000. In this same year the United States seized California, and all transactions involving the missions were suspended. Later, some of the property was returned to the Church.

Santa Inés was never entirely abandoned, though it gradually fell into disrepair. Regular maintenance was so neglected that one Sunday in the 1860's the pulpit collapsed under the astonished father while he was preaching the gospel. Although history does not record how the padre fared who suffered this indignity, damage to the pulpit was such that it was never replaced.

In 1904 Father Alexander Buckler, new pastor of the mission, with the aid of his niece, Mamie Goulet, began a twenty-year job of restoration—patching, shoveling, cleaning, and repairing. When the fine old campanario collapsed in 1911, it was rebuilt of concrete, to hold the missions' four bells, all of which have withstood most of the vicissitudes of the mission's fortunes.

ABOVE. *Campanario rises above the modest little graveyard that contains the remains of 1,600 Indians. The three bells (cast in 1807, 1817, 1818) are mounted to swing when rung from the tile-roofed platform.* ABOVE RIGHT. *The façade is less than half the width of the original, which stretched to the south for 24 arches. Promenade on top of the arcade was reactivated during restoration of 1946. It had been covered since 1817 when the roofline was extended across it to gain earthquake resistance as shown in the photograph below. Tile balustrade copied from the one at San Luis Rey. Design of church and campanario resembles San Gabriel, the mission from which the padre came who built present Santa Inés.* RIGHT. *When the Pasear Touring Club stopped at the mission in 1912, the adobe campanario had just been replaced with one of cast concrete that had only a vague resemblance to the original, which had collapsed in a storm. The new campanario shown here had four bell niches instead of three, but it was not replaced until 1948.*

JOHN S. WEIR

LEFT. *Crystal chandeliers, like this shimmering French import, were popular in Mexican churches and are found in two or three of the California missions. This one hung at Santa Inés until 1978.* BELOW. *Still-life of mission objects assembled and photographed by A. C. Vroman in 1890: small cannon used for salutes on feast days, Mexican water containers of copper, a yellow umbrella carried by the padre to ward off the sun, chant books, the neck of a cello, and a bench carved by a mission cabinetmaker in imitation of Chippendale, then in vogue.*

LOS ANGELES COUNTY MUSEUM

*Although the church interior has been restored, modernized, repainted,
and whitewashed innumerable times, it still looks the way it probably did when
the Indians knelt here on the tile floor from 1817 on. Faded green marbleized
decorations cover the walls in the altar zone, one of the most authentic examples
of a decorative element used in many missions. Trompe l'oeil, neo-classic
architectural forms grace the walls, influenced probably by the same
architectural sources as Santa Bárbara.*

San Rafael Arcángel

*Twentieth mission, founded December 14, 1817, by Fr. Vicente de Sarría as a
hospital asistencia for Mission Dolores, but given full mission status in 1823.
Named for St. Raphael, patron of good health. Church built 1818,
abandoned 1842, razed in 1870. Secularized in 1834, sold in 1842,
but returned in 1855. Located in city of San Rafael,
15 miles north of San Francisco.*

The serious mortality rate of the Indian population at Mission Dolores, which led to the need for a warm and sheltered place where the ailing neophytes could regain their health, was the reason for the founding of Mission San Rafael in 1817. Father Ramón Abella of Mission Dolores pointed out in a letter to Governor Solá that there were three causes for the high death rate, which had plagued the mission for nearly forty years. In the first place many of the dead were infants and children whose mothers lacked proper knowledge in caring for them. Then the change from wild to civilized life presented problems to cope with, and this, combined with the diseases brought by the soldiers and a few settlers, had so weakened the native people that their constitutions were prey to epidemics.

Governor Solá suggested transferring a part of the mission population to some sunnier shore. Such a site had been recommended to the Governor by Gabriel Moraga, a lieutenant at the San Francisco Presidio, who had made many trips north across the San Francisco Bay and was familiar with the land. Moraga recommended a sunny slope, overlooking the waters of the bay but protected from the chilling winds and fog by a range of rolling hills.

Accordingly, the experiment was tried. A group of ailing neophytes was rowed across the choppy waters, clutching their blankets to themselves but still shivering in the fog. After a few weeks in the warm sheltered nook, they showed surprising improvement.

Although Father-Prefect Sarría approved the measure, he hesitated to establish a permanent asistencia across the bay because communication was difficult and there were hardly enough priests available to fill the other needy mission

*A replica of the old chapel stands in place of the original
Mission San Rafael, which was razed in the 1870's.
True to the original, the modern version has star
windows, copied from Carmel Mission.*

posts, to say nothing of a new outpost in the wilderness. His prayers were answered when Father Gil y Taboada offered to serve at the new location. Father Gil was the perfect choice for the new work, because of all the mission padres he knew the most about medical science. There was no reason now to delay the project.

Preparations were made and on December 13, 1817, a launch set out from the San Francisco presidio, carrying Father-Prefect Sarría, Father Gil, and several other padres. They "planted and blessed with solemn ceremonies the holy cross" just as the sun began to set over the western hills. The first holy Mass was said the next day for the new asistencia which was dedicated to the glorious prince Saint Raphael, the Archangel, whose very name expressed the "healing of God."

On the day of the founding, twenty-six children were baptized, and two hundred natives presented themselves for instructions, wrote Father Prefect Sarría to Father-President Payéras.

The place was not supposed to be a mission: it was merely a sanitarium, a sunny spot in the rolling landscape, to benefit the Indians. Nearby missions contributed supplies for the new outpost, as was customary.

Father Gil's first duty was to erect a simple adobe building. The mission house he put up made no pretension to beauty. It was 87 feet long and 42 feet wide, divided into storehouses, hospital, and monastery, with a tule-covered corridor running along one side. The church, which had no tower, was built at one end of the mission house and at a right angle to it. A small lean-to at one side of the church served as a baptistry. The front had no decoration except for a star-shaped window above the simple door. The chapel's bells were hung on a sturdy wooden frame just outside the door. This serviceable building seems to be all that comprised Mission San Rafael except the colony of Indian huts surrounding the mission house and church. The usual quadrangle never took form here.

In the two years of Father Gil's wise management and solicitude, the Indians recovered their health so well that other missions in the bay area sent their ailing

Built during the unsettled years of the turnover of
authority from Spanish to Mexican hands, San Rafael
had little thought given to its architectural design.
The mission building never achieved a quadrangle,
nor did it acquire a belltower. As painted in the late
1880's by Henry Chapman Ford, the building was
plain indeed.

Imagining that the mission was about to be attacked by an
unknown native tribe, the Mexican padre in charge of San
Rafael in 1832 ordered his neophytes to attack them first.
When the fracas was over 21 unarmed natives were dead
and an equal number wounded. The padre was severely
disciplined for the tragedy.

SAN RAFAEL ARCÁNGEL **297**

neophytes. These, added to new converts, brought the number of Indians up to 382 in the first year.

After two years Father Gil was succeeded by Father Juan Amorós, who had been serving at Carmel. To him is attributed the leadership under which the total Indian population eventually climbed to a maximum of 1,140. This total was not reached until 1828, but near the end of Father Amorós' third year the little outpost had already attained such importance and success that it was given the status of a full mission.

With this change the records of the mission were retained on the site rather than being sent to Mission Dolores, of which it had been merely a branch. And with the added recognition Father Amorós tried even harder to see that the mission prospered, spiritually as well as physically, adding new converts as well as workshops as needed.

The Russian threat at Fort Ross may have influenced the founding of San Rafael. Once established, at least, the mission served as a buffer against the Russians who had crept down the coast almost to Bodega Bay, built Fort Ross, mounted cannons, and planted crops. Fear of Russian aggression was back of plans, supported both by the Governor and by the missions, to establish settlements farther north. San Rafael became a stop-over for military parties accompanied by padres that traveled northward. Father Gil, himself, accompanied an expedition and backed a plan to establish a presidio on Bodega Bay with missions at Petaluma and Suisun. But for one reason or another, these plans were never brought to fruition.

San Rafael had its troubles with natives. Following the death of Father Amorós after 13 successful years, Father José María Mercado took over for the last two of the mission's 17-year existence. Father Mercado had a rather explosive nature and a talent for making trouble. On one occasion he was accused of arming his neophytes and sending them out against visiting natives under the impression that they were going to attack the mission. His armed band killed and wounded a large number of strangers. Because there was reason to believe that he had acted in good faith, if rashly, he was only suspended from mission work for six months. He also clashed with ambitious General Mariano Vallejo, who managed to gather many of Mission San Rafael's assets into his own hands. When the Indians were given shares of property, they were unable to manage it, so Vallejo "protected" them by gathering the natives onto his own ranches and letting them work for their board.

The adobe buildings soon began to disintegrate, although they were still strong enough to serve Captain Frémont and his men as quarters when he found them deserted in 1846.

At last the few remains of the buildings were removed and replaced by a parish church, and for many years not a vestige of the original mission remained. Finally, a replica of the old church building was constructed, with a simple doorway under a star window and a mission bell hanging on a wooden frame just outside the door.

Because no drawings of the inside of the original chapel exist, the interior of the present chapel at San Rafael was designed on modern lines, with some concessions to mission style in the arched sanctuary and the deep-set windows. Statuary and art objects from the old mission are displayed in a nearby museum.

*Plain façade of the mission chapel has simple, rugged
dignity. Drastically restored by the state in 1911—13,
the design of the chapel approximates that of the early
1840's when this building was erected to serve as the
parish chapel for the town of Sonoma. It replaced a large
adobe church that had formerly stood at the eastern end
of the priests' quarters.*

San Francisco Solano

Twenty-first mission, founded July 4, 1823, by Fr. José Altimira. Named for
St. Francis Solano, missionary to Peruvian Indians. First church begun 1823,
dedicated 1824. Replaced 1827 by a large church east of the padres' quarters,
razed 1838. Present chapel built 1840 as parish church for Sonoma.
Secularized 1834; sold 1881, bought by Historical Landmark League in 1903.
Restored 1911–13. Located in town of Sonoma on State Highway 12.

The founding of Mission Solano, last in the chain, was the compromise result
of a grand plot by a brash young padre and an ambitious governor to suppress
two existing missions and establish a new one under the padre's supervision.

The scheme was the brain-child of one of the last of the Franciscans trained
in Spain, Father José Altimira, who arrived in Monterey in August 1819 and
was assigned to assist at Mission Dolores. He was soon dissatisfied with conditions at the mission. The soil was sterile, the climate harsh, and converts few.
Why not abandon the mission, he reasoned, and found a new one north of
San Rafael?

Instead of presenting his plan to the proper church authorities, he revealed
it in part to Governor Don Luis Argüello, who was familiar with conditions at
Dolores, having been military commandant at the presidio before being elevated
to the governorship. The Governor agreed to sponsor Altimira's plan because
it fitted in with some notions of his own. He was eager to establish settlements
farther north to push the Russians out of the province, and he saw this scheme
as offering a means to this end.

The plan, as presented to the Territorial Assembly in Monterey in 1823,
called for transferring Mission Dolores to a new site to the north. The legislature
approved the scheme and also added the transfer of San Rafael to the new
mission. Delighted, Altimira hastened to put it into effect.

Unfortunately, neither the Governor, Altimira, nor the legislature had any
authority for such an action, which had to be approved by ecclesiastical authorities. When word of the plan reached Father-President Señan, then on his death-
bed at San Buenaventura, he informed his successor, Father Sarría, and dictated a
rebuke to the Governor and the rash Altimira. The letter caught up with
Altimira, who was at Solano, just starting on the buildings for the new mission.

One of the few pueblos formed in California under the Spanish-Mexican rule, the town of Sonoma was built around a plaza in the traditional form of the Spanish town. Some of the buildings shown in this 1856 photograph are still standing. In this square the Bear Flag was raised in 1846.

Work stopped at once and remained suspended while three-cornered negotiations continued between the parties involved. Eventually, a compromise was reached. Altimira was permitted to build his mission and to be in charge of it, but San Francisco and San Rafael missions were not to be disturbed. The new mission was to be named for St. Francis Solano, a missionary to Peru.

Work was resumed on the structure, and a church of whitewashed wood was dedicated in 1824. Mission Dolores donated church necessities as well as cattle for the new venture. The Russians, surprisingly enough, donated bells, utensils, and other useful items. By the end of the year, the mission boasted a tile-roofed monastery, a granary, workshops, a guardhouse, and barracks. Orchards, vineyards, and grain fields were planted.

The mission seemed well established and all would have gone well if Father Altimira had used kindness and understanding to hold his charges. Instead, he relied on flogging and imprisonment, and many of the neophytes ran away to escape his temper. An angry band stormed the mission in 1826, looting and burning buildings, and forced Altimira to flee to San Rafael. Unable to return to his mission, he eventually went back to Spain.

The rescue of the almost-ruined mission was entrusted to Father Fortuni, who had been the faithful co-worker with Father Durán at Mission San José. Arriving in 1826, he spent seven hard years trying to restore Solano to its former strength. He replaced most of the wood and thatch buildings of the mission with an adobe enclosure, built a new adobe church, and enlarged the five-room convento into a 27-room structure. At the time of his retirement, the mission numbered over thirty structures. A succession of Zacatecan priests followed Father Fortuni. When secularization came in 1834, the last of the Mexicans fled to San Rafael, unwilling to take orders from secular authority.

General Mariano Vallejo was appointed commissioner of the mission. He dutifully carried out orders to distribute the mission properties among the Indians. But when settlers and other Indian tribes began to harrass the mission Indians, Vallejo transferred them to his own vast properties and put them to work for room, board, and protection.

Under secularization, Vallejo built up the pueblo of Sonoma to make homes for colonists brought in from Mexico to settle the town. He also largely supported the soldiers transferred from the presidio at San Francisco to Sonoma to protect the frontier, deter the Russians, and keep an eye on the incoming American settlers.

The old mission church, now without a missionary, was kept in repair by the General for a time, but it gradually gave way. Roof tiles and timbers were taken from the mission buildings by the Sonomans and nearby ranchers, and the unprotected adobe walls slowly dissolved.

A new but smaller adobe church, which is the chapel standing at the mission today, was built as a parish church in 1841 on the site of Altimira's original wooden structure. In 1845, Governor Pico offered the mouldering buildings for sale, but there were no takers.

The year 1846 marked the end of Mexican rule and saw a dramatic event take place in Sonoma that helped to hasten the occupation of California by United States military forces later that year. A group of American settlers scattered throughout the Sacramento Valley formed a loose organization to set up an independent republic in the province, in anticipation of imminent takeover by the United States. With the covert help of Captain Frémont, then mysteriously loitering in the area, they seized Sonoma, imprisoned General Vallejo and other leading Californians, and raised a flag emblazoned with the crude likeness of a bear and the proud words "California Republic." The native Californians attempted to do battle with the Bear Flag insurgents, but before the two forces could make contact, United States marines landed in Monterey, and the war between Mexico and the United States took over the stage.

After the American occupation, Mission Solano was briefly operated as a parish church. By 1881 the property was too dilapidated to salvage, so it was sold outright and the money used to build a new church in another part of town. The purchaser used the priests' house for wine-making and the former church for storing hay. The monastery later served as a blacksmith shop.

In 1903 the Historic Landmarks League came to the rescue, purchasing the property in order to restore it. The earthquake of 1906 severely damaged the church, but it was not fully repaired until 1911–12 when the state provided funds for restoration. In 1926, the League deeded the property to the state, which placed it under the administration of the Division of Beaches and Parks. During 1943–44, further restoration and refurnishing took place. The mission, now known as the Sonoma Mission State Historic Park, has a well-conducted museum, stocked with exhibits from mission days.

A delightfully inaccurate painting by Oriana Day shows the Sonoma plaza as it appeared in the memory of Mariano Vallejo in his declining years. A close friend of Vallejo, Mrs. Day painted all the missions and some other historical scenes under his sponsorship. Like most of her animated paintings, this one is more fancy than fact. The dragoons drilling on the plaza in their bright uniforms were supposed to be Vallejo's army; the tall tower is an exaggerated rendering of a lookout post. This is one of the few paintings that shows what the original old church may have looked like. The artist depicts it standing to the right of the chapel, even though it had been torn down a few years before the chapel was built.

Within sight of the old mission, the Bear Flag was raised in 1846, declaring the province a new republic, independent of Mexico. It lasted about a month.

*The chapel now restored as Mission Solano has appeared
in various guises: with squared and arched windows
and doors, and with and without steeple. The building
was built of adobe and faced with red brick. Sold in the
1880's, it was used as a winery, hay barn, and blacksmith
shop. The building was badly damaged by the earthquake
of 1906 and was not restored until 1911–13.*

*A traditional arcade crosses the front of
the old monastery wing, oldest (1825)
portion of the mission and oldest
building in Sonoma.* RIGHT. *Sole
survivor of the original complement of
bells, the one hanging in front was cast
in Mexico six years after the founding of
the mission. It carries a crown top,
the sign of a royal bell, even though
Mexico had severed all ties with the
Spanish Crown eight years before.
Evidently, the Mexican bell-founders
were so accustomed to casting crown tops
on their bells that they continued to do
so even after independence. The annual
blessing of the grapes takes place in front
of this bell in October.*

*Although the interior of the restored chapel lacks the
warmth of an active church, it is being carefully
refurbished to approximate the appearance and atmosphere
of the mission era. Local churches and organizations
have helped to create a feeling of reality by contributing
religious articles.*

Facts about the California Missions

NAMES OF THE MISSIONS

La Purísima Concepción de Maria Santísima.

The eleventh Franciscan mission was named to honor the Virgin Mary who, according to doctrine, was preserved exempt from all stain of original sin. The mission was established on December 8, 1787, the day of the Feast of the Immaculate Conception.

Nuestra Señora de la Soledad.

It is reported that when the Portolá expedition asked an Indian his name he replied "Soledad" or so it sounded. From this chance occurrence, the location of the thirteenth Franciscan mission came to be known as Soledad which was incorporated into the name of the mission.

San Antonio de Padua.

The third mission of the Franciscan chain was named after the great saint of Italy, San Antonio (St. Anthony), who was born of a noble family in Lisbon, Portugal, in 1195(?). In 1221, San Antonio became a Friar Minor, leaving the Augustinian canons regular in order to do so. Ill health prevented him from becoming a missionary but he showed brilliance as a scholar and preacher. His intense devotion to the child Jesus is invariably depicted in artistic works of his life. Death came to San Antonio in 1231 and he was canonized in 1232. He was declared a Doctor of the Church in 1946 by Pope Pius XII. His feast day is June 13.

San Buenaventura.

The Franciscan's ninth mission was named after San Buenaventura (St. Bonaventure), who was born near Viterbo, Italy, in 1221. At the age of thirty-six he was elected minister general of the Franciscans, and was nominated to but refused the Archbishopric of York. At the peak of his career of service in 1273, he was created Cardinal-bishop of Albano. He was one of the greatest scholars and theologians of the medieval period, having written numerous sermons and commentaries on the holy scriptures. San Buenaventura's chief labor, however, was in bringing unity to the friars of his order and between the Orthodox Greeks and those in the Western Church. He collapsed and died at the Council of Lyon in 1274, working to the end for reconciliation of the Christian world. He was canonized in 1482.

San Carlos Borromeo de Carmelo.

The second of the Franciscan Missions of Alta California was named after San Carlos Borromeo (St.

Charles Borromeo). Born in 1538, son of Count Gilbert Borromeo by a Medici mother, he was a cardinal at the age of twenty-two and archbishop of Milan soon after, although he was not ordained priest and bishop until 1563. The first great prelate of the Counter-Reformation, he was noted for his reforms, his devotion to the faith, and his fearless disregard for his own safety during the plague of 1576. San Carlos died in the year 1584 and was canonized in the same year. His feast day is November 4.

San Diego de Alcalá.

Alta California's first mission was named in honor of San Diego (St. Didacus), who was born of poor parents at San Nicolas del Puerto in the diocese of Seville, Spain. As a man he spent some time as a hermit before becoming a lay-brother of the Observant Friars Minor at Arrizaba. San Diego became a missionary in the Canary Islands, and in 1445 he was made head of the principal convent there. He was known for his devotion to the Eucharist. After four years of convert work he was recalled to Spain where he died at Alcalá in 1463. This saint was canonized in 1588. His feast day is November 13.

San Fernando Rey de España.

Ferdinand III of Castile, after whom the seventeenth Franciscan mission was named, was born near Salamanca. He became King of Castile at the age of eighteen and King of Leon thirteen years later in 1230. Fighting continually and with great success against the Moors, he built churches in the newly conquered territory. He is noted for his founding of Spain's great University of Salamanca in 1243. His death in 1252 ended a life of great service to the Church. San Fernando was canonized in 1671. His feast day is May 30.

San Francisco de Asís (Mission Dolores).

The sixth Franciscan Mission was named after San Francisco de Asís (St. Francis of Assisi). This son of a wealthy merchant was born at Assisi, Italy, in the year 1181. After a youth spent in seeking pleasure, he left his home and in 1209 founded the Order of Friars Minor (Franciscans). St. Francis is the most famous example of the stigmata of the passion appearing on the body. The wonderful custom of setting up the Christmas crib was started by Francis in 1223. This famous saint, whose love for God's creatures knew no limits, died in 1226. He was canonized in 1228. His feast day is October 3.

San Francisco Solano

The last Franciscan mission to be founded in Alta California was named in honor of San Francisco Solano (St. Francis Solano) who was born in Montilla, Spain, in 1549. At the age of twenty-nine he joined the Franciscan Order and was sent as a missionary to Peru, South America, where for twenty years he was influential among the Spanish colonists and Indians alike. This man of peace died in 1610 and was canonized in 1726. His feast day is July 14.

San Gabriel Arcángel

Alta California's fourth mission was named after San Gabriel (St. Gabriel), the angel of the annunciation sent to Mary at Nazareth to tell her of her destiny. He also came to Zachary and told him of the birth of John the Baptist. The prophet Daniel heard of the coming of the Messiah from this angel.

San José de Guadalupe

San José (St. Joseph) was the husband and protector of the Blessed Virgin Mary and the foster-father of Jesus. The Franciscans preached on his grace, and his name was chosen for this fourteenth Franciscan mission. He is honored by two feast days, the first on March 19, and the second on May 1.

San Juan Bautista

San Juan Bautista, the name given to the fifteenth Franciscan mission, honors St. John the Baptist. He was the precursor of Jesus and the son of Zachary and Elizabeth, a first cousin of the Virgin Mary. When Jesus was asked about John, he said that "Among those that are born of women there is not a greater prophet." St. Augustine and other doctors of the Church are of the opinion that John was sanctified from original sin in his mother's womb. His critical views on Herod led to his eventual beheading, which is commemorated on August 29.

San Juan Capistrano

The seventh mission in the Franciscan chain was named after San Juan (St. John), who was born at Capistrano in the Abruzzi region of the then kingdom of Naples in 1386. He became a leading lawyer and subsequently was appointed governor of the city of Perugia in 1412. At the death of his wife, when he was thirty years old, John joined the Franciscans and began a career of service to the Church. He preached a crusade against the Turks and he became an active leader of the Hungarian resistance under Janos Hunyadi. In 1456, during the siege of Belgrade, St. John and Hunyadi met their deaths. St. John was canonized in 1724. His feast day is March 28.

San Luis Obispo de Tolosa

The fifth mission to be founded in Alta California was named after San Luis Obispo de Tolosa (St. Louis of Anjou). He was born in the year 1274, the son of Charles II, King of Naples. The boy's uncle was Saint Louis, King of France, and his aunt was Saint Elizabeth of Hungary. After being held seven years a hostage in Barcelona, he was ordained priest, made his profession as a Friar Minor, and was consecrated archbishop of Toulouse. His life of devotion to his faith was the greatest monument that marked his death in 1297. He was canonized in 1317. His feast day is August 19.

San Luis Rey de Francia

This eighteenth mission in the Franciscan chain is one of two to share the distinction of honoring a king who became a saint. San Luis (St. Louis IX, 1214–1270), was the son of Louis VIII and Blanche of Castile. He rose to the throne of France at the age of twelve and married Marguerite, daughter of the Count of Provence, by whom he later had numerous children. His first crusade against the Infidels, after some beginning successes, came to grief in April, 1250, when he was captured by the Saracens in Egypt. He survived this trial and went on to lead a second crusade in which he was stricken with a fatal case of typhus in 1270 at Tunis. During his forty-four-year reign he was noted for being a fearless soldier and skillful administrator, as well as for his piety, asceticism, and benevolence. The Sorbonne was founded while he ruled and he was often called upon to arbitrate disputes. He was canonized in 1297. August 25 is his feast day.

San Miguel Arcángel

The sixteenth Franciscan mission is named after San Miguel (St. Michael), the captain of the armies of God, who is regarded traditionally as the chief of the archangels, a special protector against Satan's influences and attacks. In the East, Michael is a patron of the sick.

San Rafael Arcángel

The twentieth Franciscan mission to be founded in Alta California was named after San Rafael (St. Raphael), the archangel who is known as the angel of joy, good health, travelers, and happy meetings. As one of the seven who stand before the throne of God, St. Raphael is honored throughout the Christian world.

Santa Bárbara Virgen y Mártir

The tenth Franciscan mission in Alta California was named after Santa Bárbara (St. Barbara) who, according to legend, was the beautiful daughter of Dioscorus of Nicomedia. Dioscorus, a pagan, was so angered by his daughter's adoption of the Christian religion that he imprisoned her and eventually beheaded her with his own sword. For this deed it is said that her father was instantly killed by lightning. To this day, the protection of Santa Bárbara is often invoked against sudden death from lightning or explosion by seafarers and artillery men. Her feast day is December 4.

Santa Clara de Asís

The eighth Franciscan mission in Alta California was named after Santa Clara (St. Clare), who was born at Assisi in 1193 and ran away from home at the age of eighteen to join St. Francis. At San Damiano she founded the famous order of nuns called the Poor Clares. She never left her monastery except, it is reported, to dine with St. Francis and talk with him of God. St. Clare was canonized in 1255. Her feast day is August 12.

Santa Cruz

Santa Cruz in Spanish means Holy Cross. Throughout the Spanish-speaking world the name is frequently used, as it was here used to name the twelfth Franciscan mission.

Santa Inés Virgen y Mártir

The nineteenth Franciscan mission was named after Santa Inés (St. Agnes), a thirteen-year-old Roman girl who was executed in Rome in the year 304 A.D. and buried in the cemetery given her name where a basilica was built in her honor. Santa Inés is the special patroness of chastity. According to legend, she was unharmed in a brothel where she was sent by her father to break down her seemingly unassailable will to consecrate her virginity to a heavenly spouse. January 21 is her feast day.

FOUNDERS OF THE MISSIONS

Throughout the mission period, a number of padres and civil administrators came from Spain and Mexico to serve the new colony in Alta California with distinction. However, the names that have gone down in history are those of the handful of founders whose lives are briefly summarized below. (Biographies of the 100-odd padres who served here may be found in Fr. Engelhardt's comprehensive works.)

José De Gálvez

José De Gálvez never set foot on the soil of Alta California but his efforts to settle this area were the foundation of the Spanish occupation of the province.

Born at Velez, Malaga, in October, 1729, of poor parents, he managed to study law at the University of Salamanca and received a degree of doctor. His successful practice of law brought him to the attention of people of influence. King Charles III advanced Gálvez to membership in the Council of the Indies, an organization which directed Spain's far flung possessions in the New World.

Gálvez was sent in 1765 as *visitador general* to New Spain, where he undertook to extend the frontiers and establish settlements in Sonora, Nueva Vizcaya, and the Californias. The conception of occupying California was his, and Junípero Serra did not know of the plan to settle California until he was informed by Gálvez.

Since Vizcaíno's voyage to Monterey in 1602,

nothing had been done to establish Spain's claim to California. Gálvez, fearing that the Russians were planning to occupy that port, supervised an expedition to Alta California which would bring the civilization of Europe and the power of Spain to this neglected but promising outpost of empire.

Gálvez was primarily interested in the augmentation of the royal revenues of the Spanish crown. Nevertheless, his name deserves to be placed among those men who laid the groundwork for the Franciscan Missions of Alta California.

Don Gaspár de Portolá

Don Gaspár de Portolá, an able administrator and military figure of noble birth, was the capable leader of the expedition to colonize Alta California.

Born in Balageur, Spain, in 1723, he became an ensign in a regiment of dragoons at the age of 11. Some years later, he was promoted to lieutenant and then to captain. He took part in military campaigns against Italy and Portugal.

In 1767, he was appointed Governor of the Californias by Visitador-General Gálvez, who was determined to block British and Russian encroachments in the Californias. Portolá took office in La Paz on July 6, 1768, and one of his first assignments was the disagreeable task of expelling the Jesuits from Baja, where they had built up a chain of missions over a 72-year period. He performed the onerous job with such tact that he won the respect of the exiled priests.

When the expedition to colonize Alta California was proposed by Gálvez, Portolá volunteered to lead it. He organized the parties that colonized San Diego and Monterey, as described elsewhere in this book, and then surrendered his governorship and returned to Mexico in 1770.

He was promoted to a colonelcy and served as mayor of the city of Puebla in New Spain from 1777 to 1784, when he retired to Spain. His later life is unrecorded.

Junípero Serra

The name most often associated with the Franciscan venture in Alta California is Junípero Serra, whose candidacy for sainthood crowns a life of recognized achievements.

Born on November 24, 1713, at Petra, Mallorca, Spain, Serra entered the Franciscan Order at Palma in 1730. He became a doctor at the Lullian University at Palma, but he hoped to do missionary service in the New World.

In the spring of 1749, he set out for New Spain (Mexico), arriving in 1750 on New Year's Day at the College of San Fernando in Mexico City. From 1750 to 1758, Serra served in the rugged and difficult Sierra Gorda in Queretaro. Thereafter he was sent to various sections of Mexico for a period of ten years. When the Franciscans took over the missions of Baja (Lower) California in 1768, Serra became Superior and President with headquarters at Loreto.

José de Gálvez chose Serra to establish missions in Alta California. Despite an infected leg, Serra rode 750 miles on mule back up the peninsula into San Diego. On July 16, 1769, he founded the first Mission of San Diego de Alcalá, to be followed by these missions named in the order of their establishment: San Carlos de Borromeo (1770); San Antonio de Padua (1771); San Gabriel (1771); San Luis Obispo (1772); San Francisco (1776); San Juan Capistrano (1776); Santa Clara (1777); and San Buenaventura (1782).

Serra presided over the mission system from Mission San Carlos Borromeo, where he died on August 28, 1784. His devotion to his work was an inspiration to those who followed in his footsteps.

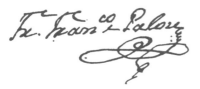

Francisco Palóu

A close associate of Junípero Serra, Francisco Palóu, is known as the author of the first great California biography, *Relacion Historica de la Vide ... del Venerable Padre Fray Junípero Serra*, written at Missions San Carlos de Borromeo (Carmel) and San Francisco (Dolores) and published in 1787. Bancroft says of Palóu's work: "It has been practically the source of all that has ever been written on California mission history down to 1784."

Born at Palma, Mallorca, January 22, 1723, Palóu received the habit of St. Francis on November 10, 1739. He studied philosophy as a pupil of Father Serra and at twenty-four he was elevated to the priesthood and given the post lector of philosophy, becoming a professor in the Lullian University at Palma, Mallorca.

On March 30, 1749, a written permit reached Palóu and Serra allowing them to join the missionary College of San Fernando in Mexico City. In 1767, following the expulsion of the Jesuits from the Spanish dominions, the College of San Fernando was directed to assume charge of the missions of Baja (Lower) California. After some time, the peninsular missions were transferred to the Dominicans and the Franciscans were given the opportunity to take over the more promising Alta (Upper) California.

On August 30, 1773, Palóu reached San Diego and acted as superior *pro tempore* until the return of Serra.

Several years later in June of 1776, Palóu and Lieutenant Moraga journeyed north. Palóu, on the twenty-ninth of June, 1776, celebrated mass, thus establishing Mission San Francisco de Asís (Dolores) at San Francisco, where for nine years he was head missionary.

On the death of Serra in 1784, Palóu became temporary president of the mission system for more than a year, until Father Fermín de Lasuén received his formal appointment.

Father Palóu spent his last days as superior of the College of San Fernando where, many years before, he had set out on his brilliant missionary career.

Fermín Francisco de Lasuén

Fermín Francisco de Lasuén was born at Victoria, Spain, on June 7, 1736. While a young man, he joined the Franciscan Order and as a deacon he volunteered for the American missions, coming to Mexico in 1759. Lasuén served in the Sierra Gorda until 1767, at which time he began six years of missionary activities in Lower California. During Father Serra's presidency of the mission system, Lasuén was stationed at Missions San Gabriel, San Carlos, and San Diego. As president of the missions from 1785 to 1803, he made his headquarters at Mission San Carlos (Carmel).

Lasuén founded nine missions, named in order of their founding: Santa Bárbara (1786); La Purísima (1787); Santa Cruz (1791); Soledad (1791); San José (1797); San Juan Bautista (1797); San Miguel (1797); San Fernando (1797); and San Luis Rey (1798).

A distinguished successor to Serra, he doubled the number of missions and more than doubled the number of converts. He also brought about an economic transformation by furthering stock raising and farming and introducing mission industries under a score of imported artisans. He introduced the now-familiar mission-style architecture of tile and stone or adobe and converted existing missions from thatch-covered structures to the newer form.

A Note about the Signatures

The quaint signatures of the Spanish-born padres and administrators are noteworthy for the characteristic flourish at the end. This embellishment—known as a "rubric"—was developed by each Spanish boy early in school, until the mid-19th century. The rubric was legally more important than the signature itself because it was difficult to duplicate or forge. Without it, a signature was not authentic. Sometimes, the rubric alone was sufficient.

Mission Recipes

The padres were not noted as chefs, but they did bring with them a number of Spanish and Mexican recipes that were subsequently used in the mission kitchens.

Recipes were for substantial dishes, mostly formed around grain and cornmeal, sharpened with chilies, and sweetened with sugar or chocolate, the favorite delicacy of the Spaniards. The recipes on these pages were gathered and tested by Mrs. O. R. Cleveland of Santa Rosa, who has devoted several years to collecting authentic recipes from the missions.

Puchero

Puchero means "a boiled pot," and there are at least eleven different versions. Here is one.

1 knuckle-bone (sun dried)	1 pound green string beans (tied in a bunch)
2 pounds veal	
2 pounds beef	1 bundle kohl leaves
3 ears fresh sweet corn	3 small summer squash
3 sweet potatoes	1 hard apple
1 cup garbanzo beans	1 hard pear
2 whole onions	2 teaspoons salt
3 fresh (or dried) tomatoes	½ teaspoon pepper
2 green chili peppers	

The knuckle-bone should be left in the air and sun to dry. Cover the knuckle-bone and meat with cold water. Bring to a boil and skim.

Place all washed vegetables and fruit over the bone and meat, carefully, and in order so that they will be whole when cooked. Simmer over a low heat for 3 hours—NEVER STIR.

To serve, lift out the whole vegetables onto a platter. Then place the meat on another platter. Strain the broth into a tureen. Carry to the table while very hot.

Quantities may be cut in half but this changes and impairs the flavor. El puchero may be warmed over, and the flavor improves with keeping.

Red Chili Sauce

1 cup red chili pulp	2 teaspoons flour
3 tablespoons fat	Dash of oregano
1 tablespoon minced onion	Salt to taste
1 teaspoon minced garlic	¼ cup water

Heat the fat in a heavy skillet, add the minced onion and garlic, and cook until golden brown. Add the flour, blend well, then add the chili pulp, oregano, salt, and water. Simmer for 30 minutes.

If the sauce seems too hot, add a little tomato sauce or a small chopped fresh tomato.

Huevas de Chili

This eggs-in-chili dish frequently was referred to in mission days as "Oxeyes," presumably because of the fact the eggs seem to stare out of the dish.

12 large dried red chilies	1 clove garlic, well mashed
3 tablespoons butter (or fat)	
	1 tablespoon vinegar
1 tablespoon flour	12 eggs
1 teaspoon salt	

Wipe the chilies clean; split, remove stems, seed veins and seeds; place in a small kettle and cover with boiling water. Steam for 15 to 20 minutes. Remove the chilies from the water and rub through a colander, adding a little of the water in which the chilies were cooked (this aids in removing the pulp from the skins). You should have a rich red purée.

Heat the fat in a kettle, stir in the flour (or if you prefer, ¼ cup of toasted bread crumbs); stir just until the two are well blended, then add salt and garlic. Pour in the vinegar, stir and add the chili purée. Cook for 20 minutes.

Pour the sauce into a casserole, drop in eggs one at a time and allow to stand in a warm oven until the eggs are set. To garnish, sprinkle around edge with finely chopped ripe black olives and onion.

Nixtamal

The Indians in New Spain taught the Spaniards and the padres how to make nixtamal and how to use it. This is the base of many mission foods as well as Mexican foods: tortillas, tamales and tacos.

- 1 gallon water
- ⅓ cup unslaked lime
- 2 quarts (8 cups) whole dry corn (maize)

In a galvanized kettle, mix the water and lime stirring with a clean stick or a wooden spoon. Add the corn and stir until the mixture no longer effervesces.

Bring to a boil, then lower the heat so that the mixture cooks but does not boil—stir frequently. When the skins can be easily rubbed from the kernels (after about one hour of cooking) and the corn is moist through, remove from the heat.

Drain and wash in several changes of cold water until all trace of lime is removed. Rub the kernels between the hands until free of hulls.

You will have a clean corn much like hominy but not so well cooked. This is nixtamal, ready to be ground into masa.

Lime Water

Quick, or unslaked, lime is used in making the nixtamal. The ratio is ⅓ cup lime to 1 gallon water.

Masa

- 1 cup nixtamal
- Water

Place one cup of nixtamal on a metate (the Indian grain grinder); sprinkle with water to keep it moist. With a small hand-stone, rub back and forth, over and over, until the corn kernels have formed a medium-fine dough. This is *masa*.

Cover with a damp cloth to keep from drying.

Torrejas

Torrejas are corn dough fritters, or sweet corn wafers.

- 2 cups corn masa
- 1 cup white cheese (dry cottage cheese)
- 1 teaspoon salt

Mix the masa, cheese, and salt to a soft dough. Mold into small balls, then pat into thin 2-inch wafers. Bake on an ungreased griddle, then fry in deep fat for a few minutes until crisp.

Torrejas are usually served with dishes having an abundance of gravy, or combined with a cooked red chili sauce. They may also be served with a sweet syrup.

Tortillas

Form the masa into 2-inch balls; press and pat with the hand into a 6-inch round cake. Bake on a hot, ungreased griddle until slightly brown and blistered on both sides.

Jiricalla (custard)

This is the nearest to ice cream that the early Californians knew.

6 eggs	½ cup masa (or 2 table-
1 quart milk	spoons cornstarch)
¾ cup sugar	½ cup water
Dash of nutmeg	

Separate the eggs and beat the yolks lightly. Scald the milk, add the sugar and nutmeg; then add slowly to the beaten egg yolks. Dilute the masa with the water, blending well. Add the milk - egg mixture and cook over medium heat, stirring all the while, until it thickens. Beat the egg whites until light and fluffy, put on top of the jiricalla; sprinkle sparingly with sugar, place in the oven just long enough to set the meringue. Cool.

Champurrado (a thick chocolate)

In the early days of the missions, the Spaniards drank chocolate, and they liked it thicker and sweeter than we know hot chocolate today.

6 teaspoons grated chocolate	½ cup masa (or 2
(or cocoa)	tablespoons
6 teaspoons sugar	cornstarch)
1 cup hot water	2 eggs, well beaten
5 cups milk, scalded	2 teaspoons vanilla
Dash cinnamon or nutmeg	

In a double boiler, combine the chocolate and sugar; add the hot water slowly, stirring until mixture forms a smooth paste. Add the scalded milk, a little at a time; then the masa which has been thinned with a small amount of the hot liquid (or the cornstarch which has been blended with some of hot liquid). Just before serving, fold in the eggs, vanilla, and the cinnamon or nutmeg.

Dulce de Calabaza

Translated, this is sweet or candied pumpkin.

2 pounds pared pumpkin
2 tablespoons (level) unslaked lime
2 quarts water

Combine the lime and water, stir well, allow to stand 12 hours, stir again and let settle. Use only the clear lime water.

Pare the ripe pumpkin and cut into strips the size of a finger. Drop the pieces into the clear lime water and let stand overnight. Drain the pumpkin from the lime water, cover with boiling water and boil 10 to 15 minutes. Drain.

Make a syrup with 3 cups granulated sugar and 3 cups water. When the syrup begins to boil, put in the pumpkin pieces and boil briskly until the pumpkin is transparent but firm (about 15 minutes).

Lift the pumpkin pieces from the syrup (save syrup) onto a large pan or platter and place in the sun until the next day. Then reheat the syrup in which the pumpkin was cooked, return the cold pumpkin pieces to the boiling syrup, and simmer until the pieces are tender but firm. Lift from the syrup and roll in granulated sugar; spread on a plate until cool.

Empanaditas

1 teaspoon aniseed	½ teaspoon salt
1 tablespoon sugar	1 tablespoon sugar
¼ cup water	3 tablespoons
2 cups flour	shortening
1 teaspoon baking powder	1 egg, well beaten

Combine the aniseed, sugar, and water in a small pan and bring to the boiling stage; cook for 3 minutes. Cool. Sift together the flour, baking powder, salt, and sugar; mix in the shortening, rubbing well together; add the beaten egg and the aniseed liquid; knead well until the dough is soft but elastic. Divide the dough into 3 portions; roll out one at a time and cut each portion into 4-inch circles.

Add filling and fold over as turnovers. Press the edges together with a fork, prick the top once or twice with the fork. Bake in a hot oven (400°) until golden.

Relleno de Calabaza (pumpkin filling)

1 cup cooked pumpkin
¼ cup sugar
1 teaspoon aniseed

Cook all the ingredients together for 15 minutes. Cool before filling the empanaditas.

Relleno de Frijoles (bean filling)

1 cup cooked frijoles (pink beans)
1 tablespoon fat
3 tablespoons sugar
½ teaspoon salt
Dash of cinnamon or nutmeg

Mash frijoles and sauté lightly in the fat. Add the sugar, salt, and spice and cook over a medium heat until the mixture is thick and separates from the pan. Cool. Fill the empanaditas.

Relleno de Carne (meat filling)

1 pound rump of beef	¼ teaspoon salt
2 green onions	⅓ cup seedless raisins
1 tablespoon fat	1 cup ripe black olives
3 tablespoons sugar	1 egg, well beaten

Cook the meat until tender, then chop (not too finely). Mince the green onions and cook in the fat until light golden in color. Add chopped meat, sugar, salt, chopped raisins, and olives; allow to simmer for 30 minutes. Remove from heat, cool, and stir in the egg. Fill the empanaditas.

CHRONOLOGY OF CALIFORNIA MISSION HISTORY

	1769-1774	1775-1780	1781-1785	1786-1790	1791-1795	1796-1800	1801-1805
Europe	James Cook circles globe	English, Dutch at war	Treaty of Fontainebleau	French revol.; Bastille fall	France at war with Europe	French wars	Bonaparte crowned Emp.
Spain and Mexico	Spain cedes Falkland Is.	Spain, England at war	Peace of Versailles	Nootka Sound affair	France, Spain war '93-'95	Spain-Eng. war; Fran. buys La.	Nelson sinks Fr.-Sp. fleet
United States	Boston massacre	Declaration of Independence	Surrender of Cornwallis	Constitution; Wash. inaug.	Bill of Rights; Wash. D.C. fnd.	John Adams, President	La. Purchase Jefferson, Pres.
1. *San Diego*	'69 Founded '74 Moved	'75 Ind. attack '80 New church	'83 Quadrangle completed	Outbuildings completed	'92 Tile roof installed	'00 Drought	'03 Earthquake damage
2. *San Carlos Borromeo*	'70 Founded '71 Moved	'78 Serra confrmtn. right	'84 Serra died; Lasuén succ.	'86 Visit by LaPérouse	'92-'93 Visit by Vancouver	'97 Present church compl.	'03 Death of Lasuén
3. *San Antonio de Padua*	'71 Founded '73 Moved	'76 Anza visit	'82 Adobe church compl.	Extensive bldg. activity	'95 Mission site search	'99 Election Ind. alcaldes	'01 Padres poisoned
4. *San Gabriel*	'71 Founded '74 Anza visit	'75 Moved	'81 Pueblo of L. A. fnd.	'90 First in livestock	'91 Present church begun	'96 1,331 neophytes	'05 Present church comp.
5. *San Luis Obispo*	'72 Founded '72 Bear hunt	'76 Indian fire raid	'83 Serra's last visit	Extensive building	'91 Tile made '92-4 Ch. built	'98 Gristmill built	'01 Quadrangle completed
6. *San Francisco de Asis*		'76 Founded	'82 Present church begun	'87 Presidio chapel built	'91 Church ded. '92 Vancouver	'98 Quadrangle completed	'04 1,010 Inds. at mission
7. *San Juan Capistrano*		'75 Founded '76 Refounded	'83 Tax for war with Eng.	'90 765 Inds. at mission	Extensive building	'97 Stone chch. started	'01 Fires, drought, epid.
8. *Santa Clara*		'77 Founded '79 Moved	'84 3rd chch. dedicated	'86 Plague of field mice	'92 Floods; Vanc. visit	'99 Willows set out on Alameda	'01 1,200 res. Indians
9. *San Buenaventura*			'82 Founded by Serra	Extensive building	'92 Ch. burned '93 Vanc. visit	'00 1,297 neophytes	'04-05 64 Ind. houses built
10. *Santa Bárbara*				'86 Founded '87-9 2 chs. blt.	'94 Third ch. completed	'00 Quake, but no damage	173 Indian houses built
11. *La Purísima*				'87 Founded	'91 Temp. bldgs. completed	'00 Adobe-tile bldgs. begun	'02 Bldgs. comp '04 1,522 Inds.
12. *Santa Cruz*					'91 Founded '94 Chch. ded.	'97 Branciforte Pueblo fnded.	'05 Mssn. aband proposed
13. *Soledad*					'91 Founded by Lasuén	'97 Adobe chch. completed	'02 Epidemic '05 Chch. enl.
14. *San José*						'97 Founded by Lasuén	'05 Ch. begun; Ind. battle
15. *San Juan Bautista*						'97 Founded by Lasuén	'03 Present church begun
16. *San Miguel*						'97 Founded by Lasuén	'04 Visits to remote tribes
17. *San Fernando*						'97 Founded by Lasuén	'02 Quadrangle completed
18. *San Luis Rey*						'98 Founded by Lasuén	'02 Adobe chch. completed
19. *Santa Inés*							'04 Founded by Fr. Tápis
20. *San Rafael*							
21. *San Francisco Solano*							

1806-1810	1811-1815	1816-1820	1821-1825	1826-1830	1831-1835	1836-1850	1851-1880
Spain seized by Napoleon	Waterloo; Bonaparte ousted	Revolt in Portugal	Spain, France at war	Russo-Turkish war	Engl. Reform Bill of 1832	Revolution in Portugal	Franco-German war; Crimea
Revolution in Mexico	Sp. colonies rebel; Mex. Ind.	Florida ceded to U.S.	Iturbide Emp. of Mexico	Panamer. Cong. at Panama	Liberal govt. in Mexico	Mex. loses west to U.S.	Maximilian in Mexico
Aaron Burr treason trial	War of 1812	Missouri Compromise	Monroe Doct.; Erie Canal	Andy Jackson, President	Abolitionist movement	Gold in Cal.; Texas as state	Civil War; Alaska purch.
'08 Present church begun	'13 Present church compl.	'18 S. Ysabel est.; '16 Dam	'21 Mission site search	'26 A few Indians freed	'34 Mission sec. '35 Dana visit	'46 Miss. sold '47 Army here	'62 Property ret. to Chch.
Extensive building	'15 Quadrangle completed	'18 Bouchard raids Monterey	'25 Cal. under Mexican Rep.	'26 Visit by Beechey	'34 Mission secularized	'46 U.S. Flag in Monterey	'56 Serra grave opened
'06 Mill blt. '09 Chch. begun	'13 Present church compl.	Extensive building	'21 Arched façade added	'27 Water system built	'34 Changed to curacy	'45 Offered for sale	'62 Property ret. to Chch.
'10 Gristmill built	'12 Earthquake downs tower	'19 Asistencia established	'22 Plaza Church fnded.	'26 J. S. Smith party	'34 Indian attack	'46 Mission bldgs. sold	'59 Property ret. to Chch.
Indian dwellings built	'15 Troops given supplies	'18 Bouchard raid scare	'24 Oath of alleg. to Mex.	'30 Martínez banish.; quake	'34 264 Inds. '35 Secularized	'45 Sold	'59 Property ret. to Chch.
'06 Measles kills 236 Inds.	'11 S. Joaquin Riv. explored	'16 Visit of Rurik	'22 Abandonment proposed	'27 Only 241 Indians left	'34 Mission secularized	'38 Smallpox epidemic	'57 Property ret. to Chch.
'06 Stone chch. dedicated	'12 Earthquake disaster	'18 Bouchard looted mssn.	'25 Hist. of Inds. written	'26 Visit by Beechey	'33 Indians emancipated	'39 Dana visit; '45 Sold	'60 Restor. attempted
'10 Padres explore Sac. Riv.	'12 Some quake damage	'18 Earthquake damag. church	'22-25 5th church built	'30 Fr. Catalá pred. '06 quake	'35 R. H. Dana visit	'36 Mission secularized	'51 Jesuits acquire mssn.
'09 Church completed	'12 Earthquake damage	'18 Bouchard; '19 Mohave rd.	'22 Oath of alleg.	'29 Pattie vaccinates Inds.	'32 Flooding '36 Secular.	'46 Mission sold	'62 Property ret. to Chch.
'06 Reservoir built	'12 Quake ruins 3rd church	'20 present church ded.	'24 Indian uprisings	'26 A few Indians freed	'31 2nd tower '34 Secularized	'46 Sold	'65 Property ret. to Chch.
'10 20,000 livestock on hand	'12 Earthquake destroys mssn.	'18 new chch. at new site	'24 Indian uprising	'30 Ind. pop. about 500	'34 Mission secularized	'44 Smallpox '45 Mssn. sold	'70's Some prop. ret.
'10 Women's dorm. built	'12 Murder of Fr. Quintana	'18 Bouchard scare	'22 Oath of alleg.	'27 Visit by DuHaut—Cilly	'34 Secularized	'40 Tower collapsed	'57 Quake destroys Chch.
'10 Lowest Ind. pop. in mssns.	'14 Death of Gov. Arrillaga	'18 Death of Fr. Ibañez	'22 Oath of alleg.	'28 Flood; Fr. Sarría arrvs.	'31 Chch. down '35 Secularized	'36 Death of Fr. Sarría; '46 Sold	'59 Property ret. to Chch.
'09 Church dedicated	'11 Padres explore inland	'17 Battle with Indians	'24 Ind. pop. 1,806	'26; '29 Battles with Indians	'34 Secularized	'41 deMofras visit; '46 Sold	'58 Property ret. to Chch.
'08 Fr. de la Cuesta arrvs.	'12 Present church ded.	'17 Doak paints reredos	'25 Death of Fr. Tápis	'29 Barrel organ received	'35 Secularized	'46 Frémont battalion here	'65 Steeple added
'06 Disastrous fire	'14 Tulare area explrd.	'18 Present church compl.	'21 Munras murals done	'30 Livestock total 12,400	'31 Indians offered freedom	'46 Sold; '49 Reeds murdered	'59 Property ret. to Chch.
'06 3rd church begun	'12 Earthquake damage	'19 40 houses for Inds. built	'22 Long bldg. completed	'27 Pueblo proposed by Gov.	'34 Secularized	'43 Discovery of gold	'61 Property ret. to Chch.
'07 1,025 Inds. at mssn.	'15 Pres. chch. compl; Pala fnd.	'20 Drought; 2,600 neophytes	'21 Mssn. supports troops	'27 Visit by DuHaut-Cilly	'32 Peyri leaves '34 Secularized	'46 Mission sold	'65 Property ret. to Chch.
Extensive building	'12 Earthquake damage	'17 Present chch. ded.	'24 Indian uprising	'28 Pattie vaccinates 900	'34 Secularized	'43 Seminary '46 Sold	'62 Property ret. to Chch.
		'17 Founded	'23 Granted mission status	'28 Ind. pop. 1,140	'32 Ind. attack '34 Secularized	'46 Mission sold	'55 Ret. to Ch.; '70 ch. raz.
			'23 Founded '24 Church blt.	'26 Indian attacks	'33 New chch. '34 Secularized	'38 Chch. razed '41 Chapel blt.	'80 Mssn. sold by Chch.

MATERIAL AND SPIRITUAL PROFILE OF THE MISSIONS

I. MATERIAL RESULTS — Livestock, as of December 31, 1832

	Mission	Cattle	Sheep	Goats	Swine	Horses	Mules	Total
1.	San Diego	4,500	13,250	150		220	80	18,200
2.	San Luis Rey	27,500	26,100	1,300	300	1,950	180	57,330
3.	San Juan Capistrano	10,900	4,800	50	40	450	30	16,270
4.	San Gabriel	16,500	8,500	40	60	1,200	42	26,342
5.	San Fernando	7,000	1,000			1,000	60	9,060
6.	San Buenaventura	4,050	3,000	16	290	200	60	7,616
7.	Santa Bárbara	1,800	3,200	28	64	480	135	5,707
8.	Santa Inés	7,200	2,100		60	390	110	9,860
9.	La Purísima	9,200	3,500	20	65	1,000	200	13,985
10.	San Luis Obispo	2,500	5,422			700	200	8,822
11.	San Miguel	3,710	8,282	42	50	700	186	12,970
12.	San Antonio	6,000	10,500	65	70	774	82	17,491
13.	La Soledad	6,000	6,200			252	56	12,508
14.	San Carlos	2,100	3,300			410	8	5,818
15.	San Juan Bautista	6,000	6,004		20	296	13	12,333
16.	Santa Cruz	3,600	5,211			400	25	9,236
17.	Santa Clara	10,000	9,500		55	730	35	20,320
18.	San José	12,000	11,000		40	1,100	40	24,180
19.	San Francisco de Asís	5,000	3,500			1,000	18	9,518
20.	San Rafael	2,120	3,000			370	2	5,492
21.	San Francisco Solano	3,500	600		50	900	13	5,063
	TOTAL	151,180	137,969	1,711	1,164	14,522	1,575	308,121

Agricultural Products, 1782-1832

Wheat Fns.*	Other** Fns.	Total Fns
91,081	67,594	158,675
26,452	66,204	92,656
60,770	23,153	83,923
127,710	105,985	233,695
78,788	16,384	95,172
73,249	62,054	135,303
90,080	61,063	151,143
126,075	53,650	179,725
111,412	79,602	191,014
97,405	31,346	128,751
72,164	32,885	105,049
45,647	39,286	84,933
41,303	27,105	68,408
79,450	24,397	103,847
51,060	18,517	69,577
46,796	11,276	58,072
76,815	21,721	98,536
75,852	146,957	222,809
37,345	29,772	67,117
41,736	32,873	74,609
6,654	4,337	10,991
1,457,844	956,161	2,414,005

*Fns. — Fanegas, a Spanish measure equal to 100 pounds.
**Included in this column: barley, corn, beans, peas, lentils, garbanzos.

The Spaniards kept meticulous records of mission activities. Each mission submitted an annual report to the Father-President that summarized its spiritual and material status at the end of the year. A comparison of the records for the missions as a whole for any given year gives a remarkable profile of the relative success of the individual missions and of the chain as a whole. By 1832, two years before secularization, the missions had reached the peak of their development. The tables on this page therefore reveal a cross-section of them at their best.

TABLE I. MATERIAL RESULTS. Figures shown in each column represent the total number of animals on hand at the date of inventory, the total volume of the crops harvested in that year. Note the dominance of. Mission's San Luis Rey and San Gabriel in the statistical summary.

TABLE II. SPIRITUAL RESULTS. The first three columns in this table are cumulative; thus, at San Diego 6,522 individuals had been baptized, 1,794 had been married, and 4,322 deaths had been recorded since the mission's founding. On the other hand, the figure for the neophytes was an annual tally; hence, there were 1,455 Christianized Indians at San Diego. Likewise notice the dominance of Mission San Luis Rey over the other missions in the number of neophytes attached to it.

(Tabular information adapted from Engelhardt's *Missions and Missionaries of California*.)

II. SPIRITUAL RESULTS (As of December 31, 1832)

	Mission	Baptisms	Marriages	Deaths	Neophytes
1.	San Diego	6,522	1,794	4,322	1,455
2.	San Luis Rey	5,399	1,335	2,718	2,788
3.	San Juan Capistrano	4,340	1,153	3,126	900
4.	San Gabriel	7,825	1,916	5,670	1,320
5.	San Fernando	2,784	827	1,983	782
6.	San Buenaventura	3,875	1,097	3,150	668
7.	Santa Bárbara	5,556	1,486	3,936	628
8.	Santa Inés	1,348	400	1,227	360
9.	La Purísima	3,255	1,029	2,609	372
10.	San Luis Obispo	2,644	763	2,268	231
11.	San Miguel	2,471	764	1,868	658
12.	San Antonio	4,419	1,142	3,617	640
13.	La Soledad	2,131	648	1,705	339
14.	San Carlos	3,827	1,032	2,837	185
15.	San Juan Bautista	4,106	1,003	2,854	916
16.	Santa Cruz	2,439	827	1,972	284
17.	Santa Clara	8,536	2,498	6,809	1,125
18.	San José	6,673	1,990	4,800	1,800
19.	San Francisco de Asís	6,898	2,043	5,166	204
20.	San Rafael	1,821	519	652	300
21.	San Francisco Solano	1,008	263	500	996
	TOTAL	87,787	24,529	63,789	16,951

VISITORS' GUIDE TO THE MISSIONS

Mission	Fnd.*	Location	Hours	Don.**	Services***	Outstanding Features
San Francisco Solano	1823 *21st*	Spain St., Sonoma; Hwy. 12	10-5	Yes	No	State His. Park; group tours; Jorgensen mission ptgs.; authentic mission garden; Blessing of Grapes, Sept. or Oct.
San Rafael Arcángel	1817 *20th*	5th Ave. & A St., San Rafael	11-4	No	Special	Parish church next door; tours; relics in Marin County Hist. Society Museum, 1124 B Street.
San Francisco de Asís	1776 *6th*	16th & Dolores Sts., San Francisco	9-4	Yes	Special	Ornate altar; Moorish-Corinthian architecture; garden cemetery: Indians, public figures; museum.
San José	1797 *14th*	Mission San Jose, off Interstate 680	10-5	Yes	No	Baptismal font; Mass bells; statues "Christ before Pilate" and "St. Bonaventure"; original olive grove.
Santa Clara de Asís	1777 *8th*	Franklin & Grant Sts., Santa Clara	9-7 museum 11-4	No	Yes	University chapel; group tours avail.; painted sanctuary ceiling; adobe ruin; exhibit, de Saisset Museum.
Santa Cruz	1791 *12th*	Emmet & School Sts., Santa Cruz	9-5	Yes	Special	Museum (open in summer; other times, apply at rectory for key) has mission books, vestments, art.
San Juan Bautista	1797 *15th*	San Juan Bautista, S. US 101	9:30-5:30 sum. 10-4:30 wint.	Yes	Yes	Parish church; picturesque town; Fiesta of Our Lady of Guadalupe, Dec.; Rodeo, July; Harvest Festival, Sept.; Mus.
San Carlos Borromeo de Carmelo	1770 *2nd*	Carmel; near Hwy. 1	9:30-5:30	Yes	Yes	Parish church; school; Moorish window and belltower; Serra cell and sarcophagus; Serra tomb; museum.
Nuestra Señora de la Soledad	1791 *13th*	3 mi. S. Soledad, 1 mi. W. US 101	10-4 closed Tues.	No	Special	Parish mission; annual Fiesta, Sept.
San Antonio de Padua	1771 *3rd*	Off US 101, 23 mi. SW. King City	9-4:30	Yes	Yes	Parish church; Padre's garden; restorations; museum; Fiesta, 2nd Sun. June.
San Miguel Arcángel	1797 *16th*	Off US 101, in town of San Miguel	9:30-4:30	Yes	Yes	Parish church, retreat hours; museum; Fiesta, 3rd Sun. Sept.
San Luis Obispo de Tolosa	1772 *5th*	Monterey & Chorro Sts., S. L. Obispo	9-5 sum. 9-4 wint.	Yes	Yes	Parish church; fine museum; collection early California photographs and religious articles.
La Purísima Concepción	1787 *11th*	15 mi. W. US 101 & Buellton	9-5	Yes	No	State His. Park; tours available; remarkably complete restoration; annual Fiesta, May.
Santa Inés	1804 *19th*	Solvang; 3 mi. E. of US 101 & Buellton	9:30-4:30 M-Sat. 12-4:30 Su.	Yes	Yes	Parish church; museum one of best: vestments, paintings, sculptures, artifacts; fine reredos; recorded tours.
Santa Bárbara	1786 *10th*	Los Olivos & Laguna Sts. Sta. Barbara	9-5	Yes	Yes	Parish church; seminary; sacred garden; museum; Crafts Show, July 4; Old Spanish Days, Aug. Outdoor Crèche, Dec.
San Buenaventura	1782 *9th*	Main & Figueroa, Ventura	10-5 M-S 10-4 Sun.	Yes	Yes	Parish church; museum; ornamented side door; wooden Holy Week bells; original rafters and tile in sanctuary.
San Fernando Rey de España	1797 *17th*	15151 San Fern. Miss. Blvd.	9-5	Yes	Yes	Seminary; museum; fine, large Convento rich in relics; Flower and Fruit Blessing, San Fernando Fiesta, June.
San Gabriel Arcángel	1771 *4th*	Mission Dr., 10 mi. E. central L.A.	9:30-4:30 after restored	Yes	Yes	9:30 a.m. Spanish Mass Sundays; museum; Indian-painted Stations of Cross; fortress architecture; Fiesta, Sept.
San Juan Capistrano	1776 *7th*	San Juan Capistrano; Interstate 5	8:30-5	Yes	Yes	Parish church; libraries; jewel-like gardens, pools; St. Joseph's Day, March 19, celebration swallows' return.
San Luis Rey de Francia	1798 *18th*	San Luis Rey; on Hwy. 76	9-5 M-S 12-4 Sunday	Yes	Yes	Parish church; seminary; sacred garden; museum; tours. Octagonal mortuary; rare dome; sunken garden.
San Diego de Alcalá	1769 *1st*	Off Int. 8 in Mission Valley	9-5	Yes	Yes	Parish church; school; tours; campanario and espadaña (false front); original tiles.

*Fnd. — Year of founding. Figure in italic indicates order of founding.
**Don. — Donation. Small donations are appreciated at the missions for maintenance and further restoration.
***Services — Missions serving as parish churches welcome visitors to services. "Special" means church used only for weddings, baptisms, funerals, special masses.

Bibliography

BOOKS

Baer, Kurt. *Architecture of the California Missions.* Berkeley, Calif.: University of California Press, 1958.

Bancroft, Hubert Howe. *California Pastoral, 1769–1848.* San Francisco: The History Company, 1888.

———. *History of California,* Vols. I, II and III. San Francisco: The History Company, Publishers, 1886.

Berger, John A. *The Franciscan Missions of California.* New York: G. P. Putnam's Sons, 1941.

Bolton, Herbert Eugene. *Anza's California Expeditions,* 5 vols. Berkeley, Calif.: University of California Press, 1930.

———. *Fray Juan Crespí, Missionary Explorer on the Pacific Coast 1769–1774.* Berkeley, Calif.: University of California Press, 1927.

———. *Outpost of Empire: The Story of the Founding of San Francisco.* New York: Alfred A. Knopf, 1931.

———. *Palóu's Historical Memoirs of New California,* 4 vols. Berkeley, Calif.: University of California Press, 1926.

———. *The Spanish Borderlands.* New Haven: Yale University Press, 1921.

Boscana, Geronimo. *Chinigchinich.* Santa Ana, Calif.: Fine Arts Press, 1933.

Chapman, Charles E. *A History of California: The Spanish Period.* New York: The Macmillan Company, 1921.

Childers, Laurence Murrell. *Education in California Under Spain and Mexico and Under American Rule to 1851.* Berkeley, Calif.: University of California Press, 1930.

Cook, Sherburne Friend. *The Conflict Between the California Indian and White Civilization.* Berkeley and Los Angeles, Calif.: University of California Press, 1943.

Corle, Edwin. *The Royal Highway.* Indianapolis, Ind.: The Bobbs-Merrill Co., Inc., 1949.

Correia, Delia Richards. *Lasuén in California.* Berkeley, Calif.: University of California Press, 1934.

Culleton, James. *Indians and Pioneers of Old Monterey.* Fresno, Calif.: Academy of California Church History, 1950.

Cutter, Donald C. *Malaspina in California.* San Francisco: John Howell-Books, 1960.

Dana, Richard Henry, Jr. *Two Years Before the Mast: A Personal Narrative.* Boston and New York: Houghton Mifflin Company, 1884.

Da Silva, Owen Francis, ed. *Mission Music of California.* Los Angeles, Calif.: W. F. Lewis, 1941.

Davis, William Heath. *Seventy-Five Years in California—A History of Events and Life in California: Personal, Political and Military.* San Francisco: John Howell, 1929.

Elder, David Paul. *The Old Spanish Missions of California.* San Francisco: Paul Elder and Company, 1913.

Engelhardt, Rev. Zephyrin, O.F.M., *The Franciscans in California.* Harbor Springs, Michigan: Holy Childhood Indian School, 1897.

———. *The Holy Man of Santa Clara: or Life, Virtues and Miracles of Fr. Mágin Catalá, O.F.M.* San Francisco: The James H. Barry Company, 1909.

———. *The Missions and Missionaries of California.* San Francisco: The James H. Barry Company, 1916.

———. Individual missions: *San Antonio de Padua,* 1929; *San Buenaventura,* 1930; *San Diego,* 1920; *San Fernando Rey,* 1927; *San Francisco,* 1924; *San Gabriel,* 1927; *San Juan Bautista,* 1931; *San Juan Capistrano,* 1922; *San Luis Rey,* 1921; *San Miguel Arcangel,* 1929; *Santa Barbara,* 1923.

Geary, Gerald Joseph. *The Secularization of the California Missions (1810–1846).* Washington, D.C.: Catholic University of America, 1934.

Geiger, Maynard J., O.F.M. *The Life and Times of Fray Junípero Serra,* 2 vols. Washington, D.C.: Academy of American Franciscan History, 1959.

———, ed. and trans. *Palóu's Life of Fray Junípero Serra.* Washington, D.C.: Academy of American Franciscan History, 1955.

———. *A Pictorial History of the Physical Development of Mission Santa Barbara from Brush Hut to Institutional Greatness, 1786–1963.* San Francisco: The Franciscan Fathers, 1963.

Hawthorne, Hildegarde. *California's Missions, Their Romance and Beauty.* New York: D. Appleton-Century Co., Inc., 1942.

Jackson, Helen Hunt. *Father Junipero and the Mission Indians of California.* Boston: Little, Brown & Co., 1902.

———. *Glimpses of California and the Missions.* Boston: Little, Brown & Co., 1902.

———. *Ramona.* Boston: Little, Brown & Co., 1939.

James, George Wharton. *In and Out of the Old Missions of California; An Historical and Pictorial Account of the Franciscan Missions.* Boston: Little, Brown and Co., 1905.

———. *Old Missions and Mission Indians of California.* Los Angeles, Calif.: B. R. Baumgardt, 1895.

———. *Picturesque Pala, The Story of the Mission Chapel of San Antonio de Pala.* Pasadena, Calif.: George Wharton James, 1916.

King, Kenneth Moffat. *Mission to Paradise: The Story of Junipero Serra and the Missions of California.* Chicago: Franciscan Herald Press, 1956.

Kroeber, Alfred Louis. *Handbook of the Indians of California.* Berkeley: California Book Company, Ltd., 1953.

———. *A Mission Record of the California Indians.* Berkeley: University of California Press, 1908.

Lummis, Charles Fletcher. *The Spanish Pioneers and the California Missions.* Chicago: A. C. McClurg & Co., 1929.

McCarthy, Francis Florence. *The History of Mission San Jose, California, 1797–1835.* Fresno, Calif.: Academy Library Guild, 1958.

Miller, Henry. *Account of a Tour of the California Missions, 1856.* San Francisco: The Book Club of California, 1952.

Mofras, Eugene Duflot de. *Travels on the Pacific Coast*, ed. and trans. by Marguerite Eyer Wilbur. Santa Ana, Calif., 1937.

Newcomb, Rexford. *The Old Mission Churches and Historic Houses of California*. Philadelphia: J. B. Lippincott Co., 1925, 1953.

Older, Cora Miranda. *California Missions and Their Romances*. New York: Coward-McCann, 1938.

Palóu, Francisco. *The Founding of the First California Missions*. San Francisco: Nueva California Press, 1934.

———. *Life of Fray Junípero Serra*, trans. and annotated by Maynard J. Geiger. Washington, D.C.: Academy of American Franciscan History, 1955.

Pourade, Richard F. *The Explorers—The History of San Diego*. San Diego: The Union-Tribune Publishing Co., 1960.

———. *Time of the Bells*. San Diego, Calif.: Union-Tribune Publishing Co., 1961.

Priestley, Herbert Ingram. *Franciscan Explorations in California*. Glendale, Calif: Arthur H. Clark Co., 1946.

———. *Pedro Fages*. Berkeley, Calif.: University of California Press, 1937.

Repplier, Agnes. *Junípero Serra, Pioneer Colonist of California*. Garden City, N.Y.: Doubleday, Doran and Co., Inc., 1947.

Richman, Irving Berdine. *California Under Spain and Mexico 1535–1847*. New York: Houghton Mifflin Co., 1911.

Riesenberg, Felix. *The Golden Road, The Story of California's Mission Trail*. New York: McGraw-Hill, 1962.

Robinson, Alfred. *Life in California, a Historical Account of the Origin, Customs and Traditions of the Indians of Alta-California*. Oakland, Calif.: Bio-books, 1947.

Sanchez, Nellie Van de Grift. *Spanish Arcadia*. Los Angeles, Calif.: Powell Publishing Co., 1929.

Saunders, Charles Francis. *The California Padres and Their Missions*. New York: Houghton Mifflin Co., 1915.

———. *Capistrano Nights; Tales of a California Mission Town*. New York: R. M. McBride & Co., 1930.

Simpson, Lesley Byrd, ed. *The Letters of José Señan, O.F.M., Mission Buenaventura 1796–1823*. San Francisco: John Howell Books, 1962.

Smith, Frances Rand. *The Architectural History of Mission San Carlos Borromeo*. Berkeley, Calif.: Historical Survey Commission, 1921.

———. *The Mission of San Antonio de Padua*. Stanford, Calif.: Stanford University Press, 1932.

Spearman, Arthur Dunning, S. J. *The Five Franciscan Churches of Mission Santa Clara*. Palo Alto, Calif.: The National Press, 1963.

Stern, Aloysius S., *S. J. Magín Catalá, O.F.M.: The Holy Man of Santa Clara*. San Francisco: Privately printed.

Tibesar, Antonine, ed. *Writings of Junípero Serra*, 3 vols. Washington, D.C.: Academy of American Franciscan History, 1955.

Torchiana, Henry Albert Willem van Coenan. *Story of the Mission Santa Cruz*. San Francisco: P. Elder & Co., 1933.

Vancouver, George. *A Voyage of Discovery to the North Pacific Ocean and Round the World, in the Years 1790, 1791, 1792, 1793, and 1795*, 3 vols. London: Printed for G. G. and J. Robinson & J. Edwards, 1798.

Walsh, Marie T. *The Mission Bells of California*. San Francisco: Harr Wagner Publishing Co., 1934.

Watson, Douglas S. *The Spanish Occupation of California*. San Francisco: Grabhorn, 1934.

Webb, Edith Buckland. *Indian Life at the Old Missions*. Los Angeles, Calif.: Warren F. Lewis, Publications, 1952.

ARTICLES

Adam, J. "A Defense of the Missionary Establishments of Alta California," *Historical Society of Southern California Publications*, (1896).

Bolton, Herbert Eugene. "The Mission as a Frontier Institution in the Spanish-American Colonies," *American Historical Review*, XXIII (1917), 42–46.

Bowman, Jacob N. "The Names of the California Missions," *Historical Society of Southern California Quarterly*, XXXIX (1957), 351–356.

———. "The Parochial Books of the California Missions," *Historical Society of Southern California Quarterly*, LIII (1961), 303–315.

———. "The Resident Neophytes of the California Missions, 1769–1834," *Historical Society of Southern California Quarterly*, XL (1958), 138–148.

Carter, Charles Franklin, trans. "Duhaut-Cilly's Account of California in the Years 1827–1828," *California Historical Society Quarterly*, VIII No. 2 (1929), 130–166; No. 3 (1929), 214–250; No. 4 (1929), 306–336.

Costanso, Miguel. "Diary of Miguel Costanso," ed. by Frederick J. Teggert, *Publications of the Academy of Pacific Coast History*, II (1911), 161–327.

———. "Narrative of the Portola Expedition of 1769–1700," ed. by Adolph Van Hemmert-Engert and Frederick J. Teggert, *Publications of the Academy of Pacific Coast History*, I (1910), 91–159.

Davidson, George. "An Examination of Some of the Early Voyages of Discovery and Exploration on the Northwest Coast of America From 1539–1603," Report of the Superintendent, *United States Coast and Geodetic Survey*, Appendix No. 7 (1887).

Judson, William L. "The Architecture of the Mission," *Historical Society of Southern California Publications*, VII (1909).

Polley, Frank J. "Shipbuilding at the San Gabriel Mission," *Historical Society of Southern California Publications*, III (1895), 34–39.

Schanzer, George O. "A Russian Visit to the Spanish Franciscans in California 1836," *The Americas*, IX (1953), 453–458.

Smith, Frances Rand. "The Mission of Nuestra Señora de la Soledad," *California Historical Society Quarterly*, XXIII No. 1 (1944).

———. "The Spanish Missions of California," and "The Burial Place of Father Junipero Serra," Reprint, *Hispania*, VII Nos. 4 and 5 (1924).

Index